The Imam and His Islamic Revolution

1982

THE SNOW MAN PRESS
Victoria, British Columbia

The Imam and His Islamic Revolution

A JOURNEY INTO HEAVEN AND HELL

Robin Woodsworth Carlsen

ISBN 0-920910-17-3   paperback edition
ISBN 0-920910-20-3   clothbound edition

Published by
The Snow Man Press Ltd.
1765 Rockland Avenue
Victoria, British Columbia
Canada   V8S 1X1

Designed and printed in Canada by
MORRISS PRINTING COMPANY LTD.
1745 Blanshard Street
Victoria, British Columbia

For the warriors who live on Annapurna

Prefatory Note

Through this book the terms "mythology," "mythological" and "mythic" are used; this does not imply any sort of fictitious reality, but rather those rich systems of divine revelation and codified meaning that link man to God. The word "mythology" carries the resonance of imaginative power worthy of the highest poetry and truth within Creation. It is, then, absolutely non-pejorative in its application to the Islam of Iran. In the absence of direct mystical experience, great mythologies such as Islam, Christianity, Buddhism, Judaism, and Hinduism carry the most integrated expression of the meaning of existence. They are man's—potentially at least—most enduring achievements.

Preface

It should be noted at the outset that the author has made no attempt to present the story of this revolution against the background of twenty-five centuries of complex history, for it is obvious that the present cosmological structure (Shi'a Islam) does not reflect the multi-faceted reality of ancient and modern Persia; it is as if a particular individual were to be interpreted on the basis of one single moment in the successive moments of having been so many different characters: the only proper evaluation of the totality of that individual's nature would be an analysis which explains the present emphasis (profoundly meta-physical) in terms of the overall evolutionary pattern of character that he (Iran) has manifested. The most authentic expression (or rather pre-sentation) of a given personality is one that sees that personality in terms of the integrated presence of everything that has ever been; thus, for someone to truly understand Iran (and make that understanding avail-able to others) one would have to have a grasp of the whole historical, social, and cultural consciousness of Iran; this the author does not have. Indeed one could go as far as to say that the validity (and enduring reality) of the present system of government in Iran should—ideally—be determined by the extent to which that system, that cosmology reflects and integrates the totality of experience of Iran—from its beginnings 2500 years ago. It is doubtful whether most Iranians could claim that the present leadership (and its absolute imperatives) is a pure expression of the personality of Iran; indeed there will be many Iranians who dispute the claims of the universality of justice and meaning that the current establishment in Iran has appropriated to itself—on behalf of the inhabitants. The very individualistic and pluralistic nature of the script of Iranian history and culture precludes the possibility of a consummat-ing mythology that would do justice to the variegated, intricate nature of that history and culture—and thus the genuine cry of pain and sorrow among so many Iranians today—especially those who have gone into exile.

However it is the author's specialized sensibilities that are pertinent to the understanding of present-day Iran, for the author, while remaining only modestly acquainted with the nature of Iranian history and culture, nevertheless feels himself able to seize the particular meaning of the present juncture Iran has reached in her own becoming, and to translate that meaning in terms of a meaning that extends well beyond Iran. The author thus takes a profoundly intuitive approach to this subject; operating on this level it becomes especially clear that what is manifesting through Iran today is something that gives some basis to interpreting history and present-day political realities allegorically, that is, in terms of significant archetypes of meaning. Such a view does not ignore complexity; indeed it welcomes such complexity. It does, however, treat the events of history somewhat symbolically, and it especially seeks to understand why great myths (such as Islam) periodically assert themselves. The meaning of the present revolution is central to the meaning of the whole script of human existence. The author has sensed—in his intensive involvement with the current events in Iran— the intention of something marvelously dramatic that, sacrificing (apparently) the strains of Iranian uniqueness, takes Iran and bends it to fit into a demonstration of metaphysical and mythological meaning that, paradoxically enough, tells us much more about the final pattern and meaning of human history and human consciousness. This, at least, is the rationale of the author. Experts in Iranian history and culture can give a picture of present-day Iran which does justice, in the words of one reader of this book, to "the rich resources of tradition in the history of Iranian secular and sacral leadership to define the role of power in Iranian society . . . [and the] interplay over the centuries of the tension between official doctrines of Twelver Shi'a Islam and the practical exercise of power by secular and religious forces."

What is taking place in Iran today is something which attempts to transcend culture and history; in the present circumstances it may seem ludicrous (and even cruel) to force the Iranian people into a mould of socio-historical belief which does not reflect the character of Iran over its twenty-five centuries of experience and striving identity. Nevertheless the affirmation of this metaphysic of Shi'a Islam has been remarkably successful, and its current dominant and monopolistic status is suggestive of reasons that transcend a purely scholarly and rational analysis. That element within reality that gives meaning to events, events which lie outside of the intellect's or ego's ability to comprehend them—such an element is given full sway in this book. The author feels qualified to give a portrait of present-day Iran because of the overwhelming—and spontaneous—sensation of having been accessible to those impulses of meaning and integration that manifest outside of time and space, the impulses that order themselves into the great mythologies that constitute the living basis of the world's great religions. A time has come when

8

there is a re-assertion of these impulses—at their genesis, before and beyond the dogmatic crystallization of those impulses—and the events of modern Iran are calculated to provide the experiential justification for the continued existence of such mythological systems of belief. It is as if modern man had successfully exiled God from the domain, the stage, of international politics, history, and culture. In the intuition of the author the sequence of events in Iran constitutes proof that something mysterious—even numinous—is behind the ordering of those events; that something has everything to do with the invention of Islam and—it is boldly asserted here—the ability to understand that context within which that invention seeks its vindication.

Therefore although there will be those (the experts in Middle East history and culture) who will attempt to explain the meaning and reality of this revolution within a socio-historical perspective it will be found— especially by those who have given themselves utterly to the mythology that grips Iran today—that such an analysis does not touch the fundamental spirit of this revolution. Shi'a Islam can never "succeed in becoming totally exclusive as the custodian of an acceptable cosmology for all Iranians."* Nevertheless, for those unable to participate in the exalting ceremony of Islamic renascence it remains absolutely imperative to give an analysis that does not a priori deny the possible ontological reality of the Islamic perception of the universe. The Islamic Revolution in Iran aims at ultimate truths; the Western, secular historian cannot (and must not) vitiate the objectivity of his methods by succumbing to the notion that the religious impulse is the one impulse that adequately explains and makes meaningful everything that happens (and has happened) to man. He therefore must see the attempt to arrive at ultimate truth as itself a manifestation of something that is intrinsically relative and conditional. He must therefore (and in many instances this is virtually an unconscious presumption) reject any analysis that is itself subject to the same absolutist mentality that is at the basis of a mythological view of man, God, and the universe. However, in the present instance the author feels confident in asserting that the analysis of this book takes within its circumference the delimitations of the purely mythological view, while at the same time accounting for the relativistic and critical attitude toward such a view—i.e. this book attempts to explain both the mythological and the secular view of Iran and its revolution—or at least why two such divergent views could come into existence. It is not, however, the analysis which will fully satisfy the academician or specialist in Iranian history; there will be others who will

* Unpublished review by one Iranian expert in conjunction with an appraisal of this book in its manuscript form.

attempt this project. So far, however, no Middle East specialist has adequately conveyed the complexity of this revolution, and within the intuitional mode of analysis there may be some inspiration that draws to itself those same imaginative elements that have given birth to the mythology that such an analysis seeks to explain—but which inspiration is rooted in the pure source of what creates such mythologies, and thus, like the Sufi, can explain the meaning beyond the exoteric content of that mythology; in other words, place the revolution—and its adherents, and its critics—within the context of wholeness and multiplicity of meaning that is the actual context, the context of reality.

If such a thesis seems presumptuous in the extreme, it is enough that it become judged within whatever terms are agreed upon as constituting what is excellent, mediocre, and inadequate. The author feels he under-stands the revolution (this is a continuing part of an overall epiphany of understanding as to the nature of life itself as a sacred script) and he understands its critics. What is presented in this book are the impressions of one writer who deeply trusts in the integrating intelligence that has arranged all the terrible and beautiful movements of human history, both individual and collective.

Contents

Appendices

Introduction

Light travels 186,000 miles in one second, or seven times around the earth. In one year light travels about six trillion miles.

A galaxy is composed of billions of stars. There are some hundred billion galaxies in the universe; there are perhaps as many planets as there are stars, or about ten billion trillion planets in the universe.

We live on one of those planets within a galaxy that is several million light years across. Each one of the four and one half billion human beings on our planet possesses a brain with a hundred billion neurons, about the number of stars in our galaxy. Each neuron has thousands of connections with other neurons, about one hundred trillion million such connections existing in the cerebral cortex alone.

Ayatollah Khomeini has declared that Islam and the Islamic Revolution of Iran is inspired by the Creator of this vast universe, and the universe within our brain. That which has created these astronomical distances, this almost infinite number of atoms (about ten billion billion billion) is alleged to have sent down revelations of absolute truth through a human being, the Prophet Mohammad. These truths have become the cosmology of the consciousness of revolutionary Iran. During the month of February of 1982 I visited Iran; this book is the story of my experience there, inside this powerful metaphysic of Islam.

It is also the story of a single human being who is the center of the galaxy of Islam, and the source from which all the neural connections of the revolution have their inspiration. This is the story of a universe unfamiliar to us, but a universe that desires to touch eternity, and therefore to overcome all these enchanting, awesome statistics about the size and complexity of the physical universe. The Islamic universe of revolutionary Iran is composed of absolutes; these absolutes can not and will not compromise with the startling and relativistic implications that we draw from the galactic, neurological facts I have described. The scientific implication is that we must remain humble in the face of the tremendous unknown of this universe; the religious implication of Mohammad's revelations is that such a universe, no matter how staggering are these distances and sizes, is explained by the Creator through these revelations; and by obeying the laws that emerge from revelation, one can come to know the Creator of the hundred billion galaxies in the universe, the one hundred trillion million neuron connections in the brain.

Now I had been to Iran before[1] and had, ever since the seizing of the American Embassy ("the den of spies" according to the Iranians) in November of 1979, maintained a fascinated albeit ambivalent attitude towards events in Iran. The invitation to come to Iran was the opportunity for me to see for myself whether the charges of torture, persecution, peremptory executions, and medieval repression, were true, whether this revolution has become perverted by the morbid spiritual preoccupations of Ayatollah Khomeini, whether the revolution had, as many insisted, been betrayed.

During the three weeks I was there I was able to come into contact with those facts, experiences, and personalities that enabled me to confidently assume that I had touched the pulse of this revolution. I did not set out to have any kind of hypothesis or moral judgement fulfilled; I did not set out to find the evidence to support a one-sided view of the revolution. In effect I looked both for the best and for the worst, for I knew that any attempt to describe this revolution outside of the extremes of competing values would be to miss entirely its significance. While I was sympathetic with what I had come to know as the supreme spiritual sincerity of many of the leading revolutionary forces in Iran (I had been, for instance, impressed with the vision even of the student leaders who had held the American diplomats: while I did not agree with everything that they said, I could not deny the tremendous sense of purpose, the sense of total surrender to this religion called Islam) I had nevertheless, especially since the allegations of wanton executions, persecution of Baha'is, intolerance of all opposition, and devastation of cultural pluralism, become doubtful as to whether the revolution had not gone completely off course and become a victim of forces of hatred and narrowness that were as evil as the forces identified as the enemies of Iran: imperialism, the CIA, infidelism, capitalism, Marxism. Something had marred the reputation of the revolution and what the Iranians interpreted as Islamic justice I tended to think was the convenient method for releasing the hostility and frustration and impoverished sensibilities of those masses of people who had suddenly found an identity in this revolution and now found it possible to blame all their troubles on forces outside of themselves.

---

[1] In March 1980 I gathered material together for a second book on Iran: *Seventeen Days in Tehran: Revolution, Evolution, and Ignorance* (Victoria, B.C.: The Snow Man Press, 1980).

There was, then, in my visiting Iran, the awareness of the polarity of views; Muslims whom I had come to know in Iran and North America assured me the revolution was on track, that I was simply a victim of the propaganda of Western media; however other Muslims had become disenchanted with the Islamic Revolution and had indicated to me their criticisms, their doubts about Khomeini, and the Iranian assumption of the pre-eminence of Shi'a as opposed to Sunni Islam. I had also many friends who were connected with the first impartial coverage of events in Iran during the revolution, and during the hostage crisis; these people were often critics to the left of center and once the full weight of Islamic law was brought to bear upon all oppositional groups in Iran these critics became deeply disillusioned and openly hostile to the regime. And there had of course been many moderate, even apolitical persons who had seen the distorted picture given by the Western press to this revolution, and who had therefore sympathized with the beleaguered Iranians; however once the executions began and the Islamization of all culture, ideas, and institutions in Iran, there was the nagging sense that even the innocence of this revolution had been corrupted, that perhaps the Shah was not so bad—in comparison with what was now happening in Iran. Soon I found myself pretty much isolated—and feeling that I should be quiet until such time as I could determine for myself how it was that a revolution that had so much promise and spiritual resonance, how such a revolution could be taken over by purely retrogressive forces and turned into a nightmare for all persons with any sense of allegiance to freedom of expression.

I take it as the very most important part of my own personal philosophy that life can be seen aesthetically—even within the realm of politics. I do not seek to have certain moral, political opinions confirmed by the experiences that present themselves to me; what I have sought since arriving at my own view of man and the universe is the actual, sometimes momentary meaning that seems to be organizing itself at a given time, in a given place. Since I do intuit there is an order and creative purpose behind the working out of the script of human existence I know that I need not rely upon a particular idea or hypothesis that is either validated or invalidated by subsequent experience. Somewhere that purpose seeks to make known its essentially mysterious and infinitely complex intention; such an intention can be comprehended sometimes only on the level of the heart; what I knew was that there was a message in this revolution, a message that was just as meaningful if it proved upon observation that the spiritual power of the revolution had been utterly corrupted, or that the evil that was identified and resisted during the Pahlavi dynasty had now transferred itself to the Khomeini regime, that revolutions, no matter how idealistic, inevitably become subject to the violent distortions and base motives that seem to confirm the notion that man is utterly incapable of pursuing a vision of the world based upon millenarian objectives. The Iranians had sought to bring God into their society; they had, according to their growing number of critics merely given God an even worse name by attempting to implement their theocratic ideas; the attempt to place Allah at the fount of Iranian society had resulted in atrocities that confirmed the inadvisability of joining the secular with the sacred. Belief in God taken to its extreme limit ends up perverting the purpose of life.

Well, I exposed myself to the evidence and did in fact conclude that those who opposed the Islamic Revolution did so for—at least in many cases—the most idealistic reasons; it was entirely obvious that Iran could be experienced as a hell, and one would have to sympathize with those who could not see it any other way; on the other hand one had to come to terms with those very different dynamics of consciousness which made millions of others anticipate through this Islamic Republic the Kingdom of Heaven.

On the Method of Observation Used to Describe the Revolution

The reader will sense, from the start, that although I include some of the most relevant facts necessary to make an appraisal of present-day Iran I place these facts within a cosmological context, a context which is at once highly subjective and metaphysically consistent; the reader will only forgive such a personal and speculative approach if it becomes clear that such subjectivity, such metaphysical wandering does not distort the facts necessary to make a judgement about what is happening in Iran. In other words, the reader may disagree with the context within which the facts receive their interpretation; he should not, however, experience that my rendition of my experience necessarily prevents the reader from drawing his own conclusions, and from finding out facts that just may not be available from other sources. It is the very individualistic nature of my presentation of Iran and my experience that enables the reader to objectify for himself the meaning of the Islamic Revolution, the particular way in which this revolution acts upon the sensibility of the reader in order that he might discover where some of his own unconsciously held biases exist. Naturally this book is written with a bias, but that bias is rooted in the idea that Creation is itself going on within a bias, the bias aptly described by Wallace Stevens: "the actual is a deft beneficence."

18

It is with a sense of that agile and aesthetic beneficence that I seek to draw myself and the reader into some of the more disquieting and complex facts about this revolution, and more particularly about the man who is the official leader of that revolution. For it was within the experience of meeting Ayatollah Khomeini that I began to understand what this revolution was all about.

A reviewer described my second Iran book as "a Dante-esque trip into Iran and the Islamic mind."[2] If that book was Dante-esque this present book is nothing less than the attempt to forge a crucible of experience within which the essential meaning of the world can be understood. It goes considerably further than the second book and attempts to locate precisely the significance of the revolution in relationship to the whole spiritual and political direction of the modern world. It is quite conceivable that I have failed to communicate this context; nevertheless for those readers willing to open themselves to a journey in which their cosmologies may be disturbed, the experience of the book will be a meaningful one—even if it is just to clarify why they cannot assent to the perceptions that articulate themselves within the dominant and domineering subjectivity of the book. For other readers the whole sense of the book will be frustrating in the extreme; and for some the book will appear to be as insane as the revolution in Iran itself. For the intuitive, mythologically sensitive reader, however, I think I can guarantee an experience which will enrich consciousness and allow us to see connections between events previously thought to be categorically disparate.

The arrangement of the book suggests a series of impressions, much like a journal; there is no attempt to join these impressions together in any systematic way, or to tell a continuous story. There is however a definite sequence, a sequence which was determined by the chronology of my experience. At the end there is an attempt to summarize the meaning of the revolution.

[2] The Victoria, B.C. *Colonist*, August 31, 1980.

Heaven and earth do not contain Me, but the heart of my faithful
servant contains Me.

Hadith of the Prophet

The Journey

*In Frankfurt with Muslims,
Awaiting Flight to Tehran*

I suppose if one takes seriously the idea of God, and one submits oneself to the notion that obedience to one of the systems of belief—such as Islam—brings with it a natural piety and disciplined way of perceiving the world outside of its secularized forms—if this is the case then one comes to expect that an encounter with a devout Muslim would demonstrate the benefit derived from acknowledging the presence of Allah, and following his rules. In other words if there is a God (and we presume that if he does exist he figures in most everything—even politics) it is likely that he enjoys being recognized by those whom he has created, and if the great world religions have been inspired by him—through his chosen prophets: Moses, Jesus, Buddha, Mohammad—then a sincere believer should give evidence of the superior connectedness he has with the Creator—this in contradistinction to the unbeliever, or the rabid secularist.

Well my experience with several Muslims (and one in particular) in Frankfurt who were accompanying me to Iran left me disappointed: even when a tour guide (a charming and articulate woman) told us of the fire bombing of Frankfurt during the month of March in 1944 and pointed out how the tower of one of the great cathedrals (built in the fourteenth century) was the only monument to survive the Allied attack, there was little registration of the significance of this fact, for the implication was, somehow, that, as in the German bombing of London where St. Paul's cathedral stood erect while all around this magnificent edifice buildings were levelled, a kind of miracle had happened. And this resonance was palpable when one viewed the tower of the cathedral. And yet one felt that the Muslims (and there was one outspoken socialist as well) did not possess that sensibility that could derive the religious pleasure from the obvious causality implied in the commentary of our guide. In the mosque, at prayers, reading the Qur'an, discussing Islam, there could be a reverence and indeed a deep commitment to God; but outside the confines of the regulated idiom of Islam there was, as in the case of many religious people—but with a specific meaning when applied to these Muslims—, no spontaneous response to the intrinsic religiosity of life (if one assumes it is possible to perceive the impulses of feeling that substantiate and give articulation to the empirical evidence of a Designer to this universe).

One Muslim, a former architect and now entrepreneur (from the Middle East) expressed himself perpetually within a standardized mode of humour, and this systematized and uncreative method of adapting himself to the world (at least in a social sense) greatly diminished his opportunity to enjoy the more universal, aesthetic, and spiritual meanings contained in our guided tour through Frankfurt—including an hour inside Goethe's house, the very symbol of Western European culture and intellect.

I wondered to myself whether there was something inherent to Islam which made it less likely that the worshipper of Allah could innocently perceive and appreciate the finer expressions of intelligence and beauty that, while unattached to a specific religious mould, nevertheless celebrated something transcendental and pure. This would be one of my specific concerns when I visited Iran.

On Iran National Airlines, destination Tehran: Some Observations on Chadored Stewardesses

When I had travelled to Iran in February of 1980 the stewardesses did not wear chadors. Now here in the plane stewardesses waited upon us, their bodies and hair concealed by the dark blue gowns[3] (only the face was permitted to show) that seemed almost stridently opposed to Western colour and fashionable attire. And yet, when I gazed upon the women (and there were many passengers also clothed in this traditional Muslim dress) I noticed the absence of sexual provocation, the absence of attention on the outlines of the body, the absence of emphasis on the sensual differences between man and woman; in this the energy flow from the chadored women was pure, simple, and free of contrivance. I thought to myself: we are almost unconscious of the extent to which seductive possibilities are going on all the time between woman and man, that the Western mode of dress for women accentuates the physical distinctiveness of woman so that in expressing herself she has to rise

[3] In actual fact the stewardesses wore the *rusari* (head-scarf) and not the chador. The chador is the traditional Iranian covering for women but is inhibiting for the performance of certain tasks since it is a single piece of cloth covering the woman's body from head to foot, held in place by the hand which grasps it under the chin, or by the teeth if the hands are otherwise engaged. "Chador" here simply refers to the veiling of the woman's form so as to eliminate the reality of eros.

22

above her physical form to assert an identity that is based purely on her womanhood. Stripping away (to paradoxically emphasize what had happened here) the outward garments that reinforced the idea, the reality of woman and sexuality, and making the whole woman breathe her identity through her face made one much more conscious of the 'character' of the woman, and the miracle of uniqueness that displays itself through the countenance of a person. Cutting off (and I am making clear that much of this sensual content is absorbed unconsciously when we are with a woman who does not wear the veil) from our attention everything but the physiognomy there is the clarity of the lines of the soul that expresses itself, and whatever loveliness and beauty is hidden— which is highlighted and glorified by the variety of costumes permitted in the West—there is a commensurate increase in the sense one has of a fresh mode of communication, that here a woman can be a person and one must devote one's attention to that dignity of personality that ignores the physical form in which the soul has been clothed.

At the same time the sensuality, the feminine power and attractiveness is silent and unmanifest; yet one senses the coiled potential underneath the concealed dress of the chador and this in a sense 'transubstantiates' the sexual energy, keeping it in balance, retaining its unexpressed vitality and, if I can use the word, virginity. One senses why, under these conditions, there is the familiar reference to "brother" and "sister," that only in this situation can a woman assert her dignity free of distracting the man, free of entering the ancient ritual of seduction, free of taking the energy from the concentrated focus of attention that comes from talking to someone and looking right into her face. On the one hand one might wish to see the 'performance' of ceremonial beauty enhanced by the deliberate emphasis on the woman's hair and physical form; and yet—in the absence of this—there was some more spiritual and cleaner form of experience just not possible (at least in its purest form) without submitting to this tradition of covering the woman's hair and body. A woman's hair, I had been told by a young Muslim some years ago, is considered to be one of the most potent sources of sensuality and is, for the unconditioned Middle East male, a deliberate enticement to sexual advance. (I mean here that there is an instinctive reaction to the uncovered, flowing hair of a woman on the part of the man.)

One stewardess in particular—I should note here—was exceptionally beautiful, poised, and commanding. Alert, confident and in full posses-sion of her womanhood she made the chador simply the form of herself —as if God *chose* to clothe her in this way. I sensed how the chador defines, gives dignity and certitude to a woman. It becomes the vesture for the archetype of herself and in association with this traditional dress comes the sense of surrender, the laws of the universe, the reality of good and evil. There becomes a dominant sense of absolutes (whereas in the West the variegated forms of attire relativize and therefore reinforce the sense of the anti-mythic, the merely individualistic, the separateness of the self). Here, just watching the stewardesses (and even some of the passengers) one realized that dress does not necessarily have to be solely for aesthetic reasons; it can be that which turns the attention to something else; it is decisive; it is authoritative; it is—finally—submission to something higher.

I wondered if this law were universal: What would a Western European, an American woman look like in a chador? Was there the sense (implied in the fact that none of the other great religions prescribed this dress code: their prophets were content to look upon women freed of this constraint) that it was only in the context of Islam (and the Middle East) that such a convention gathered the power and authenticity that gave to it the imprimatur of something ordered from above? There would be many more encounters with and reflections upon the Muslim women's dress in Iran. For now I was relieved that the strain in understanding this seeming (at first) brutal defacement of the female form—this strain had reversed itself and become, surprisingly, a revelation of order and, yes, beauty.

Alcoholism—German style—
Among Devout Muslims Travelling to Iran

As we were preparing to disembark there was some angry shouting, and it became clear that a German businessman (obviously a non-Muslim) who had boarded the plane in Istanbul had become excessively drunk and even obscene with some of the Muslim women on the plane. Finally a Muslim man ordered him to stop, and scorned him for his disgraceful behaviour, appearance, and odour. Indeed, although I had many times witnessed drunkenness, it was especially dramatic here among almost all Muslims (and therefore strict teetotalers) for their religion expressly had forbidden this 'pleasure' and here was a spectacle that seemed to give absolute credence to the wisdom of their prophet, for he was grotesque, an animal, senseless and in absolute violation of the laws which governed the conduct and atmosphere of this circumstance (on a plane with Muslims headed for revolutionary, Islamic Iran). I was able to view this condition of possession through the lens of Islam; it was as if God himself had arranged for us to see what distortion of the human soul is wreaked by alcohol consumed to the point of inebriation—arranged here in the disciplined, uncompromising light of Islam. In this moment one could not but agree that alcoholic substances were truly given over to demonic powers, for I believe I have never seen such a contrast between the drunk German and his fellow, Muslim passengers. The whole indulgent appetites of Western, de-mythologized man seemed cruelly yet appropriately exposed. At that moment if one were to gauge the laws of the universe according to what contributed to the harmony and upliftment of life, one could, without being a prophet, determine it was God's will that such activity was evil.

The Role of the Stewardess on Iran National Airlines

Once there was the Islamicizing of the government-owned airlines of Iran, instituted after the revolution, it became obvious that the whole rhythm and intent of the role of the stewardess (to give full comfort and service to the paying customer—the passenger) played upon the background of Islamic piety was strangely contrived, for clearly the invention and the style of this organization (hostessing on a plane) was Western. It was a subtle feeling, but nevertheless an unmistakable one: there was no alternative to the serving of meals, the announcing of various items in sequence to soothe and inform the passenger; Islam had arrived in a situation in which the traditions had already been set. Nothing could be substituted, for all passengers had been conditioned by this kind of treatment, and although one could imagine the whole thing as being rather arbitrary, there could be no reversal and revolutionizing of the decorum required by the stewardess, required to satisfy the customer. But all the while one felt how artificial it was here among Muslims and chadored (and presumably—at least is some cases—revolutionary) stewardesses. They were carrying out a sterile Western ritual; the food (and the number of meals) was excessive. It was as if everything would have to be rediscovered in the context of Islam; that is to say, the form, the style of service would have to be defined so that it naturally accorded with the spirit of Islam. In the mean time there was no substitute and one felt the clashing of myths in the stewardesses being forced (however conscious they were of this dissonance) to carry on with a tradition already set down and inherently out of synchrony with the vibration of Islam.

Islam de-emphasizes comfort, wealth, and luxury; perhaps on a truly

Islamic airplane the customers would be satisfied that God had arranged to get them to their destination, that for the sake of their own souls it was purely indulgent to give to them a service which they might not be spiritually entitled to. Islam constantly sanctions sacrifice and the elevation of the oppressed; while many live in poverty and hunger this act of receiving meals for merely sitting on a plane, and the constant solicitude of the stewardesses seemed to be an embarrassment to the simplicity and self-sufficiency required by Islam. At least this is the way I began to work out the problem as I instinctively felt the incommensurable facts of Western travel comfort and chadored Islamic stewardesses—on the way to Ayatollah Khomeini's Iran.

Praying while in Flight

Since Muslims pray five times a day there were a number of Muslims that had still to complete their afternoon prayer, and various Muslims would rise from their seats and, instead of going to the back of the plane to use the restrooms (as one expected was their purpose), would prostrate themselves in the narrow space that separated the final seats from the passageway behind, turning towards Mecca. This determination to complete one's duties as a Muslim in circumstances that did not lend themselves to that completion (after all Boeing did not design an airplane with the idea of building some sort of mini-mosque near the back)—such determination was very much part of the almost physical resilience and 'primitive' (I use that word in its strictly non-pejorative sense), timeless integrity of Islam.

Cigarette Smoking Among Muslims

Even when I encountered the Canadian Muslims that were travelling to Iran I was surprised at the proportion of heavy, compulsive smokers. Here on the plane to Tehran (we had joined hundreds more Muslims in Frankfurt, where we had been in transit) there was again the sense of addiction to something other than Allah. And my experiences in Iran (and the inordinate number of nicotine addicts that I met there) of necessity drew out from me a hypothesis about smoking in the context of Islam. It is essentially this: it was observable to me that many of those

Muslims who smoked appeared to do so with a slight self-consciousness, that is to say, while they inhaled and drew the smoke through their
lungs and withdrew the rolled, burning tobacco from their lips there was
some evidence of conflict somewhere. Now this conflict was not likely
understood by the psyche, but deep in the consciousness of the devout
Muslim smoker was some registration that he was perhaps violating
some inner albeit unformulated law of spiritual integrity. After all
Islam emphasized purity as well as piety, and the temple of the soul was
part of the design of Allah—and needing to be purified. It became clear
to me that perhaps the Muslim was more inclined to smoke than even
his secular counterpart. Why? Because of all the other proscriptions:
gambling, drinking, pork, sexual freedom—and the prescriptions: fasting, prayers, obedience to the Qur'an, the emulation of the behaviour
of the Prophet. There was, as I watched many Muslims (not all) who
smoked, the sense of compensation, as if in God's mercy He might just
permit this one indulgence, this one minor sin against the physiology.
While Mohammad had not forbidden cigarettes (after all the nicotine
demon was then still hidden from civilizations in the Middle East) still
there was the tacit understanding that one was encouraged not to smoke,
indeed, one was enjoined to abstain altogether. Still in a religion in
which everything else was legislated, codified, and formalized—with
regard to right and wrong—this absence of explicit and legal prohibition
constituted the licence to indulge, and there was almost the sense of an
orgy of delight, an orgy that drove off the energies of frustration that
may have built up in the denial to the appetites of other forms of
'pleasure' and freedom.

The sense of sin remained self-conscious, that is, it had not—at least
in many cases—transferred itself to the plane of intuition, where the
impulses of conscience become more immediately and spontaneously
discriminating, where one recognizes the laws of religion and the thou
shalt nots as being the systematized expression of a more universal Law,
the Law that leads to spiritual evolution, to higher consciousness, to the
awareness of something absolute. The Prophet had not said "no" to
tobacco: ergo, one could take it in whatever quantity one wished, and
even if one instinctively felt it was injurious to one's health—or even
spiritually unaesthetic—still, there it was; Allah had not denounced it,
and one thus was defended against the consequences that counted, i.e.
Judgement Day. It is the conception and not the perception that counts
—no matter what ugly sediment covers the delicate membrane of the
lungs as the nicotine continues to be absorbed into the body.

But the more sensitive of the Muslims who smoked did not entirely
escape from the knowingness that the microcosmic reality of man was
perhaps being slightly desecrated by this ritual, a ritual incidentally

that in its Middle Eastern and Muslim expression seemed, externally at least, as notoriously self-subjugating (determined by the need being fulfilled and the outward manner of feeding that need) as opium smoking —or the taking of any kind of drug on which dependence becomes acute. It became a ceremony of gratification of the senses, but inwardly something rebelled against the effects—and even the style of fulfillment, which of course was the worship of something other than God.

In any event what interested me was the high visibility of the smoker living within the idiom of Islam; it was a kind of tribute to Islam that these smokers stood out so much and appeared in this one act to be incongruent with the whole intention of their religion—which was one of submission to Allah and a war against the lower self (what the Prophet had called the "Greater Jihad"; the "Lesser Jihad" was the fight against the external enemy—these days, American and Soviet imperialism).

Of course I challenged and prodded various Muslims (this during my visit to Iran) about this matter of smoking, and some became extremely and irrationally defensive, employing all kind of casuistical arguments to extricate themselves from the natural revulsion their conscience (and even the physiology possesses a kind of voice of protest) felt in "being smoked" by a need they could not rise above. On the battlefield I would have a modified perception of this ritual; here on the plane however where life and death did not coalesce, the universe itself seemed to declare the judgement about tobacco. And even in the West I sensed there was, paradoxically (especially if we view the West as the Muslims do: a place of infidelity and animalistic indulgence) a much greater sensitivity to the inner and outer ecology of smoking; most Westerners were much more willing to be responsible to the non-smoker; here, until some edict was passed that enunciated the spiritual as opposed to the merely physical dangers of smoking (and only Ayatollah Khomeini could do this; then, as someone said to me, the tobacco trade would dry up in one day!), Muslims would continue to blithely blow their fumes in front of one's eyes, in spite of the subconscious (at least in many cases) knowledge that a minor sin was being committed against themselves and the rest of Creation.

And from the tone of this entry one can see the author has a bias against this drug. This comes however from a convincing perception that the actual light around an individual's face and body becomes obscured and in some sense clogged through continued and unbroken dependency upon nicotine. The very perfume of the soul is—at least on a physical level—dulled, and one perceives some kind of violent resistance going on within the body against the activity that is being forced upon it through this habitual feeding. The molecules that dance around one's countenance and which form the physical 'presence' and illuminated gestalt of the individual attenuate, wither, and even seem to become tiny corpses that keep the physical consciousness in a state of perpetual gloom; never do the fragile, fresh morning-rosed molecules of vitality manifest.

Of course there is the sensitivity that the non-smoker has towards the environment he must live in if others smoke. In this context the author reacts strongly—or rather finds his body reacting strongly—to the effects of burning tobacco. While steeping himself in Islam and surrounding himself with all the spiritual influences that accompanied the particular truths and applications of Islam, it always became ironical that he, a non-Muslim, was often driven away by the noxious influences that seemed merely to soil and stain the white scriptures of the Prophet's revelations.

On Muslim Surrender and Technological Progress

As we disembarked and touched the concrete of Mihrabad Airport, and as I gazed back at the Boeing 747 I wondered: with the absolute emphasis on surrender (Islam is derived from the root '*salama*' in Arabic, which means both surrender and peace) and Unity (*tauhid*) is it possible the Muslims must invent their own technology, for there was the sense of power and competitive urge, the lust of individual genius and intelligent aggression that seemed embodied in the form of this awesome machine? The consciousness that had created this airplane had been nurtured on the sense of conquest and striving, and therefore I had the intuition that Boeing 747's were the manifestation of Western non-surrendered intelligence— magnificent in its autonomy from mythology. Therefore I could not see how Islam (especially the resurgent form now expressing itself in Iran) could appropriate this form of technology (at least in this style, with its Rolls Royce engines and streamlined efficiency) without imaging itself with something that was foreign to its nature. Islam was an image of the imageless, but in that image the scrupulous regard for the imagelessness that it represented (Allah, the Absolute) seemed to demand a whole universe of attitude, value, and behaviour that would not tolerate forms of technology (or anything else) that had been the results of an antithetical image, especially when that image denied, at least implicitly, the existence of the imageless, and therefore had the stamp of the individual, the Renaissance urge for self-expression, for experience, for emancipation from inherited shibboleths of religious doctrine.

Of course the Iranians could not ignore the conveniences that sustained the externals of their existence—such as this Boeing 747 jet—but one felt the awful burden of attempting to recharge a religious system, a pure and classical mythology, when all around was the impress of the forms of a system—Western scientific secularism—that implied the obsolescence of such mythologies. IBM, Chase Manhattan, Exxon consciousness was something that emerged out of a matrix that was fundamentally anti-Muslim (at least in spirit, for according to Islamic belief all beings are '*muslim*,' that is, existing by virtue of their submission to the Divine Will; only man can stop being a Muslim, for he can defy the laws that brought him into being, the laws which sustain the whole universe: he can even deny his origin in God)—because all these American firms had their inspiration in a constant search for progress, profit, and control: surrender, piety, and reverence for a Creator were not the working elements in success. For a Muslim these came ahead of everything else.[4]

The essence of the argument: if Islam had continued to dominate the Middle East and much of Europe what would have been the forms of technology it spawned? Would there be some intrinsic difference between a Muslim-inspired airplane and secularist-inspired vehicle for defying space and time? As it is, having absorbed the climate of Islam in Iran and having come to know the intimate workings of the revolution I discerned the great struggle all Muslims would have (at least those who agreed with Ayatollah Khomeini that Islam must rule the politics and not just the mosques of the Middle East) in developing their revolution in the midst of the fruits of Western technological progress. Technology did not in this vision seem as neutral as I had thought, although on the battlefield I would have cause to see how American tanks could be transformed into weapons of the Prophet—provided that a portrait of "The Imam" was affixed to one side of the tank and displayed prominently to the aggressive and infidel forces which opposed the purification of world Muslims.

---

[4] Western readers should be aware of course of the superiority of Islamic civilization to Western civilization for a period of seven centuries, and that a large and important part of that superiority was expressed in science: "...one is struck by the magnitude as well as importance of the contributions made by the Muslims to the various branches of science... The magnitude of these achievements is so vast that it is giving rise to another tendency among the historians of science. It is incomprehensible to them that the Arabs who were so backward and ignorant in the centuries preceding the advent of Islam could have become so enlightened and scholarly in such a short time after adopting the new faith." (M. M. Sharif, *A History of Muslim Philosophy* (Wiesbaden: Otto Harrassowitz, 1966), II, 1277.)

A Tanzanian Muslim's Explanation for
the Anti-American Rhetoric

For some time I had been aware of an exaggerated (and, at times downright fictitiously based) accusatory stance towards the United States on the part of the Islamic Government, emphatically represented in the rhetoric of Ayatollah Khomeini himself. Yes, the United States had plotted the coup against Mossadegh, had trained and supervised the hated SAVAK, had discussed the possibility of another military coup against the provisional revolutionary government, had generated hostility towards the Islamic leadership of Ayatollah Khomeini,[5] and yet, now it seemed that the constant reference to the plots of imperialist America did not coincide with the actual reasons for what was happening in Iran today. The terrible assassinations of government leaders (in one case seventy-two government officials were killed in one bomb explosion) were said to be the work of "American agents." This just was not a credible explanation for the indigenous opposition to the present regime, especially the activities of the Mujahaddin e Khalq, who were generally thought to have been responsible for the violent, sometimes suicidal attacks on religious leaders and even civilians who were known to support the regime.

I had, however, misunderstood the intent of this rhetoric, and an intelligent, shrewd explanation was provided to me by an articulate Tanzanian Muslim. I had felt that this obsessive concern with the plots of the United States—and the hatred of its government—was an incorrect assessment of the spiritual realities of the revolution: after all, a revolution made in the name of the Absolute, made in the name of God and righteousness would necessarily have to manifest that level of purity and wholeness that could only come from the deeds, from the consciousness of the individual members of that society.[6] To blame all the misfortunes on some external power seemed to misdirect the energy towards something which prevented the Muslim from taking responsi-

---

[5] Recently, it was revealed in the *New York Times* (and other newspapers, including the *International Herald Tribune*) that the United States (through the C.I.A.) is covertly helping to finance exiled Iranian paramilitary forces that are opposed to the present government, in Turkey, France and Egypt; see: David Kline, "Bani-Sadr fears U.S. aid to Iranian dissidents will hurt his cause," the Toronto *Globe and Mail*, April 22, 1982.

There is also evidence that the U.S. has taken steps to woo Iraq and take its side against Iran in the war; see: Thomas A. Dine and Aaron D. Rosenbaum, "Steer Clear of Iraq," the Manchester *Guardian*, April 11, 1982.—Ed.

[6] "God changes not what is in a people, until they change what is in themselves." Qur'an, Sura XIII, 12. (Passages quoted from the Qur'an, except where otherwise indicated, have been taken from: Arthur J. Arberry, *Koran Interpreted* (New York: McMillan, 1955).)

bility for his own destiny, his own contribution to the problems—in so far as he himself was not yet pure. The Prophet himself (and even Imam Khomeini) had counselled Muslims to work on themselves, to conduct a revolution against the Satan within; only through such work could a larger, Islamic revolution succeed:

One who seeks to purify a society will not be able to achieve one's goal if one's self is not purgated and purified.[7]

And yet, the overwhelming impression I had in following the revolution of late and even landing here in Tehran was that the single most threatening force in the world was the United States, that the enemy was fundamentally external, that ceaseless and adamant enmity towards the United States was central to the success of the revolution. It all seemed too simple, and worse: a deception. Was it not the positive rather than the negative emotion that could generate the spiritual power necessary to draw out from Allah that grace that would lead to success?

The Tanzanian explained that the antipathy towards the United States (the antipathy that was in excess to the real danger posed by U.S. policies and strategies) was itself a strategy, a propagandistic device that actually strengthened the revolution. His explanation went like this: the United States had installed the Shah (after the coup in 1953), trained the torturers of SAVAK, and proceeded to impose its culture upon the people of Iran, gradually dominating the tastes and values of the people. The influence of the United States and all the values and conditioning which went with that influence had to be totally extirpated from the soul of the people. That de-conditioning could only take place through hatred of all that smacked of U.S. influence. The hate was generated to remove all traces of domination, to reverse the tendencies of the people (from McDonald's hamburgers to television sitcoms to total dependence on American technological expertise) so that the Iranians created their own culture, their own values—which would of necessity have to be Islamic. According to this Muslim (who spoke non-defensively and with considerable sagacity and calm) the policy of the United States had not changed; to relent from this campaign of hatred of the United States would mean the probable re-assertion of U.S. might and the cultural wasteland (according to Islamic criteria) that prevailed during the time of the Shah. Besides, he said, Imam Khomeini himself has declared that "what had been achieved thus far in Iran is only a breeze of Islam." It would take twenty years before there is a truly Islamic society. Iran may

---

[7] Ayatollah Khomeini, speech of September 20, 1979, in *Imam Khomeini's Views on Ethics and Spiritualities* (Tehran: Council for the Celebrations of the Third Anniversary of the Victory of The Islamic Revolution, 1982), p. 5.

appear extremist in its views, he said, but this extremism is working against the long-standing habituated sensibilities of the people who are utterly alienated from the impulses which would restore Islamic culture—as a result of the Shah's (to the delight of commercial and industrial interests in the United States) determination to destroy the hold of Islam and substitute the materialist/capitalist values and goods of the West.

What existed now was the ABC of Islam, but the desperate need for self-sufficiency, the need for autonomous identity was not taking place within a neutral condition of awareness. The people had been soaked in Western and especially American culture; it had even reached down into the unconscious of the people so that even a devout Muslim might be unaware of how much he still was a victim of this influence. To adopt a friendly attitude towards the United States, to welcome diplomatic relations, and to reduce the invective against American imperialism was to seriously undermine this whole process of cultural transformation. Only by firm opposition, supported by the implication that the United States was behind all the troubles of the new regime—or most of them—could there be the gradual eradication of the impressions of the West and therefore the ripening receptivity to Islamic impressions, impressions that were, in the minds of the leaders of the country, the impressions of God.

Thus this was an implied admission of deliberate dissimulation on the part of the Iranian government, but this strategy was the functional equivalent of truth in so far as it led to the possibility of inculcating that much more efficiently the values that were considered to be divine. It was possible to draw the inference that it was God Himself who countenanced, nay even recommended, this propaganda. To bring the people to Islam, to build Islamic consciousness: anything that would hasten this Allah-ordained circumstance was justified.

Visit to Islamic High Schools

On my first day in Iran I visited a high school for boys, and a high school for girls. There were a number of impressions I had: the girls, while projecting their deep Islamic faith and decorum nevertheless, as they chose a spokesman, and I received the translation, exhibited that universal female, adolescent mood of laughter, shyness, togetherness as they whispered among themselves and displayed their spontaneous self-consciousness, revelling in the unusual circumstance of being interviewed by a Western, non-Muslim writer. But as I gazed at those faces (and within the chador the configuration of uniqueness—against the black outlines of their dress—becomes so vivid) I experienced the ancient beauty that blessed the appearance of the Iranian female. I might have been imagining this, but I experienced the sensation that the soul that inhabited each one of these creatures was happily free of that adolescent scourge of shallowness and conforming mindlessness that dominates the world of the North American adolescent, a world that does not ennoble nor revere the traditions, the mythology of the Tribe. Adolescent life is in our culture bereft of commanding models of behaviour which young people seek to emulate: a rock star like Alice Cooper is likely to be a more exciting image than that of, say, St. Augustine. Here in Iran at this high school for girls the faces were set in a mould that fitted the archetype of the revolution, and one recoiled naturally at the idea of noon hour sock hops. Was it just wishful thinking—or perceiving—on my part, or was it part of the design of a Creator that these girls were spared the excesses of a culture which virtually turned over its authority to the individualism of the adolescent? To be sure, one felt, as in many other instances, a certain imposed limitation on the degree of spontaneity that was permitted in an inter-action with a foreigner—to the point of arbitrariness; naturally abiding by the rules of Islam did not permit the discovery that perhaps might be made were the impulses of life itself allowed to have their say. But within this restriction there was an order and one had to respect the dignity that seemed to flourish within such order and rectitude.

At the second school (we were told that we had gone to the wrong school: the revolution was still in a state of improvisation: the systems of efficiency were yet to be developed) the girls had been prepared to see us, and before the obligatory mass slogan-shouting—from "Allahu Akbar!" (God is Great) to "Death to America! Death to the Soviet Union!"—I had spotted the classrooms where the girls were gathering before coming outside to perform. Furtively, faces would appear just behind the cur-tains, and there was a considerable exuberant anticipation and much giggling as I felt the energy coiling itself, ready to release itself at the command of the headmistress. When they did gather in the courtyard to chant their ideology they were a surprisingly disciplined and im-pressive group, with a genuine religious power and conviction that would fearlessly march onto a battlefield if that was demanded. That girlish delight and excitement that was bursting inside the classroom as they huddled before making their entrance had been transformed into a psychological determination, a spiritual wakefulness that sang its joy and devotion into my consciousness. They were fully politicalized; they seemed fully Islamicized. This was the generation that would make the revolution blossom. Martyrdom was close at hand, for the daughter of

34

assassinated President Mohammed Ali Rajai, was one of the prominent students at the school, whom I had the occasion to talk with after the assembly.

Praying in a Mosque Inside a Boys' High School

At the boys' Islamic high school we were taken into the mosque which was part of the center of learning within the school. As it was noon the guests (those who were Muslims), the teachers, and the students, washed themselves, removed their shoes, and then prayed. Attending a private school for boys which was strongly Anglican I had been forced to take chapel services twice a day. I recall the level of participation at that time in these services, the decided absence of any reverence or intuitive feeling for the homilies we were served, or even the hymns we were obliged to sing. Here, however, as I scanned the faces I saw only a handful of students (out of perhaps 350) who were reminiscent of my fellow students, for in contrast to the others, these boys performed their movements of prostration with the most perfunctory obeisance, and—as we had done at old St. George's—placed their minds on other topics than the one at hand: Allah. But for the others there was a remarkable investment in the solitary act of honouring their God, for when a child or young man is contriving his piety it is obvious to the discerning on-looker. I am quite confident of spotting the faked Islamic submitter, and rather than formally carrying out this midday duty, many of the boys I watched turned within themselves, into a world in which they genuinely gained the satisfaction of communicating with a power beyond them-selves—or so is the conclusion one must draw from the fervency yet the serenity with which they spontaneously performed their rites. The con-sciousness of the mosque changed as the ritual continued, until one felt there was a kind of beneficence that charged the air. And these were mostly—apart from the Muslim guests that had accompanied me—adolescent boys. Certainly there was still the thought as to whether it might be premature to ask so much from someone so young—that is, to ask them to become totally absorbed in the Qur'an, in the world of Islam—and yet there was the sense, perhaps as with no other major religion, of the possibility of doing this without seriously inhibiting the instincts, the impulses of youthfulness. Still, I said to myself: it is a particular kind of historical situation that is reinforcing this surrender to Islam, since there has been a revolution, there is a war, and there is a peerless leader who is thought to embody the truth of Islam.

In spite of the success of the religious program within the school (I should not call it a religious program: it was the very *raison d'être* of the school), in spite of the apparent happiness of the students there the stark, barren, and institutionalized aesthetics disturbed me, for apart from the multitude of posters of the revolution and the Imam, there was almost a complete absence of colour, of texture, of warmth. Absolutely no attention had been placed upon the decor of the school: quite obviously surrender to Allah did not bring with it a growing awareness of The Beautiful, for the sensory deprivation a student would experience here would, at least to my imagination, be almost detrimental to his learning efficiency. It was not even properly monastic. There simply was no sensitivity to the environment, no design, no awareness of the interaction between the human being and the physical forms within which he moved. It was a destitution that indicated that Allah was without artistic sensibility, and I knew that somewhere spirituality could not be the excuse for aesthetic obtuseness. How I yearned—and it would not have cost much—to brighten, to enliven the environment where these sweet children learned about Creation. Austerity should be deliberate, and not the outcome of simply a failed antenna for beauty. The rejoicing would have to be entirely from within. For the rest, the school could be converted into a shooting location for Ken Kesey's "One Flew Over the Cuckoo's Nest."

Of course one might explain this away by saying that an obsession with spiritual, i.e. invisible, truth necessarily obscures, especially among a class of people who have not inherited (most of the boys and girls attending these schools came from the poorer section of Tehran) a tradition of art and culture that emphasizes the felicities of exterior beauty, obscures from the vision the inessentials; for after all one can pray, one can serve, one can martyr oneself, one can eat, one can perform one's duties without adherence to the laws of visual artistic integrity. Furthermore most of Iran consists of such flat, arid land which does not invite the soul to contemplate the richness of vegetation, the verdant beauty that is so familiar to those populations accustomed to trees, lakes, and flowers. The Shah lived in an extravagant and surfeited aesthetic style: perhaps the absence of light and play of colour is an unconscious reaction to the potential corruptibility of the instinct for what is beautiful. Could the teachers at this school still admire the Chagals hanging on the walls of the Shah's palace? It poses some interesting questions, and I suppose one should not push too far the idea that with the sense of the wholeness of life (the essence of the religious point of view) comes an awareness of and desire for allowing the creation around one to become organized so as to let Beauty shine through. In the mean time the stirring speech delivered by the headmaster of the school, a turbaned member of the *'ulama* (clergy), perfectly summarized the essence of the Imam's priorities, with its denunciation of American and Soviet imperialism and its celebration of the eternal Truth of Islam. The students seemed to understand, and there were becoming good Muslims who would die for their religion and their leader. Perhaps the negligence of the interior of their school was something that would just distract their attention. But my fetish was there, nevertheless; and I was not about to be cured.

Thoughts on Religious Tradition
which Circumscribes the Freedom of Communication

Since the woman in Islam is, because of her well-defined role, not permitted to range too freely in her responses to a man who is unrelated to her, it becomes permissible to ask the question: where does innocence really end, and desire, temptation begin? Cannot a man and woman interact without any a priori ideas of what is possible to discover in this connection? I remember catching the eyes of a fourteen year old girl in the playgrounds of the school, holding her stare and experiencing the objective delight that both our souls felt in that intermingling—a delight that had little to do with the fact of my manhood, her budding woman-hood. A meaning (and I should point out here that of any peoples I have met, the Iranians have an extraordinary capacity for innocent recep-tivity, for spontaneous warmth and tenderness) structured itself in that ingenuous ease of eye contact, but then, when it (the meaning of that contact) seemed to be articulating itself (we were two souls recognizing our universal closeness to one another, discovering our specific feelings as our uniquenesses met), she recovered her formal reticence and dropped her eyes away from me. And yet I wondered how a strongly individual-istic girl in these surroundings would fare. Has not God created certain souls to assert their autonomy, their essential selfhood outside of the constraints of dogma? But then I thought of the alternative—complete licence, the absence of divine laws—and I realized that even such an innately irrepressible creature (and I had seen one in this assemblage of chadored teenagers) would still learn something in having to have her bountifulness of personality discipline itself through the medium of

Islam, and perhaps something would compensate for the slight loss of individualism. I was grateful that the forces at work in this situation allowed this question to come to the surface, for it indicated the pressures of ultimate meaning and value that were making Iran and, through its revolution, Islam, the basis for an allegorical play. Here in Iran life was mixing with death, time with eternity, good with evil, and the stakes—immortality, the resurrection of an Islamic civilization to counterpoint the West—were of the highest order. Secular man was meeting his Nemesis.

A Bus Ride Through Tehran

One couldn't help noticing that the dominant sense in Tehran was that things were in a state of idleness, that great numbers of the people had no living connection to the revolution, that so many of these people simply whittled away their time wandering the streets. Indolence: it was a disease that had reached epidemic proportions. How to rouse these people, how to inflame them with the spirit of the revolution—these were questions of acute importance to those now governing Iran. Their very torpor drained away the sacred energies needed to win the war, and to build a civilization on Islamic values. Of course with a work force of eleven million people, three million were unemployed, and this was a devastating statistic for the regime to deal with. With all the enthusiasm for the revolution that I had been exposed to it was a shock to realize that so many millions of Iranians had, in a sense, not been touched by the cataclysms of that last three years, or if they had, they had managed to anaesthetize themselves; thus they were simply like children who had become bored playing in their sandboxes.

Visiting a "Construction Jihad" Site

The revolution has launched a building program that creates a purely Islamic context in which hundreds of people in certain villages gather together under the direction of some appointed guardian of the revolution (selected by Imam Khomeini) and construct a building without any assistance from foreigners. We visited a hospital being built in Veramin, sixty kilometres south of Tehran; the people had been working on this project for months and it was still being completed. While we walked through the partially finished building we were asked to note that "the people" did this with their own hands, and that the "spirit of Jihad"[8] in this situation meant the people were motivated by Islam and the leadership of Imam Khomeini. We were told that an American company could build the structure in less than one month. However even if it took the people of Veramin a year it would be much more spiritually successful since it is not the efficiency which goes into constructing a building, it is the consciousness that is important. Here every brick was laid with a sense of devotion to Islam and therefore the hospital possessed (or would possess) an integrity absent from a hospital built without a sense of surrender to God. I wondered whether this same intention could create the generations of religious adoration that manifested in Westminster Abbey, where the reverence of the worker was seen in the consciousness produced by the architectural form. The mosques of course were a magnificent testimony to the power of Islam to evoke forms of architecture that glorified Allah; however one wondered whether that impulse was sophisticated and vital enough now to soar towards the transcendent. Things still seemed primitive, inchoate, inarticulate. However the people were genuinely proud of what they had done, and their commitment to Islam and to Imam Khomeini was indisputable. Was there some basis in fact for the claim that the quality of motivation of the builder could play a decisive role in the actual consciousness that finally expressed itself in the form of the building? There was every suggestion at least that such a conception fitted into the design of the Creator, and one would have to wait to see whether the Gothic cathedral complex applied here. I rather thought that it would; Allah would have to reward such enthusiasm and sacrifice.

Celebrating in the Veramin Mosque

We walked through a shouting, hand-gripping gauntlet of Veramin Muslims on our way to the mosque. There before the prayers we were served tea and cakes and treated to a chorus of young girls singing revolutionary songs, and afterwards some recitation from the Qur'an and some fiery political diatribes against the United States and the Soviet Union. I never quite got used to the idea of the mosque, the place of worship, as being for a communal gathering, where there were no

---

[8] *Jihad*: the Muslim struggle against the visible enemy in the battlefield.

distinctions of class and wealth, where in this holy shrine a common denominator of brotherhood was the dominant tone, and where cracking walls, unpainted ceilings, and even deterioration of the interior of the mosque seemed to matter much less than the consolidating presence of each Muslim brother. And in totality the ambience seemed to point towards this interrelatedness, although one could well suggest that the interior of a traditional Catholic church, or, for that matter, Buddhist temple, was more conducive to the flight of the soul towards the celestial regions of heaven. Nevertheless the religious intention was there. It was just that it came from the earth, was rooted also in the body, and included everyone who was willing to pray. Only in the height of the prayers, however, was there the sense of deep absorption in what was Absolute; before and afterwards the conversation, the atmosphere here easily accommodated itself to topics and feelings that were not explicitly religious.

A Division in the Shi'ite Community

One of the Muslims from Canada told me of a controversy over the status of the Twelve Imams, the divinely ordained guardians of Islam according to the Shi'a. Apparently many of the Shi'a community near Toronto believed the Imams—like the Prophet—were made of light. Such a conception of the Imams was, according to a scholar brought into the community by the president of the Shi'a community, incorrect and even detrimental to understanding the nature of spiritual reality. Of course such denial of the divine perfection of the physical structure of the Imams irritated and hurt the sensitivies of those believers in miracles and the president of the Shi'a community suffered considerable opprobrium as a result. It very much reminded me of a statement of Ludwig Wittgenstein (this in response to a comment by a student, on the Modernist movement within the Church): "People who call themselves Modernists are the most deceived of all. I will tell you what Modernism is like: in *The Brothers Karamazov* the old father says that the monks in the nearby monastery believe that the devils have hooks to pull people down into Hell; 'Now,' says the old father, 'I can't believe in those hooks.' That is the same sort of mistake that Modernists make when they misunderstand the nature of symbolism."[9]

[9] Rush Rhees, ed., *Ludwig Wittgenstein: Personal Recollections* (Oxford: Basil Blackwell, 1981), p. 122.

40

Indeed even the Prophet himself in a well-known *hadith* (the sacred tradition of sayings reputed to have been spoken by the Prophet and his family during his lifetime and recorded by those around him) has given support to this literalist interpretation of his own physical purity. His grandson, Imam Hassan, is reported to have said:

I heard my grandfather, the Prophet of God, declare: "I was created from the Light of God, the Glorious and Exalted, and my family was created from my light."[10]

Now light here may refer to absolute Being, that his very being was created in the Being of God, that his own being gave perfection to his offspring.

The scholar in question was a blind Lebanese professor who had taught at Harvard and was currently at the University of Toronto. He was one of the most respected Muslim intellectuals in the Western world, and unquestionably one of the most devout members of the Shi'ite community. Yet, despite his piety and erudition he ultimately saw himself as the final authority on matters related to Scripture, and one tended in conversation with him to sense he was blind to a form of communication that might actually be a revelation to him. He also tended to discount the more miraculous and spectacular aspects of Islam, those elements of belief that might create superstition, or a too unearthly vision of Islam. Thus the professor's discounting of the transparent nervous system of the Prophet and the Imams. One felt in the narration of the story of the president and the scholar the actual devastation to the vulnerable side of those who professed a contrary belief to that of the professor.

There is a kind of final intuitive grace and power that comes with what the medieval theologian Tertullian said, namely that: "I believe because it is impossible." Some ideas that are associated with religious truths can be comprehended only by the suspension completely of profane intelligence. The Prophet may not have been made of light, but to deny this belief to others, even if one feels such a belief is harmful to the proper reception of Islam, is a step to be taken with the greatest of discretion and delicacy. I would have cause to sense the at times arbitrary judgements of truth by the professor during my three weeks in Iran, this, despite the fact that he possessed perhaps the most remarkable insights into Islam of anyone there and was a scholar who knew the Bible perfectly, having been a devout Christian for fifteen years before returning to the Muslim faith.

[10] Javad Nurbakhsh, *Traditions of the Prophet* (New York: Khaniqahi-Nimatullahi Publications, 1981), p. 40.

But the rift in the Shi'ite community had never really healed after that, and the president of the community had continued to bear the censure of those believers whose faith had been violated by the more moderate and sensible interpretations of the scholar.

Observations of the Prime Minister of Iran: Mir Hossein Musavi

Prime Minister Musavi addressed us one morning at our Hilton Hotel (and many Muslims had protested at the luxury of the hotel and the sumptuous meals, declaring such comfort to be *taghooti*, that is, anti-Islamic: as long as there are others suffering one cannot afford to enjoy such luxury). He recounted Iranian history according to the Muslim viewpoint and delineated the ways in which the Shah had attempted to de-spiritualize Iran, to weaken the power of Islam, to exalt the values and ideas of pre-Islamic Iran.

Musavi emphasized that the removal of Islam from politics was a deliberate and systematic strategy carried out by the Shah and the colonialists. He then described the characteristics of Imam Khomeini as those which justified his leadership: he was the embodiment of what Islam stood for; no leader had been closer to his people in 1400 years (since the Prophet); Imam Khomeini had revitalized the people's consciousness of their proper destiny, that the real source of power was Islam and the Qur'an, and that now the people understood this.

There were more important things than standard of living, than in having factories running smoothly. The important thing was to make these factories "our own," so that the Iranians became entirely self-sufficient and gained the confidence necessary to make them independent of all foreign influence. The factories must belong to the people. The people would be prepared to fast so as not to deviate from the slogan of "neither East nor West." For over one hundred years the Iranians had been bombarded by Western values; now the culture was to become one hundred percent Islamic. Only through this orientation would the people of Iran find their proper dignity.

He then excoriated the Western press for its biased reporting of the revolution. Zionism and imperialist arrogance controlled what was said about the revolution, and this combination made it necessary to always portray Iran in the most hostile light. No mention, he said, was ever made of the sacrifices of the people, the courage of the martyrs. All the pictures show the revolution as savage, bloody, and destructive.

42

There was a deliberate intention to ignore the real meaning of Islam. He then gave the example of the bravery of the people, where a twelve year old boy and an eighty year old man would insist on going to the war front. The soldiers ("brothers") were fighting in the day and worshipping at night. This indomitable will, this willingness to be martyred was simply the result of the spiritual power of Islam. The "world devourers" would never understand this, for they sought only to manipulate the events of the world through means that were amoral, through motives that opposed absolutely the dictate of Islam, the laws of Allah. "We regard our revolution as the prelude to world revolution" was the most dramatic affirmation of the confidence of the Prime Minister.

Musavi denied that Iran was trying to expand its territory of influence. Export of the revolution meant simply the enlivening of true Islam and the consequent realization by Muslims in the Middle East that their countries were not Islamic. The revolution spreading across Iran's borders was the spontaneous and natural result of an authentic understanding of Islam; it would be Allah himself who would bring about the export of the revolution—through the instrumentality of devout Muslims.

But whatever his rhetoric, Hossein Musavi spoke quietly, and with considerable self-assurance and aplomb. Since much rhetoric was fierce and hostile coming from Iran's leaders it was peculiar—or rather, disarming—to hear Musavi speak the convictions of his government and yet within such calm and even serenity. Musavi was a natural; and his heart easily integrated itself with his mind. He was no fanatic, yet his surrender to Imam Khomeini and Islam was absolute. Still I felt it was a good sign that a leader could emerge—after all the assassinations— with so much inner strength and a kind of purity of intelligence (measured by the subtle amalgam of intensity and detachment that projected itself in his manner). Whatever one felt about the content of his ideas nevertheless it was undeniable this was a good, noble, utterly honest human being. Nothing angular; if there was a grace somewhere in this revolution, certainly Musavi was standing in that grace.

Celebration and Rally at the Martyr's Cemetery: Beheshte Zahra

Perhaps half a million people had gathered on this afternoon to celebrate the third anniversary of the revolution. Chanting in unison their allegiance to Imam Khomeini, denouncing the superpowers, and radiating their enthusiasm for the revolution, the people seemed lifted on a wave of undiscriminating devotion and energy: were they meant to see the world in the more complex way it really was? Perhaps not. After all what was essential was to understand three things: first, that God wanted an Islamic revolution; second, that Imam Khomeini was the embodiment of what God desired in an Islamic leader; and three, that evil was whatever opposed that desire of God (i.e. the Islam promulgated and acted out by the Imam). To see the world allegorically as a great play of light versus dark, good versus evil—this against the background of Shi'a martyrdom where, as the poster proclaimed: "'Ashura is now; Karbala is the whole world."[11]—this became necessary in order to supplant the images left impressed upon the people by the Shah and his American supporters. The cleansing had to be simple; there was no room for sophisticated analysis. Awaken the people to the glorious message of the Qur'an; make them see that the struggle for justice and truth takes place outwardly as well as inwardly (i.e. in the struggles of 'politics'), and give them the simple images which will deface all those which might qualify their ardour, their intention of total sacrifice.

Standing on a platform overlooking these fervent believers and soldiers of Allah I felt that rush of energy that comes (at least in my own scrutiny of the human soul) when there is ultimately something right and truthful at the heart of a certain response to existence. However much the people were blind to the more subtle relationships of cause and effect that operated in the cosmos (and even in politics) there was a justification in their black-and-white, Manichaean vision of things, for in this manner they achieved their purpose for living; they achieved some awareness that the pulsation of the universe itself vindicated the revelations of the Prophet and a time had come for the full revival of Islam and an Islamic civilization. All the faults, all the alarming simplicities, all the sheer distortions could not eradicate the validity of the main theme of their intentions, which was surrender to God and the overcoming of evil. Whether there were perfect candidates for setting up these archetypes (i.e. whether there were people and forces in the political world which were out and out evil; whether the Iranian citizen could say he represented pure good) remained to be seen. But standing there feeling the energy that stormed towards me I could sense something lifting up this people, and the quality of that supportive vibration was pure.

[11] 'Ashura: the tenth day of Muharram, the first month of the Islamic year; the day of the martyrdom of Imam Hussein, the son of the first Imam, Ali, at Karbala in Iraq. On 'Ashura the Shi'ite participates in the tragedy at Karbala, and he identifies himself with the holiness of the martyrs who have given their lives for Allah.

*Impressions of the Interior Minister,
Hojjatoleslam Nategh Noury*

The turbaned leader of the Beheshte Zahra rally was the Interior Minister, Noury. Noury was a member of the *'ulama* and a personality with tremendous force and command. He carried the brightness of not only his convictions, but the brightness of his own integrated selfhood. In shaking his hand and looking into his eyes there was the evidence of a heart that drew upon the resources of goodness, harmony, and vitality. He was fearless and, in the furrowed wisdom of his face, happy. Again, a good sign that there was something healthy happening to the revolution. If something is fundamentally wrong, such persons would be less likely to rise to the top. (Calculating of course that the moral intention of this revolution bears some relationship to the teleological intention of the universe—i.e. is God supporting—for the most part—this revolution and its aims? Noury symbolized the positivities of the revolution.) For the people his authority to represent them resided not just in his religious credentials but in the successful way in which he presented the results of his religious commitment: he was blessed.

Stories of the Imam

While driving back to the hotel with my translator, the guide for all members of the Canadian delegation to Iran, Reza Husseini, I learned of an incident concerning Imam Khomeini which gave sustenance to the notions of the Imam's special sensitivity; it might be called cosmic intuition. The morning that Mohammed Ali Rajai, the successor to Abolhassan Bani-Sadr as President of the Islamic Republic of Iran, was assassinated, Imam Khomeini asked his son Ahmad to send for Rajai, for, as the Imam said, "I miss Rajai." Now Khomeini had never uttered this request before, and it was calculated that just shortly after that moment Rajai was martyred. The implication? That Imam Khomeini makes his calculations according to the computations that are taking place in the universe; somewhere the universe was anticipating the death of the President; this impulse touched the Imam and he translated his feeling into a request to see Rajai. The "missing" of Rajai was because he was about to leave the earth; Khomeini was thus aligned with that anticipation and the consequent results.

A visit to a hospital for men and boys who had suffered wounds during
the revolution against the Shah, and those who had been injured in the
war revealed the inexhaustible commitment of thousands of young men
for martyrdom. Each wounded patient recounted how he had just
missed making it to martyrdom; that his friends had been luckier (that
is, had successfully lost their lives for Allah); that his one regret was that
he had not achieved his goal.

A thirteen-year-old boy, Abdul Reza, told how he had been guarding
the mosque at Dezful when the Iraqis attacked the mosque and killed
ten of his friends. He had apparently gained a taste for martyrdom
during the revolution when he was just ten years old. There, seeing the
Shah's troops gun down the people, he sensed that there was something
beautiful in dying, and that the love that his leader gave him for Islam
filled him with a feeling that guaranteed his ascent to heaven if he was
brave and surrendered at the same time. He had gone to the war front
when he was twelve; learning that the mosque was essential in obtaining
victory he vowed to protect this holy building, and when the Iraqis came
he fought until felled by a bullet into his neck which left him paralyzed
in both the upper and lower parts of his body.

I asked him how he learned to become a martyr, that is, how to gain
the faith that makes martyrdom and its promises real. Abdul told me
that Imam Khomeini and the feeling he received from the Qur'an and
Islam gave him the faith he knew was his protection against evil, the
faith that would take away all fear, and leave him, according to his
own description, feeling no pain and out of time and space—yet fully
conscious. The whole world, he said, was changing: there were his
friends dying around him, and he could sense the mixture of remorse
and joy that accompanied the fact of the martyrdom of his friends. His
parents, he said, were proud of his contribution to Islam.

Valiallah ("friend of Allah") was an older victim (or, should we
say, beneficiary—spiritually) of the revolution. Twenty-one years old,
Valiallah had been tortured by SAVAK and then had joined, after the
overthrow of the Shah, the Revolutionary Guards. He was sent to
Kurdistan where he spent eight months fighting against the Kurdish
Democratic Party which sought, according to him, to destroy the cities
there, wishing to sabotage the revolution. It was the Iraqis that had
supported the rebellion there, deliberately trying to deceive the people
into believing that the Islamic revolution was trying to take away their
rights. As it happened most of the people supported the Revolutionary

Guards, but nevertheless the number of martyrs was high. He had spent the whole time in mortal danger (or should we say, on the verge of immortal bliss) and one night the rebels opened fire on him and his friends, killing thirty-five Revolutionary Guards. Previously one of his friends had been martyred but the body was never returned. He survived the attack but was left, as Abdul was, paralyzed from the neck down. Like Abdul he too regretted his inadmittance into Paradise. Asked about fear, Valiallah replied his only fear was that *he might not get martyred.*

These warriors from *jihad* were treated as heroes who were linked up to the armies of the Prophet; the nation honoured them, revered them next to the martyrs whose bodies lay in Beheshte Zahra Cemetery. Their status was derived almost entirely from their having been wounded in that great revival of the glories of Islam, and they lived in this formal esteem. I thought of the contrast with those American soldiers returning from Vietnam, a war which could not be said to be holy and for the cause of Allah. But even the victorious North Vietnamese did not include the idea of eternity and blessed peace in their conception of bravery; the individual lived for a social not a metaphysical end. The individuality of the Iranian Muslim was drowned in the ocean of Allah; the Vietnamese Marxist's individuality was effaced in the duty to the people. One aimed at the transcendental; the other at the purely material. When the West understood the categorical difference in temperament between the revolutionary who seeks to do the will of Allah and he who seeks to do the will of utopian socialism, it will begin to act with more wisdom in devising its strategies in the Middle East. Alexander Haig would have to visit with these wounded soldiers to understand the enemy with whom he was dealing. West Point did not hold copies of the Bible over their tanks, nor did a picture of Ronald Reagan get affixed on the front of the tank. The Qur'an and the Imam, however, were talismans applied in just this powerful way, and besides, all the martyrs stood around invisible to the human eye, giving the benefit of their deaths to the cause of the revolution and the war.

This at least was the thinking, nay, the experience of the Iranian Muslim devoted to the revolution in the manner prescribed by Imam Khomeini.

Jihad *Versus* Murder in the Cathedral—*a Difference*

On the bus back to the hotel I engaged in a discussion about martyrdom with a Muslim from the United States, a Pakistani-born writer who had previously written a book about Ayatollah Khomeini. He said that the martyrdom of a Muslim is not a passive martyrdom like Thomas à Becket's as depicted in T. S. Eliot's *Murder in the Cathedral*; martyrdom in the line of the Imams, especially Imam Hossein, was a martyrdom of striving against injustice, a martyrdom which came in the act of opposing evil, even a martyrdom in which one slew for the sake of Allah. Only in this form of martyrdom could there be said to be an actualization of the intent and meaning of martyrdom. The more secret mechanics of martyrdom at the point of death were less understood, for clearly when one is being consecrated by the ritual of death into some kind of immortal kingdom of bliss there must be the right approach. And here, Ayatollah Khomeini's description of the attributes of the martyr deserves to be quoted in full:

The first is that a martyr is absolved of all his sins as soon as the first drop of his blood is shed on the earth . . . But most important . . . is that a martyr looks in the direction of God. This is said both of all the Prophets and of all martyrs. It might be thus explained perhaps, that all veils which separate man from the direction of God all end in the veil existing within man himself. Man himself embodies all veils. All veils originating from darkness or light convene in the veil which embodies man himself. We ourselves embody the veils which separate us from the 'direction of God.' Once a person should give away this veil for the cause of God, and for Him alone, and once he should defeat this veil and offer his life, which is his own veil, he has broken down the origins of all veils. *He has destroyed his ego* [emphasis added]. He has destroyed his egoism and his selfishness and he has offered himself. And since he has fought for God, and defended for God, and risen to safeguard a land of God and His Divine decrees, and further since he has offered generously and sincerely whatever he has had, including his own life, he has torn down this veil.

The martyrs who offered their lives for the cause of God generously and sincerely, and who do so solely for the Blessed and Supreme Lord, who have offered everything within their possession including the most [precious] thing which they have, will see God's Epiphany, as did the Prophets before them. The Prophets who wanted everything for the cause of God. They did not see themselves except as being from God. They were free from individuality, and from 'self.' And so did they unveil the shroud which separated them from God.[12]

To understand this interpretation of martyrdom is to understand the essential consciousness of this revolution and the irrepressible courage of the soldiers and Revolutionary Guards on the battlefield against Iraq.

---

[12] *Tehran Times*, January 13, 1981, p. 3.

It is also to understand the metaphysics of Imam Khomeini's mind, and therefore the basis upon which to erect some form of response to this revolution.

As for the mechanics of martyrdom, it seems obvious that what makes a martyr 'succeed' is that in the moment of his death he has the sudden opportunity to instantaneously master the art of surrender to God, the art of giving up his separateness. In other words the difference between the Iranian Islamic revolutionary fighting and losing his life, and those other millions who have died (and even the Iraqi enemy) is that the Iranian is steeped in the ideology of Islam, steeped in the idea of self-sacrifice in order to experience transcendence of his ego. He dies in a context of extreme alertness, and in that moment when the shell blows up his body (assuming there is a soul, there is a God), his dramatic confrontation with his own surrendering up of his life enables him to turn towards God and extinguish the selfhood that separates him from God. It is by "looking in the direction of God"—consciously and with complete willingness to spontaneously accept no form of existence except in God—that the soul capitalizes on the moment of his death to come purely into relationship with what is Absolute and beyond his ego. Martyrdom in this sense is the most efficient technique of "removing the veil" that is the basis of man's alienation from his Creator. The martyr learns, as it were, everything necessary to reach God in a single flash; what the mystic may take decades to master is grasped organically in the annihilating bliss of the death of the ego, offered up by the martyr on the battlefield.

This document on martyrdom is more acutely germane to understanding Islam as it is manifesting in Iran than is *The Communist Manifesto* germane to understanding Marxist-inspired revolutions. The psychology of this document goes deeper down into the consciousness of man than any possible strategy devised outside of religious mythology. The Japanese finally uttered the word "surrender" after the Americans had bombed Hiroshima and Nagasaki. The Muslims in Iran would celebrate their invisible deliverance even if all that was left in Iran was dust and ashes. Nothing, absolutely nothing, could be more enticing to the soul than this promise of immortality achieved by virtue of a single act, and it is therefore the ideology of Islam that is esteemed of even higher importance than the knowledge of modern warfare, and the Revolutionary Guards who have distinguished themselves for their bravery even in the eyes of the Iraqi generals spend eighty percent of their training in ideology and, when they come to the war front, they train the professional soldiers in Islam. On the war front prayers are as vital to the concern of the Iranian fighter as are his armaments.

Martyrdom as delineated by Imam Khomeini would seem a powerful methodology for extreme and sudden expansion of consciousness, a climaxing 'satori' that could be achieved (with the proper intention) in the moment when the ego faces its death through the grace of God, since, as Khomeini has pointed out, it is the ego which is the microcosm of resistance, the source of the veil of ignorance. Khomeini as mystic: this is more critical to understanding Iran than Khomeini as demagogue, as politician. All significant religious experiences come from the surrender of the ego; Shi'a Islam had a whole symbology which built into the present circumstance: a war with Iraq, a continuing pressure for real Islam in Iran against all opposition—the necessary procedure for accomplishing this final transcendence. Of course only God and the martyrs could ever verify whether the Imam's words (and the Prophet's: "Count not those who were slain in God's way as dead, but rather living with their Lord, by Him provided" Qur'an, Sura III, 164) were an actual description of the reality and not just the compulsive urges of an imagination seeking escape from the awful fact of man's mortality. The war front would tell me more.

Imam Khomeini's Estimation of the Sepah Pasdaran, the Revolutionary Guards

To be admitted into the Sepah was, according to the officials I spoke with in Iran (and many non-Sepah persons who were desirous of becoming a Sepahi), even harder than getting into university; every true revolutionary yearned to pass the rigorous tests of the Sepah, which included not only a past history of devotion to noble pursuits (the absence of signs of a weak or indulgent character) but a thorough understanding of the basic principles of Islam and a vivid, awakened and articulated sense of the purpose, the moving inspiration of this revolution.[13] Khomeini himself, I was told, uttered his appreciation for these Islamic warriors:

I wish I could be a Pasdar. I would like to kiss their hands. I envy you.[14]

When I asked why it was that so many thousands of young men appeared on the streets of Tehran, without any perceptible commitment to the revolution, to Islam, or to joining the Sepah, the young Revolutionary

[13] From the actual charter of the Sepah are the following requirements:
  1. Belief in the noble Islamic ideology.
  2. Faith in the Islamic nature of the revolution and the Islamic Republic.
  3. Having bravery and spiritual valor as well as necessary physical and mental power. (*Message of the Revolution*, June, 1981, p. 51.)

[14] As quoted to me by Husseini, my interpreter, and later verified by others.

Guard told me, "They have not yet smelled the revolution." I thought this an apt metaphor indeed—or perhaps it was not even a metaphor! In any event it conveyed the instinctual, extra-rational level of commitment required to divine the secret of the power of this revolution. The point became: how will the Imam and the Revolutionary Guards go about inspiring the flower of Iranian youth, so many of whom seemed to be content to wither their energies in idleness on the streets of Tehran.

Whirling Dervishes Performing in the Festivities for the Third Anniversary of the Revolution

One afternoon we visited a stadium which was packed with Iranians celebrating the revolution. A schedule of events included singing, wheelchair races, juggling, gymnastics, and dervish dancing. There was a decidedly amateurish tone to these activities; the sense of professional grace was, for the most part, absent. But everything was being seen within the intimacy and brotherhood of the revolution and this light gave a kind of lustre to each act (and the juggler dropped his sticks and had to discontinue one of his more dextrous balancings) that saved each performance from the ignominy it would suffer if the audience were there to register an objective appraisal of the show. However, the whirling dervish display was the single most beautiful and intoxicating display of Iranian grace that I had witnessed. Once turned into full motion, the dancer was like a top that spun with its own power, only in this case it seemed the intention of the dancer had been taken over by another intention and he was simply held in that eternal anti-inertia. His body was being whirled into a different sphere of forces, and he defied the laws of motion that govern this earth. I could see how it could become a religious exercise, as everything would disappear in the absoluteness of concentration necessary to overcome dizziness and the weight of the body. The vibration of the dance actually seemed to refine the consciousness in the stadium and then I truly experienced that grace that is achieved in any aesthetic act that aims at something absolute.

As a reminder of the Islamic schools, however, the floor where all the various skills and competitions were enacted was covered with a thin layer of dirt that cast a shadow under each performance. In my judgement the discerning organizer of this event would have chosen to wash the stadium floor as almost his first act of preparation. I could not be whirled out of this stationary perception.

The Blind Lebanese Professor of Comparative Religion and the Concept of Shirk

La ilaha illa 'Llah is one of the testimonies of Islamic faith (the *Shahadah*) and translates as "There is no god but God." The implication of this is that the Absolute cannot have anything associated with it. *Shirk* is thus coming to associate God with anything other than Himself. Taken literally the Christian concept of the trinity is *shirk* since it equates God with an individuality that took a human form. The Qur'an in Sura CXII summarized the reality of the Absolute and the imagelessness of truth by having the Prophet utter, when asked about the nature of God:

> Say: He is God,
> The One and Only
> God, the Eternal, Absolute.
>
> He begetteth not,
> Nor is He begotten;
>
> And there is none
> Like unto Him.[15]

Now while we were finishing dinner a splendid conversation began about the meaning of *shirk*. The blind and beautifully articulate professor explained that loving *anything* other than God was wrongful association, and in his judgement the veneration of Imam Khomeini (with the multitude of pictures, posters, portraits) bordered on *shirk*, and thus endangered Islam. Not that he was alarmed that such danger had already posed a threat to the unity of Islam, but that he grieved that it might. Only by bypassing all that was relative (and Imam Khomeini was, despite the instincts of the people to the contrary, an expression of relative life) could the believer achieve union with God. The professor pointed out that the Sufis guarded this absolute knowledge through their spiritual wholeness, for what they sought above all else was to become one with the Absolute, thereby transcending the exoteric forms of Islam itself. This could reach a point of such perfect unity that

> All the Lights of Infinite Life may penetrate the soul of the Sufi, and make him participate in the Divine Life, so that he has the right to exclaim: "I am Allah."[16]

---

[15] Abdullah Usuf Ali, *The Holy Qur'an: Text, translation and commentary* (State of Qatar: Presidency of Islamic Courts and Affairs, 1946), p. 1806.

[16] Sheik 'Abd al-Karim Jossot, quoted by A. Berque, *Un Mystique Moderniste*, p. 750, in Martin Lings, *A Sufi Saint of the Twentieth Century* (London: Allen and Unwin, 1961), p. 136.

As Professor A. enunciated this concept and the consequent need to focus ultimately on God, he remarked, "My final loyalty is to God not to Islam. Islam itself is a form of *shirk*." What Professor A. was keen to point out to the Muslims (and myself—and he was speaking in the provocative esotericism of the Sufi mystic: he would never utter this statement outside of this context) who were gathered at the table was that Islam was a system of worship which was there ultimately to be transcended, that the Absolute (or God) was not Islamic; merely that He had arranged a form of surrender to Him that efficiently brought man closer to Him. Once having known Him, however, or rather once having brought about that condition of universality of awareness, then Islam dissolved and all that was left was the presence of the Absolute. "All is ephemeral save the countenance of the Lord." (Qur'an, Sura XXVII, 88.)

What was interesting in this discussion was that no one disagreed with Professor A.: it seemed that contrary to a Christian gathering where symbols become realities, Muslims recognized the concept of ego-transcendence and the ultimate illusion of all forms of duality. As for the display of Imam Khomeini (implying that as it were he embodied the imageless truth of Islam, i.e. the Absolute) there seemed little that could be done to erase this image or this need, and that such an image probably led people towards a concept of imagelessness (as contained in the Qur'an) that would not otherwise be there in the absence of the portraits of the Imam. Imam Khomeini breathed the fragrance (or so his people thought) of God; to see his picture everywhere was to catch that sublime fragrance, was to capture an essence (the Absolute) which manifested through the being of the Imam.

This was pretty much like the concept of the guru in Eastern religions, although the orthodox Muslim might consider this an invidious comparison.[17] There, the guru was worshipped not in his personal form, but in his impersonal and 'realized' form, as the Self. By serving the guru, by even worshipping the guru, one achieved an orientation that brought one into contact with a microcosm of the Truth. The Truth lay beyond the guru, but the authentic guru embodied, was himself the manifestation of, the Absolute. The only place in Creation where what was "uncreated and uncreatable" could be known was in the self of the Guru, for he had, as had the Prophet, turned his satan-self into a good Muslim,[18] i.e. his actions were determined by the Absolute and not just

---

[17] Yet the Qur'an acknowledges the diversity with which God has revealed his truth: "Every nation has its Messenger." (Sura X, 48.)

[18] The full *hadith*, according to Professor A., went like this:
    The Prophet: "To every man there is a Satan which is his double."
    Friend of the Prophet: "What about your Satan?"
    The Prophet: "My Satan has become a Muslim."

the ego. Imam Khomeini had become a sort of Master, an individual whose life was guided not by the intelligence of the small and isolated self, but by the creative intelligence of the universe itself. This at least was the implication of the status Khomeini enjoyed, although the professor and others were quick to abjure any insinuation that Khomeini was anything other than an ordinary human being. In any case, through this discussion of *shirk*, the features of Islamic mysticism and the ontology of human perfection became topical subjects of interest, here in the midst of a great political upheaval. I was grateful to Professor A.

The Palace of the Shah

The Niavaran palace of the Shah in North Tehran posed an interesting question: since Islam seemed against any display of extravagant beauty and wealth, how could they reconcile the fact of some of the splendour of the palace (for instance a silk carpet woven by hand, that covered 145 square metres of floor space) being that which brought great pleasure to the soul—how to reconcile this with evil? Well, according to the Iranians (and everything was left just as the Shah had left it when he fled Iran in January of 1979) they were not against the "existence of these things"; indeed "we take pride in the fact that we can make something beautiful; however in the case of the Shah, this reality was abused." While people starved in their mud huts in South Tehran, the Shah flushed his gold-plated toilet bowl; the Shah's sister washed her poodles in specially made gold-plated bathtubs. According to Islam one is not permitted to enjoy any form of luxury as long as one person in the world suffers from want. The pain, the suffering, the impoverishment of one soul is the responsibility of he who seeks to do justice, is, in fact, the responsibility of everyone. The Shah displayed his wealth with such abandon and profligacy[19] in a country in which there was a violent extremity of wealth on the one hand, and abject poverty on the other. The point was that the Shah just did not possess the nobility or aristocracy of character (not to mention wisdom or intelligence) to merit enjoying and displaying his

---

[19] Even the Central Intelligence Agency, as indicated by documents seized by the students occupying the American Embassy, had judged the Shah and his family as corrupt, wasteful, and ostentatious: "The Royal Court has traditionally been a hotbed of byzantine scheming. In the Shah's family are an assortment of licentious and financially corrupt relatives, notably his twin sister, Ashraf, a lady possessed of a greedy nature and nymphomaniac tendencies." *Research Study: Elites and Distribution of Power in Iran* (February, 1976), p. 10.

monarchical status. His royal lineage went only back to his Cossack father, who had been installed upon the throne by the British.

But in looking through the palace and all its magnificent splendour and opulence one could not imagine that the actual construction and decor were satanically inspired. Perhaps no human being was beautiful enough to live here, and yet man had created this brilliant elegance out of his own sensitivity to Creation itself, for the act of creating such beauty was itself an act that glorified existence, that humbled and exalted man. The Imams were the rightful inheritors of all the riches of the world since their purity was unblemished, their nobleness of purpose superior to any king. In paradise there might be palaces such as the Shah's, but here on earth such luxury was to be shunned by the good Muslim. The Shah had given material beauty a bad name; it would forever be linked in the minds of most Iranians with something that was evil, with a 'dynasty' that "sucked the blood of the people." And yet, as I wandered through the rooms I thought: could there be a pure monarch, a pure patrician who could rise to the level of this luxury and live it beautifully? The beauty was innocent, neutral; that a weak and deluded man had possessed this beauty did not finally efface the intrinsic radiance of the fact of the possible pleasure that even Allah himself might take in the dazzling chandeliers, the exquisite furniture from Napoleonic France.

Originally the hierarchies of power may have been based upon the "Great Chain of Being" in which angels, then kings, then noblemen, then serfs formed the expression of the distinctions of intelligence and talent, an echelon of authority that was the reflection of life itself. Now, however, with the dictatorial rulers such as Somoza and the Shah, it seemed the tendencies within Nature that would offer up suitable royal candidates had been thrown off, that perhaps the correlation of power with intrinsic merit was no longer actual, and thus that revolutions would continue until that rebalancing could occur; then the egalitarian notion of man would be seen to be a deception. The Shah—what if he had been a human being with great dignity and self-possession? What if his moral stature had competed with Ayatollah Khomeini? As it was, however, the Shah fitted into the Shi'a allegory of good and evil, and never contacted the moral power that would have convinced even himself that he deserved to be addressed as "God's shadow on earth," as "The King of Kings." There he really committed *shirk*.

Four hundred architects and engineers had worked on the design and construction of the Shah's palace and its surrounding buildings. If the Shah had built one mosque among all his palatial surroundings he would have succeeded in countering one of the prejudices against him, revealed in his admission, "I am a Muslim only inside my own country."

Instead he spent a million dollars just creating a small palace to accommodate the visits of Anwar Sadat and King Hussein of Jordan.

Wouldn't one be embarrassed in one's soul to have all this wealth unless one knew one deserved such things? That, it seems to me, is the issue. If one is to accept gratuitous riches one must feel one is superior to others and therefore more deserving of special treatment by the gods, or God. The Shah and the Pahlavis were not pure enough to prevent some outrage in Creation that such luxury was being enjoyed by those who perhaps, if their souls were the judges, should have been consigned to the mud huts in South Tehran.

Visit to Exhibition of Technology

As part of the celebration of the Third Anniversary of the Revolution we visited an exhibition in which the present technology of Iran—especially with regard to war—was displayed. There I talked to young technicians who had designed and built the spare parts that had previously been ordered from Bell Helicopter. Before, under the Shah, all spare parts were supplied by the United States, and even the Iranians who worked in the plants where helicopters were built and serviced found themselves under the direct supervision of Americans. In those days if something went wrong with a helicopter there was no attempt to repair the plane; a spare part was ordered from the United States. The Iranians knew no independence, and, according to each technician I talked to, no Iranian was given the authority that the top Americans were given. Bell had said: "Change parts; don't repair," but now, as the Iranian told me, "We are happier because we are free to think!" The basic policy encouraged the Iranians to "Just watch; don't touch." Now, however, the war forced these people to come up with spare parts, and although the repair process has been understandably slow (they had to build these spare parts from scratch) the Iranians were able to keep the war going, to service the planes and helicopters, and to repair parts. They even asserted that they now worked much more efficiently than before; that indeed they accomplished more work than the Americans, although they acknowledged that there had been some brilliant American technicians who supervised them.

But they had experienced their sudden emancipation from American tutelage as a gift, for the pressure of the war had created tremendous inspiration to devise ways of combatting the severe handicap of no longer having a supply of spare parts for all the war armaments (everything had been designed in America; all breakdowns depended upon American spare parts). They felt more creative, more useful, and even more knowledgeable about their given area of expertise. For instance, a computer specialist explained that even the most sophisticated forms of computer technology were now being used and developed in Iran, despite the fact that here too, most of the experts had left and that they were short of components. But all agreed that it had been a kind of miracle, for even at the beginning, when the word came down that they would have to make the spare parts themselves, that no effort would be made to reach agreement with the United States in order to facilitate the outfitting of the armed forces,—at the beginning they did not have the confidence that they later found in abundance. They said that the Imam had inspired them to believe they could turn this adversity into a blessing and so prove to themselves and the Iranian people the real meaning of self-sufficiency and independence from both superpowers. Some of them were more explicitly religious in their analysis of the cause of this development; all, however, agreed that they had taken an evolutionary step that had transformed their attitude towards their work, their own abilities, and even their own country.

I had thought that perhaps this was all a set-up, that they were forced to put up a good front; but, upon more searching questions and further contact, it was obvious their claims were authentic, that indeed, contrary to Western assumptions, this part of the revolution was unfolding in the right direction. The war was, from an Islamic standpoint, a sacred cause; even if the people would have to fast, this was more acceptable than the collapse of their war effort because of a lack of spare parts. The fundamentals of the revolution were in place. The miracles that counted continued to happen.

A Conversation with an Iraqi Student Secretly Attending the Conference in Iran

A young Iraqi student, studying in Germany, had come to Iran, and was anxious to keep his identity hidden. Here he was supporting a country that was at war with his own country. But his description of the rule of Saddam Hussein Takriti and his war of terror on devout Muslims left little doubt that many of his people resented his policies, were terrified of his actions. According to him, the majority of the people did not want the war with Iran, were anxious to avoid a war that pitted them against other Muslims. Saddam Hussein had already arrested, expelled, tortured, and executed thousands of Shi‘a Muslims, and those with Iranian ancestry were driven from the borders of Iraq. Conscription meant that anyone who refused to fight would be executed. The Islamic Daawa Party (sympathetic to the establishment of an Islamic Republic) was banned and membership in this party meant certain death. According to the Iraqi student who was himself a member of the Daawa Party, 7000 young people, especially young professional, educated men, had been executed. For one member of a family to join the Daawa Party meant imprisonment for the whole family. Because of his affiliation with Islam the family of the Iraqi student now lay in prison in Iraq. He had six brothers; two were doctors, two were engineers, and two were economists. He had heard nothing from his family now for one year and three months. In Iraq 100,000 people (opposing the regime of Saddam Hussein) were in jail.

If he was to be believed the picture was grim for everyone who criticized the Iraqi regime. As he said it, each person had two choices, "Either to fight against Saddam, or be killed by the hand of Saddam." There was a censorious attitude in Iran towards criticism of Khomeini's regime, and yet this censuring was of a different sort unless one equated religious intolerance and the authority of Scriptural revelation with state terrorism based upon political power. The Iraqis feared the Muslim devotee who identified with Imam Khomeini, and Saddam Hussein was determined to forestall and ideally to eradicate the influence of Pan-Islam, substituting instead the idea of Pan-Arabism, with Iraq being the center of Arab power.

The Iraqi student spoke with passion and clarity; he was convinced that the people of Iraq desired a revolution that was similar to the one that had happened in Iran, that the West was making a grievous error in supporting the present Iraqi regime. He announced that if the site for the Conference of Non-Aligned Countries in September of 1982 was not changed from its present location in Baghdad there would be an explosion set by the Daawa Islamic Party in the building where the conference was scheduled and that all those who did not defy the agreement to hold the conference in Baghdad would have their lives endangered. He urged me to announce this, to write about this in the West. For the non-aligned countries to have agreed to hold the conference in Baghdad was tantamount to recognition of the legitimacy of Saddam Hussein's rule. The murders Saddam Hussein had committed even within his own party —over one hundred Baathist Party members had been killed on his personal instructions—and the persecution of conscientious Muslims (the Iraqi student was adamant that Saddam Hussein was a traitor to Islam, was in fact an infidel) made him unworthy to represent his country. He was convinced that the greater the intensity of persecution, the more heinous the crimes committed by Saddam Hussein, the more likely was his fall from power and the overthrow of the present regime.

He gave one startling statistic: the ratio of soldiers killed versus soldiers captured. He insisted that where 1000 Iraqi soldiers are being killed, 1500 are being captured. On the other hand very few Revolutionary Guards were being captured. Many of the Iraqis will give up their arms without a struggle, shouting "Allahu Akbar! We are with you!" There was no will to fight, whereas on the part of the Iranians, fighting was an act of worship, of devotion to Islam. The Iraqi student said that Saddam Hussein knew he was losing the war, but that all the Gulf States that were frightened of Khomeini and militant Islam were coming to his rescue. The Iraqi president was reported to have uttered, "Even if we do not win the war, we will not lose the spirit of victory"—a virtual admission of the successes the Iranians have had, especially recently.

Naturally, I knew the Iraqi student to be biased against Saddam Hussein but intuitively one could sense his loyalty to Islam and Imam Khomeini was an impulse supported by a moral sensitivity not part of the calculation of power in Baghdad. One could say he was fanatical in his adherence to an absolutist kind of Islam in which secular rule would be eliminated but this fanaticism co-existed with a profound sense of surrender to Allah. In my observations there was an unmistakable correlation between the intensity of one's commitment to Islam and one's loyalty to the revolution in Iran. It seemed that a willingness to become totally absorbed in Islam—at least at this historical moment —produced spontaneously an intuitional understanding of what the Islamic Revolution in Iran was all about. There were major obstacles, even excessive contradictions, but on the non-rational mystical level of comprehension, the basic intention was known to be true, and therefore worthy of being defended. The Iraqi student whose actions had threatened the lives of his whole family, whose actions now might cost him his life lived only to bring about the vision of Islam that he held uppermost in his mind, that was at the core of his heart.

I wondered: could an Iraqi student absolutely loyal to President Hussein provide me with a moral credibility and intensity that had been impressed upon me by this young Iraqi? Can two absolutes be equivalent in their degree of truth? The Islamic Revolution in Iran depended to a great extent upon villains. The Shah, the United States, and now Iraq fulfilled the role of evil since they had opposed the leadership and policies of Ayatollah Khomeini, someone whom the Iranians (and many Muslims throughout the world) believed had the mandate of Allah.

One morning early we left for the war front in the southwest part of Iran, near Susangerd. Our method of transportation was a military plane accompanied by a convoy of F14's (to protect us from Iraqi fire), and once boarded one could feel the warmth of feeling, the alertness of consciousness created by the currents of anxiety in the air. The belief in Allah (most of those on the plane—there were about sixty of us—were Muslims), the acceptance of his will, the almost appropriate fatalism that characterized these individual Muslims, transformed the fear into something creative—the sense of aliveness was heightened, the sense of possible death brought into an immediacy the real meaning of religion and the soul's promised judgement and immortality. While these Muslims could die with some sense of purpose and even serenity (if the plane was actually fired upon) I experienced the desire to accomplish something more, that my life was unfinished, that it had an individual texture that these Muslims could not know about. At the same time it was worth competing with them in terms of making certain I stayed steady and fearless, else they might attempt to prove to me the perils of remaining a non-Muslim.

I suppose that the orientation of Islam is one that minimizes the significance of the private, subjective world of the individual, reminding him instead of the oneness of God and the need to submit absolutely to His laws. For me, however, I felt that a non-demonic side of the Western experience (with its loss of mythology and consequent glorification of individualism and selfhood) could, with the necessary acknowledgement of the Absolute, deliver one of the secrets of God's Creation, that individuality might even be (in its purer form) one of the means of self-expression of God. At least some of these thoughts formed in my mind as I thought about the possibility of being annihilated in mid-flight to Ahvaz, Iran. How precious is the human personality? Can the finite be said in some sense to be as sacred as the infinite? Are images part of the reason why the imageless has manifested? Meanwhile I contemplated how I might too master the technique of martyrdom if that possibility presented itself suddenly. There would always be something one could die for, something to bring to one's attention at that moment of extinction, something that would in a posture of surrender and innocent discrimination give one a sense of completion.

We touched down on the landing strip in Ahvaz, where the Iraqis had sent mortar fire and destroyed many civilian targets such as hospitals and schools. The landing strip and the terminal building were near where the war was being waged. Here near the front one could feel the brightness in the air, the tension and sensitivity that carried with it the sense of a holy war. By this I mean that not only could one smell death and destruction, not only could one feel the pain and the suffering, not only could one realize the heroism and bravery required to fight this war, but, as I saw several stretchers bearing severely wounded soldiers to a waiting helicopter, I was certain I was experiencing the living impulse of Islam as it purely translated itself into this encounter with 'evil,' with the sense of sacrifice and surrender to God. It was only here on the battlefield that one could judge whether one possessed the requisite faith and courage to be a fighter for Islam. And apparently the soldiers and Revolutionary Guards all responded with invincible confidence and even joy at the prospect of risking their lives for the Imam and Islam. And I was certain that something was in the air that was not the injection merely of the psychology of war; the Imam was right: here martyrs were gaining their glory; here was the testing ground for Islam; here one gathered more and more power and faith in facing death, in facing the 'infidel' armies of Iraq (as defined at least by their purpose in fighting to resist Islam).

Viewing the Bombing Damage by Iraqi Shells

In the city of Ahvaz, there were dozens of buildings that had been levelled. Obviously the Iraqis had attempted to terrify the civilian population in the hope that they would panic and create problems for the Iranian defenders. The strategy backfired, however, and these people—many of whom were Arabs—became more Islamic and revolutionary than they had been before the attacks, and mourning their martyrs (thousands of civilians had been killed in the bombing attacks), they began to identify with the script as interpreted by Imam Khomeini, where good and evil battled for the soul of man, where Islam could be triumphant and change the face of the earth. Saddam Hussein did not know it at the time, but he may actually have saved the Islamic Revolution by invading Iran; Iran was sinking into the doldrums after the revolution, to be revived momentarily by the seizing of the hostages. With the attack by the Iraqis suddenly the people and their forces were mobilized: they had a fresh enemy, and they needed this enemy to forge the soul of their revolution. So many of these young men were fulfilled as they would be in no other situation: they knew how to surrender to Allah and give their lives for Allah. There was little faith; it had become a biochemical reality in their perception and feeling. One could sense their certainty about their fate if they were slain in battle—this certainly seemed virtually a gift from Allah himself, so natural, so imbibed were the soldiers and Revolutionary Guards with the impulses that had articulated themselves in the religion of Islam (and all the great religions): the confidence in the soul's immortality; the knowingness that one could die nobly and could therefore give power to a holy cause.

Visiting a Graveyard for Martyrs of the War in Ahvaz

The graves were covered with the dust and dirt of the surrounding desert, but the people placed their flowers on these graves—fresh graves; this cemetery had been created since the war and was designated only for martyrs. Photographs of each martyr had in many cases been enlarged, and one could gaze upon the face of each body that now lay under the ground. Were these faces standing all around us? A father and mother were weeping without restraint; was this Islamic? After all, these martyrs were, according to the prevalent belief, happier than those left on earth; therefore it seemed there was a contradiction, but a purely human and necessary one. The promise of Paradise did not obviate the need to express one's sorrow, one's extreme pain in the absolute separating of the dead from the living. Even God, one felt, wanted people to experience this grief, else what would death be but a mockery of life. It was something for all time; it was something final, and something that gave to life itself a sacredness. One person dying in a war was too many. Here hundreds of civilians and soldiers had been honoured and had become the cause for outrage against Saddam Hussein, and the proof of the evils of the United States who were, in the minds of all these people, collaborating with the Iraqis, giving them encouragement to weaken the dangerous regime of Imam Khomeini.

Closer to the War Front, Meeting the Soldiers

We drove in a bus towards the front lines and there was evidence all around us that the Iraqis had been driven back: tanks lay abandoned; the Iranians had diverted a river and had flooded the land so that Iraqis were held up in their advance into Iran. Hundreds of tanks had got bogged down in the marsh and they now reinforced the sense of eventual victory for the Iranians. Once we arrived in Susangerd, which had been the scene of fierce hand-to-hand fighting and had eventually been recovered by the Iranians—under the inspired courage of Revolutionary Guards—we stopped to eat lunch with the soldiers and to listen to an army lieutenant explain through various maps (superimposing maps: one, of the area captured by the Iraqis; the other, the areas now recaptured by the Iranians: there was the indication of steady and irreversible progress) the fortunes of the war. Strangely enough, this commanding officer had the archetypal military bearing and one realized that so many—the majority—of those fighting in the war lacked this professional manner of the soldier. And one knew that these professional soldiers were absolutely vital to the success of the Iranian forces; the lieutenant knew the art of warfare; he was moulded in the destiny of war, and he breathed a confidence and knowledge that seemed indispensable for the war effort. War was still won by combat ability and not just Islamic ideology. The Iranians were grateful to possess real soldiers and not just freshly made warriors for the Imam. In watching the lieutenant one experienced the more objective aspect of war; that is, the element of success that was determined by the extensiveness of one's knowledge of warfare, one's knowledge of military fact and strategy.

A bridge and river divided the two parts of Susangerd, and I discovered in my conversation how a group of Iranian soldiers had built a makeshift bridge (the larger one had been destroyed) and in the night had attacked the other side of Susangerd which had been held by the Iraqis. The soldiers that guarded the bridge—it was a checkpoint for all vehicles—had fought in that battle and now proudly recounted their surprising successes, acting out the moment when they landed on the other side and ambushed the Iraqis. Susangerd had become one of the symbols of victory and martyrdom in the revolution; the Iraqis had been once again driven from this territory, thus vindicating the faith in Islam and the cause of the war. One wondered if even the land itself resisted the invasion from a foreign power; the atmosphere was already so strong with religious feeling; perhaps the consciousness of Iran was inviolate, and that outside enemies who sought to conquer it were cursed by their very presence. This notion at least fitted into the prevailing mood of the surroundings. Here were these soldiers fighting a war, and yet they seemed so exuberant, so buoyant, as if they could not wish to be anywhere else. I thought of the American forces in Vietnam and how in over one hundred cases the men of certain divisions had killed the commanding officer in order to avoid being sent to an area that was considered to be recklessly dangerous. Here there was an anticipation of immortal happiness always near one's very breathing, and the belief was that the martyrs stood all around, now giving their freshly gained grace to the still living warriors. This was the conception of martyrdom; the martyrs actually altered the balance of power, for the energy that accompanied their deaths actually charged the energy of those living, giving power and divine strength, weakening the enemy.

The Atmosphere at the War Front

I have never been in a combat zone before, but even a number of kilometres from the actual fighting there was the presence of something in the air that signified the consequences of this war, for a victory or loss (and it was inconceivable how the Iranians could 'lose' this war since even a nuclear bomb—or several—would never induce the Iranians to surrender or to silence their Allahu Akbars [God is Great], would mean the life or death of the revolution. The objective assessment of the adequacy of the forces and arms on both sides was not the critical factor in the outcome of the fighting, for the Iranians, as I have alluded to before, were possessed; that is, their faith in Allah, in martyrdom, in the wisdom of their leader, Imam Khomeini, had become an ontological fact; they fought and died in a kind of grace, and one could sense that in the absence of this war, these young men would not have found the intensity, nor the joy that now filled their activities. Of course in the West there is little attention on the 'vibration' of intention or behaviour, but those discerning enough will realize that a polarized vision of values which leads to fighting inevitably will pit one side (which has more of the support of Nature) against another side (which will—at best—have much less support). Without visiting the Iraqi side I knew that the grace was all on the side of the Iranians, that no matter what severe criticism was directed against the present regime, no matter how many political leaders continued to be assassinated, the universe itself relished the idea of a mythology, a great religion being vindicated through an allegorical (that is, symbolical, archetypally-defined) interpretation of the Script. The essence of Islam—seen as a system of revealed truth which commanded total allegiance to the laws of God (and the division of politics and religion was, in the argument of Khomeini, a false and destructive division; even in the absence of the Twelfth Imam, there was a shadow of the Imam on earth; that shadow of the Imam was none other than Imam Khomeini himself)—this expression of Islam was the vindication of the religious point of view, the Nemesis for the rapacious secularism and *Realpolitik* which threatened to give empirical validity to the idea

64

that there were no divinely ordained cause and effect relationships in the universe of politics. The Kissinger view that morality was irrelevant to politics meant that God had (if He indeed did exist) no preference for what was good over what was evil. Ayatollah Khomeini, on the other hand—and those Iranians graced enough to be given the insight into the divinely irrational reality of this revolution (with all its extravagant rhetoric, with all its simplistic categories of good versus evil, with all its absolutes)—opposed the secular, *Realpolitik* conception of politics and international events, and the success of the Iranians so far indicated there might indeed be something in the anti-Kissinger argument, the argument that affirmed God's will, God's bias within each event—especially when one of the contestants or actors aligned itself with the laws of God (as assumed from the revelations of "The Seal of the Prophets"—i.e. the final prophet).

These soldiers (and young boys of fifteen) rode the waves of this grace; they were quickened by the perfect roles they assumed in the war: they were following in the line of the Prophet and the Imams: they were doing battle with infidelism; they were the warriors of God, those ready to give up everything for Allah. There could be no stain upon their motivation, even if this intention dwelled in the relative absence of sophisticated knowledge of the world. It was enough to have surrendered to the Imam; as a child one enters the Kingdom of Heaven—at least this was one way of explaining what was happening here on the battlefield.

In the most simple terms, if there was a God, and if He permitted Khomeini and the Muslims to be defeated, there would be the end of any attempt to impose a theocratic system, to insist that God's laws were of relevance to everything; that the religious view of Creation did not confine itself to one's private life, it had great consequences and meaning for the world at large, and particularly now that the institutions of diplomacy and hegemonic manipulation took place in a moral void, or rather excluded quite specifically the relevance of revealed truth. Islam and this revolution inspired by Ayatollah Ruhullah Khomeini would continue to defy all predictions of the secularists, would continue to draw upon sources of power that had been relegated to the category of outmoded mythology and superstition; to believe in Khomeini was to believe in miracles, angels, the Scriptures, and the Day of Judgement. In the mean time the unfolding of events in the Middle East (most especially in Iran) seemed to conform to an empirical rebuttal to the cynical, CIA-determined view of reality. The Scriptures were being enacted on this battlefield, even though one realized that most of the Iraqi soldiers were entirely innocent, did not share in the adamant hostility of their president towards Imam Khomeini, and whose deaths merely compounded the sorrow of the universe. But they had to play their role, and that role meant fighting on the side of evil; they thus sacrificed themselves (unconsciously) for the cause of the good, and thus the allegorical reality could be sustained. but until someone understood this power of the irrational, one could never understand let alone accept the extremist views and actions of the present regime in Iran. Ayatollah Khomeini's charisma and grace was insured by his decades of piety, sacrifice, and spiritual knowledge; without being called one of the Imams, without being called a Prophet, he nevertheless commanded the allegiance and devotion of a Christ figure, and in the context of this whole revolution one could only go back to the Bible to understand the forms of reality that dominated the consciousness of the people. Liberalism, communism, socialism were, to devout Muslims, the aberrations of Western infidelity; the policies of the Baathist Party of Iraq, and the ruthless authority of Saddam Hussein were the expression of that force which sought to resist the holy mandate of Islam and the Prophet. No matter how genuinely the Iraqis believed the regime in Iran was plotting to spread its revolution across the border, no matter how provocative the Iraqis believed the Shi'a population had been in Iraq, still the final decision to invade Iran was the perfect gift to the Iranians and to the cause of militant Islam. Without that invasion I am willing to bet that the revolution in Iran might even have spent itself, so dependent has it been upon adversity and opposition.

In the mean time, despite my abhorrence for war and for all the killing that was going on, I had to marvel at the electric feeling in the air, in the exuberance, the serenity, that dominated the consciousness of the Iranian soldiers. Their ideology was consecrated here in the confrontation with death; and it seemed—at least to my vision—that the angels did indeed wish to assist Islam.

A Visit with Iraqi Prisoners of War

An extraordinary phenomenon greeted me when I entered the compound where thousands of Iraqi prisoners were being housed. At the beckoning of one of the former officers in command of an Iraqi unit, all the prisoners shouted all the slogans that had been so familiar to me: from "Allahu Akbar" to "Long live Khomeini!" to "Death to Saddam!" I studied the faces closely to determine whether this apparent unconditional support for their captors was genuine, or whether it had been orchestrated by enthusiasts of the regime who promised rewards for any Iraqis that demonstrated their allegiance to Islam and the regime of

Ayatollah Khomeini. There were, it is true, examples of prisoners who sullenly refused to give their hearts to this exhibition of solidarity with the Iranians, but the vast majority of the faces were filled with undeniable loyalty and sincerity; it was not contrived; the response was spontaneous, and even in the discussion I had with three of the Iraqi prisoners—selected randomly—it was apparent that they had indeed thought out their position, that there was nothing to compel them to defend the cause of Saddam Hussein, that they had, under the influence of their captors, come to respect the revolution in Iran, had come to accept the form of Islam which the revolution (and the war) expressed, and finally had come to embrace Imam Khomeini (who met with many of the prisoners) as the authentic leader of Islam.

Most of the prisoners expressed a strong desire to return to the war front and fight against their own troops! However, the Iranians thought better of the idea and have told them that they should stay in Iran, under the control of the Iranians, and absorb the meaning, the spirit of the revolution. This meant to intensify their understanding of Islam and the particular expression of religious leadership provided by Ayatollah Khomeini, whom, as I have said, they seemed to revere. How could all this be true? Well, the Iraqis explained that on the war front they had no will to fight, that their forces were dispirited, that they were fighting under coercion, that they knew their Iranian 'enemies' possessed courage, conviction, and absolute determination. This is why, they explained, they would often give up their arms without a struggle, allowing (and this was quoted from two sources) five Iranian Revolutionary Guards to capture twenty Iraqi soldiers. Here, they said, they were learning more about Islam, were becoming unified with their Iranian brothers, and were preparing to return to Iraq after the war, and there to lead the revolution, a revolution made on the exact model of the Iranian revolution, that is, pure Islam freed of all compromises with modernism. While all this was going on the Iranians insisted that the Iraqi prisoners were "not prisoners, but brothers and our guests!" They were free to roam around the camp and they were encouraged to attend lectures on Islam and to join in the prayer services.

The Iraqis did remind me of one most important truth: "We would have fought to the death if it were anyone else but our Iranian brothers" —meaning that they were brave soldiers, eager to fight for a just cause. Here, however, they evinced no loyalty to the aims of their own leader and appeared content with their lot: "The only thing we don't have here is women!"

I wondered whether any Iranian soldier captured by the Iraqis would commit this act of apostasy—an apostasy against what they viewed as the infidel. Here thousands of Iraqis were willing to denounce their

country; they insisted that they had not been tortured; they insisted
that this was their own decision; that they supported absolutely the
revolution in Iran, and all yearned to return to their country to bring
about the expansion of the revolution. My intuition about the dynamics
of this revolution would be severely weakened in its credibility if
anything like what I witnessed here in the compound of the prisoner of
war camp was taking place in a similar camp in Iraq. In the mean time I
wondered why no Western journalists had investigated this phenomenon. These were not mindless victims of torture or brainwashing; they
were, for the most part, simple soldiers from the country who had been
forced to fight inside the borders of Iran, and who now, under the
persuasion of their captors, had come to recognize the absurdity of this
act and the consequent 'truth' of the Iranian cause. I suppose there could
be some sort of test devised to determine whether a change of position
(and the starting point of the soldiers when they went into battle was
tenuous at best in its commitment to the cause of Saddam Hussein) was
the result of factors intrinsic to a greater knowledge of the issue, to a
more discriminating understanding of the context of this conflict, or
whether the change was induced by mental pressure, by enticements, by
pure propaganda, relentless in its message. Although strongly tempted
to assume there had been some form of subtle manipulation in this
unalloyed enthusiasm for the Islamic Revolution in Iran, in this rapid
denunciation of their own government, I had, except in isolated cases,
come to the conclusion that here too the grace of the revolution (despite
all its serious flaws, its excesses, its crude over-simplifications) reigned,
that the attitude of the Iraqi prisoners of war was a natural and
inevitable outcome of being exposed to the revolution and to the
mentality of the Iranian, Muslim captors. And I had been told that the
audience with Imam Khomeini had transformed many of the Iraqi
prisoners, greatly intensifying their allegiance to Islam and to all the
goals of their revolutionary brothers in Iran.

It all seemed a part of a great strategy, for by capturing thousands of
Iraqi soldiers and persuading them of the virtues of the revolution and
the need for total commitment to Islam and the spread of the Islamic
revolution, they had created potential fifth columnists on a scale that
probably was unheard of, considering that the fever of martyrdom now
dominated even these Iraqis. They would—when the war was finally
over (and whether Iran actually 'won' the war; it was impossible to
imagine their 'losing' it, in so far as I knew they would fight to the
death; and even perhaps these Iraqis would, in the improbable event of
the Iraqi troops moving across Iran)—undermine the support, whatever
level there was in Iraq, for the Baathist Party and create painful pressures upon Saddam Hussein until he was overthrown and a true Islamic

state was established. I pitied those poor Iraqi soldiers on the battle-field who were risking their lives in a war that, according to the most conservative estimate, only twenty-five percent of the soldiers believed in. The Iranians on the other hand were assured of glory if they survived, immortality and bliss if they were slain. Ayatollah Khomeini had appropriated the conditions for martyrdom and Saddam Hussein was confined to defining the purpose of the war in terms of Arab nationalism. Whatever one thought of Khomeini, one had to recognize that his adherence to Islam was absolute, his lust for power non-existent. But one could only understand this through the grace that came or didn't come as the revolution took its course.

The Islamic Revolution's Program for Education

From the Ministry of Culture and Education came an official appointed by Imam Khomeini to describe the conception of Islamic education. The very idea of teaching knowledge, of exploring the universe, within the severe and carefully delineated parameters of Islam seemed, a priori, a closed system of education, one that would necessarily compromise the 'value-free' atmosphere necessary to do research, to discover how the universe worked. And yet these Islamic educators were determined to impose a truly Islamic system of education regardless of whatever 'Western' reactions they might encounter. The universe *was* known; its laws had been revealed by the Prophets and the Qur'an was a divine description about how the laws of God worked, and how man should conduct himself in order to take advantage of the fact that God had revealed his own nature, his own intention, his own desire for man to live in accordance with his laws. Everything would have to prosper within this frame of reference, and any educational system that was predicated on the tacit assumption that the ultimate questions about God, man, and the universe were unanswerable, or remained perpetually problematical, was a heresy against God and an insult to Islam, and a method of inquiry that was corrupted by the devil. While one might argue the point that such assumptions were bound to restrict the range of exploration of man and the universe, nevertheless if the prophets were not liars or hallucinating, then the Scriptures would have to stand as the ultimate truth, and they had clearly—in the Old Testament, in the New Testament, and then, most perfectly, in the Qur'an—answered the Big Questions and had laid down a strict code of behaviour, an all-embracing system of ethics that necessarily would influence the activities of the educator—and his student. Simply put: one either accepts God and the revelations of his prophets as being the manifestation of his will (and therefore the blueprint of his Creation) or one questions the existence of God, and obviously the final ontological, spiritual, and scientific validity of the contents and implications of the Scriptures. For the Iranians to compromise to the secular bias (or non-bias) was tantamount to denying to the people that the truth of Islam was absolute, a truth that was not about to be up-dated by modern liberalism, science, or positivism. Of course the greatest villains were the Marxists, for these people posited a doctrine of reality that ridiculed religious faith as being merely a deception, created out of superstition and, of course, economic struggle. One could not over-estimate the revulsion, the hostility, the suspicion these revolutionaries had about all Western intellectual inclinations, especially those that had grown into prominence through secular humanism, a word that finally became even more hated in Iran than it was in the pews of Jerry Falwell's Liberty Baptist Church.

In what way does a doctrine of religion affect the psyche differently than a doctrine of materialism, a doctrine of existentialism, a doctrine of classical liberalism? One would just have to come to Iran to see that there was an irrational power in Islam (as rational as this system of devotion was) that unified the deepest level of consciousness and created a certainty and an emotional loyalty that was immovable. Demythologized Western man can never understand this; and this is why he cannot understand the revolution in Iran, or the expansion of conservative religion in North America. Relativism, secularism, humanism has become itself a kind of absolute mythology in the consciousness of especially the educated; the older mythologies, the real mythologies were considered dead, unverifiable, and discredited superstitions, which only the unliberated would continue to espouse. Here, however, in Iran secularism found its Nemesis, and those unable to grasp the innate truths of Islam would only find the revolution an intolerable aberration, in the words of the former Iranian ambassador to the United Nations, "a coercive reversal of Iran's socio-cultural development of the past century... [a] regressive transformation... a quick return to an imagined puritanical past."[20] These are the words of an educated, courageous, and rational individual, someone who opposed the Shah with great eloquence, someone who even defended the revolutionary regime right up until the departure of Abolhassan Bani-Sadr. They are, however, the words of an Iranian who cannot suffer the irrational death of his liberal

[20] Mansour Farhang, "Ruling Iran by Fanaticism and Fear," *Christian Science Monitor*, March 5, 1982.

70

consciousness enough to receive the throbbing power of puritanical Islam, and the literalism of Qur'anic law:

He [Khomeini] believes there is only one legitimate mode of being and doing; and he knows to the very last details what the norms of behavior within that mode ought to be. Khomeini's puritanism is a joyless and morbid devotion to a God who demands constant sacrifice.[21]

This perception cannot be questioned: neither as to its sincerity, nor to its accuracy—*as seen by the relativist*. For the devotee of Khomeini's Islam, however, it is neither "joyless" nor "morbid," although it certainly may appear this way to someone who cannot participate in "Born-again Islam." Just as V. S. Naipaul could not, in his journey into Islam,[22] understand the fasting, the denial of pluralistic truth, the total subjugation of the ego to an Absolute that encouraged the annihilation of the 'self,' neither could this former Iranian ambassador (and millions of others: Iran was either heaven or hell; there were few Iranians who viewed the situation in relative terms) understand the yoking of the individual to the invariable, unchanging, and invincible laws of Islam. And of course an educational system that emerged out of this "joyless and morbid devotion to a God who demands constant sacrifice" would necessarily extirpate whole areas of the universe of experience and ideas that tended to encourage autonomous, self-created, self-affirming dispositions of the intellect—and even of the heart.

This was the awful dilemma for anyone contemplating the meaning of this revolution: if one *knew* that God and not one's self mattered, that the subjective play of imagination and free will was a danger to the spiritual well-being of man, then one readily acceded to all the edicts of the revolution—even the banning of famous poets who were not Islamic enough for the puritanical tastes of the present rulers of Iran, the self-appointed guardians of the pure strain of Islam. The only justification for the direction of the revolution (and in the transformation of the educational system) was that God indeed had decreed that Ayatollah Khomeini governed under His (Allah's) mandate, that obedience to Islam led to the divine perfection of man and to his eternal happiness:

Human beings have been created in this way: unlimited in anger; unlimited in animal passion; and unlimited in selfishness, and nothing satisfies them unless they are correctly trained and educated. With this training, they will enter a path that human beings seek to achieve and that is absolute perfection. When they reach that perfection, they find themselves in peace and calmness and will enjoy

---

[21] Ibid.

[22] V. S. Naipaul, *Among the Believers: An Islamic Journey* (London: André Deutsch, 1981).

confidence, reliance and reassurance. This reassurance comes with their approaching God, for having confidence in anything else such as "an open socio-
political order" will not bring them peace."[23]

Clearly then, an educational system that is based upon Islam promises
that "joyless and morbid devotion" will eventually lead to a transformation of man, for man in his present state (his un-Islamicized state) is
subject to the influences of evil; for Khomeini, "All the efforts of the
Prophets were aimed at turning human beings *into true human beings*
[emphasis added]; to turn a creature of nature into a divine human being
in this very world."[24] This—the altering of man's mode of being—was
an absolute proposition; there were no compromises possible, even if
one felt—as millions of Iranians did—that such conceptions of transcendental joy and self-actualization were chimerical and abused man's
earthly destiny and purpose. As long as this affirmation of religious
truth remained a dogmatic and not an empirical reality so long would a
significant minority of Iranians remain sincerely appalled at what was
taking place in their country, and they would be disposed to exaggerate
the undeniable excesses and even sins that had been committed in the
name of Islam. But what was critical was whether the archetypal
impulse of this revolution—as embodied in the personhood and pro-
clamations of Imam Khomeini—resonated with the impulse of divine
intelligence, or the teleological nature of the universe. If it did not—or,
more obviously, if there were no God, or if this God did not require
such slavish obedience to a specific creed—then the revolution and
Ayatollah Khomeini would have to be resisted to the death. If, on the
other hand, Allah smiled upon the revolution (despite its distortions),
then no matter what appeared to be the character of the regime in Iran,
nothing could be done to destroy it, and unremitting criticism redolent
with extreme accusations of torture, rape, pillaging, and corruption,
would simply weaken the final potency of such criticism since, at the
most important level, this revolution was being conducted by the force
of evolution itself, as anti-progressive, as regressive as it seemed to be.

As the Deputy Minister of Education told us: "Today our aim is
Islam and we consider the students as people to be trained by God and
we must place our children in the hands of devoted teachers fully aware
of Islamic thinking." In other words any teacher who had the least
doubts about Islam or the current practices of the regime would be a
harmful influence on the innocent souls of children who needed only to

<hr>

[23] Ayatollah Khomeini, speech of September 6, 1980, Council for the Celebrations, p. 19.
[24] Ibid., speech of July 7, 1979, p. 18.

72

be nurtured in the wisdom of Islam: all other forms of education would blossom out of the garden of Islam; any remnant of Western education which was contrary to Islam was to be eliminated from the educational program of the country. Adherence to Islam was pleasing to God; it was God who would reward such devotion by making certain that an Islamic civilization would compete in all the ways that counted: technologically, culturally, scientifically, and certainly, philosophically. This had been the case centuries before when Islam swept Asia, North Africa, and parts of Europe; then, for several hundred years, Islam was the dominant and superior civilization, making the West seem barbaric by comparison. Now all that had changed and it was time for Islam to be vindicated; the deputy minister even proclaimed that "we expect the entire world will respond to the message of Islam and thus be freed from 'world arrogance'" (a reference to both Soviet communism and American capitalism).

Clearly if Allah had not convinced one that Islam (and especially the way it is presented by Imam Khomeini) was the truth, then, if one were a professor or teacher in Iran, one would, by virtue of one's skepticism, be forced out of work, for one did not have the eyes to see, one was under the powers of darkness. In the mean time, those who were given (or forced themselves to imagine) the joy of faith in Islam and Ayatollah Khomeini were more than content with the changes in the educational system. Writing anonymously in the Manchester *Guardian*, an Iranian intellectual in exile described the "psychology" of the present regime by quoting the Grand Mullah of the Isfahan revolutionary committee:

All my life I have only been giving sermons on God's Paradise. I have sometimes had occasion to doubt whether it's true. Now, when I see my merest wishes come true as soon as they are expressed, when flying up in the former Army commander-in-chief's helicopter I look down at the city at my feet, I see that Paradise does well and truly exist and that I am in Paradise.[25]

Others see hell in Iran; to one whose vision is informed by Islamic realities it is, apparently, Paradise itself. One questions whether the Imam would subscribe to the notion that Iran has already become "Paradise," since, as mentioned earlier, according to Khomeini, what exists in Iran now is but "a breeze of Islam," that it will not be for twenty years that Iran will truly become Islamic. In the mean time the fact that a religious leader such as the Grand Mullah of the Isfahan revolutionary committee can experience such heavenly fulfillment means that the revolution is unfolding in the center of God's desire, and there-

---

[25] "An Eyewitness to Khomeini's Terror," *The Guardian*, March 7, 1982.

fore within the design of man's bliss. This is extreme; it is, however, the precise thinking (or rather feeling) of those such as the *pasdaran* (Guardians of the Revolution), the *hezbollahi* (Party of God), and the *Mostaz'afin*, great masses of the "oppressed," i.e. the underprivileged. those who lived in destitute poverty under the reign of the Shah. The *Velayate Faqih* (government of the religious guide) took its orders from Islam, but Islam and the Twelfth Imam had a representative on earth who, through his unequalled piety, his unfailing wisdom, transmitted the true impulses of divine knowledge and procedure as these impulses came from God and articulated themselves through the purity of consciousness of the Imam. Education was thus necessarily a part of achieving Paradise; it was ultimately to acquaint an individual with God's laws and with the potential divine purpose of man's life, with the potential divine manifestation of the wholeness of existence, the Oneness of God, the immortal substance of man's soul. The secular—or even the relativistic religious—position was utterly incommensurable with the *Velayate Faqih*, and with regards to education that incompatibility, that antagonism was the difference between (at least in terms of emotion) the astronomer gazing at the stars with his telescope and the poor but pious shepherd, whose gaze fills him with reverence for the Creator of the stars. Individuality as determined by God; individuality as determined by the interpretation by that individuality. And, for the time being, it was clear that even God himself did not make any sort of unequivocal and unambiguous declaration of his intention, of even his existence. He had made it possible to doubt him, and for those who sincerely questioned whether God would condone the divine fiat of the Imam, or questioned whether there was even a basis in divine revelation and law, support for or acquiescence in the present government of Iran (along with its educational system which aimed, in the words of the Minister of Education, "to consolidate the *hezbollahis'* reign in the schools") was an act of existential, not to mention political, extinction. Why, if there was a God, did he not make his existence (and, in the context of this revolution, his predilections for the pattern of Islamic government—after all even some of the prominent ayatollahs disagreed with the *ijtihad* (interpretation of Islamic law) of Ayatollah Khomeini, and for their outspoken criticism were placed under house arrest)—why did this God not make evident his existence to each individual soul that was sincerely moved by moral values, by moral instincts? Did it necessarily hold that those who accepted Allah and the authority of Imam Khomeini were superior human beings, superior in the sense of being more conscious of Creation and its meaning? This was one of the vexatious issues that would plague any honest analyst of the revolution who recognized the deep and authentic spirituality at its basis.

Perhaps piety was as important as I.Q. in the ultimate education of the human soul. Certainly the present scheme of the Islamic government, as enunciated by the current Minister of Educaton, Ali Akhbar Parvaresh, rewarded and took as the supreme qualification this piety and surrender to Islam.In this context one might ask: who was a wiser man, a more educated man, St. Augustine or Lionel Trilling? For the Iranians the St. Augustine model (and Ayatollah Khomeini was not very different from this great Christian divine, at least in his absolute devotion to God, his intolerance to heresy) dominated; the liberalized man was a corruption of satanic forces. Besides, the greatest human being had been an illiterate: the Prophet Mohammad, an individual whose lack of education made him like the Virgin Mary: he could receive innocently the impulses of intelligence of the Creator. If the Prophet could survive and distinguish himself in the eyes of God by his untutored wisdom, how necessary was it after all to seek after a Harvard or a Cambridge education? What counted was one's closeness to God; everything else was, in a sense, superfluous.

Visit to Fayziya Theological School in Qum

Qum was considered to be a holy city because it was the center of a number of Islamic schools and the residence of most of the senior ayatollahs. I was told there were upwards of 60,000 religious students studying in Qum, and that the center of the identity of Qum was its religious consciousness. Upon arriving in Qum we immediately visited the most famous theological school, Fayziya, where in 1975 the Shah's Imperial Guards had thrown mullahs and students from the rooftops (the students and teachers had barricaded themselves inside the school and were shouting "Long live Khomeini!" from the same rooftops) leaving dozens of broken bodies and streams of blood on the concrete courtyard below. Those who had died and those who had survived the fall were then taken by helicopter and dropped from the sky into a salt lake just outside of Qum. The school was closed down, not to be re-opened until the revolution was victorious.

The account of this massacre had been described to me by a twenty-year-old student who at the time was only fourteen. He told how the police in Qum had originally placed a sharp barrier around the school and then had thrown tear gas at the shouting teachers and students. The people who had gathered to watch the confrontation had thrown sand and stones inside the school for the students and teachers.The police had then cut the electricity and water. The Shah then phoned and announced that any teachers or students not willing to swear allegiance to the Shah and support his party would be barred from the school. Then his Imperial Guards arrived by helicopter, broke the door down with a ramming rod, and with ladders scaled the roofs and picked up the protesters and threw them down upon the pavement below. Heads were smashed and Holy Qur'ans were tossed onto the road outside the school. With blood running over the pavement and streaming even out of the police cars the injured and dead were driven away to be carried into the helicopters and dropped into the salt sea.

It was inconceivable to me how the Shah would not realize that this desecration of religious property and the violent murder of beloved teachers and students of the most famous theological school in Iran would cause a deep scar—no, an open and unassuageable wound—deep in the consciousness of the people and the religious community. The deaths of these teachers and students, whose only sin was to publicly proclaim their loyalty to Ayatollah Khomeini, could only be vindicated in a violent overthrow of the monarchy and system of military rule that made such an atrocity possible. Those that had been sacrificed had died not just for an "open society," for equal rights, for a higher standard of living; they had died for Allah, and what would happen after the revolution had succeeded would not be according to predictions of lukewarm Muslims, or the liberal social democrats—nor, of course, of the Marxists. Blood had been shed—and within a ceremony of martyrdom that was part of the whole mythology of Shi'a Islam; these martyrs now demanded (or so was the surmising of the religious leaders and the believers) justice; their power had become greater in their martyrdom, and even those souls who had perished brutally on the pavement inside the courtyard of the theological school were giving their grace, their *barakah* to those still clothed in their human flesh. The mythology was absolute; the aftermath of the revolution would have to be similarly absolute. Would the Prophet Mohammad have attempted to form a democratic state based on ideas of individual freedom and pluralistic ideologies? No, and this revolution was not situated in time; it was going on in sacred, not profane, time and therefore the fact that this was the latter half of the twentieth century was not a calculation that meant anything. Modernism meant nothing in the context of eternity—and eternal truths. These people were even more conservative than Pope John Paul II.

Surrounded by Theological Students in Qum

After watching the prayers and having heard three prominent ayatollahs speak to us: Ayatollah Montazeri, the proposed successor to Ayatollah Khomeini, Ayatollah Golpayegani, and Ayatollah Mar'ashi—three out of the six or seven most prominent ayatollahs in all of Iran (each was impressive in his own way; each radiated, in varying and distinctive manner, the serenity and conviction that seems to accompany the spiritual evolution that presumably takes place from—in the case of Ayatollah Golpayegani—sixty years of religious devotion)—having visited these ayatollahs I found myself surrounded by students from the Fezeih school. We were actually on the street by this time, and about forty students began to ask me questions—or rather began to answer some of my own questions, which prompted questions of their own. They were absolutely dedicated to their studies and when I inquired whether they ever felt bored, whether they experienced some of the cycles of frustration or lassitude that students experience in high schools and universities in the West, their immediate reply was this was impossible. Studing the Qur'an with outstanding teachers, steeping oneself in this sacred knowledge, mastering Arabic, the language of the Qur'an, learning the many aspects of Islam—these activities brought one closer to God and therefore to one's true self. Islam existed as the method God had revealed to the Prophet for man to harmonize himself with the universe and to rise above his weakness and selfish desire in order to transcend the ego, which was "a prelude to the perfection of man-kind."[26] No matter that they had stopped asking questions about ultimate matters; these had been decided; the object was not to skepti-cally examine the merits of competing arguments about the nature of reality and man's purpose on earth (or if indeed there were a purpose); no, the object was to receive, integrate, and consolidate this divine knowledge into one's very being, and in this way to "come to true and eternal life through divine life."[27] In their faces was the undeniable joy in what they were learning; in their faces was the confidence that they were soldiers of the Prophet, that Islam was indeed the very highest Knowl-edge that existed; and that this revolution was the purest outcome of the sincere desires and prayers of all true Muslims in the world. Nothing could convince them they were deceived, or that their faith was merely a determined affirmation of things unseen; no, these young men saw the

[26] Ayatollah Khomeini, speech of February 26, 1981, Council for the Celebration, p. 19.
[27] Ibid. p. 4.

acquisition of knowledge as the source of man's fulfillment, and all the knowledge necessary to realize one's destiny on earth—and in heaven—was contained in the pages of the Qur'an. I remembered what a contrast I felt in talking to students at Cambridge, or just seeing the effect of the knowledge they were gaining —in the classics, in sciences, or whatever it might happen to be—; the students at Qum had a humility, a *pietas* towards the universe and God, and this surrender and faith gave to their countenances a glow and happiness that was not present at Cambridge, as impressive and brilliant as that other more cerebral glow might be. No, the intellectual presumptions of Western, non-religious thought tended to isolate the ego, tended to increase the sense of pettiness and pride, and thus seemed to severely limit the expression of the heart. One couldn't help but notice how these contrasting systems of education revealed themselves as one walked through Caius College at Cambridge, and as one walked here, through the corridors of the theological school. And the comparison even holds true when applied to theological students in the West. Here, the emphasis on the rational, the still culturally conditioned primacy of the ego and the intellect meant that most students of religion in the West lacked the all-out rhythms of surrender and self-extinction which were at the heart of the procedures of Islam. No, my prejudices were not the sole determinant of my observations: even Confucian knowledge had much more resemblance to the system of learning that expressed itself indirectly in the attitude, in the demeanour and presence of these young Muslims. Before the revolution Islam did not have much relevance to the power and authority that governed Iran; now it was from these students that eventually Iran—if the revolution survived and flourished—would be governed. And someone who had studied Islam for many years was looked upon as a human being who possessed the most treasured wisdom, and therefore these religious leaders who had been assassinated by the Mujahaddin (in retaliation for executions, alleged torture, and massive repression) were considered priceless sources of power and integrity for the country. It was clearly implied that to assassinate a member of the 'ulama was more destructive to God's purposes and to the balance of good and evil in the world than to assassinate a citizen.

The students told me they had all visited the war front where they found their Islam tested, where they actually fought and taught and prayed with the soldiers. This had brought them closer to Imam Khomeini and to Islam, and they confirmed that the atmosphere at the front had a kind of ecstasy to it. Some of the students at the school had been martyred, and these students were acclaimed to have reached their highest station. I asked them about their fear in going to the war front and being in danger. They said that there was no attempt to suppress their fear since that fear did not exist. The ideology of Islam was too much impressed into their consciousness to even permit some feeling that was not part of their devotion to God and Islam, and therefore they took no credit for this equanimity in the face of possible death; it—the state of fearlessness and joy—was the outcome of their intimate association with the highest knowledge on earth. Whatever one may have thought about the revolution it was impossible to understand its central impulse without talking to those young students who would some day occupy prominent places in the Islamic Republic of Iran. There was nothing really that I could give to them; God had not made them feel any deficiency; they were fulfilled in this and only this activity, an activity that had empirically demonstrated its truthfulness, its ultimate benedictive grace.

An Encounter with an Irish Muslim

I was told by some of the students that there was a Muslim student from Ireland who now lived in Qum, who studied at the school, and who was someone with whom I should speak.

When I asked how this Irish youth (he was now twenty-seven; he had become a Muslim in Pakistan four years ago) had come to the Muslim faith he explained that what life offered in the West was a violation of his humanity, that until he found Islam he had been "not much more than an animal; no: worse than an animal." As he went from country to country, searching for a fulfillment that he had not yet found, he felt guided by some beneficent force. Once he had embraced Islam his spiritual hunger, his quest for ultimate meaning and purpose spontaneously began to be satisfied, until he became convinced that Islam, more than any other religion, represented the most perfect system of belief and practice."As I progressed in Islam I felt the sense of certainty that Islam had been sent down for the benefit and perfection of mankind. I had always felt that life was eternal; Islam convincingly told me it was the key to eternal felicity."

Islam consisted of three things: "belief, purification, and action." All three were necessary to fulfill God's will: believing in God, purifying one's self, and acting in accordance with God's laws. Once Mohammed Salaman Tawheedi (he would not divulge his pre-Islamic name) had become a Muslim he felt confirmed in his perception that England (where he received his schooling) was a society of "aggression, injustice, and conceit." There was no humbleness before God; the society structured its priorities according to moral criteria which were anti-Islamic, and therefore anti-divine. English society had "contempt for those feelings that are at the basis of religious awareness." It was a cold and heartless society, one not given over to those values that would have fulfilled this articulate, wounded, brooding, devout Irishman. He was "disgusted with the English system" and here, living in Iran, he experienced a common aspiration and life style, living for God, living to come near to God: this was the only real basis for fulfillment of life.

I asked what he thought about the metaphysic of individuality in the West, the glorification of subjective experience, of privatized reality that came from emancipating oneself from any sort of traditional religious mythology (such as Christianity). I contrasted this with the notion of surrender in Islam. But the moment I mentioned the principle, the human tropism of surrender, he immediately attempted to clarify what surrender in the context of Islam meant:

Surrender in Islam does not mean you surrender 'to what is happening.' Surrender in Islam is surrender to God's will. It means what God says you have to do, you do. And this is not some one-sided thing. Why does God say it? God says it not because he needs us, because he needs our help; he doesn't need our worship. He wants it for us to perfect, so that we can become clean enough to come near Him. And if we don't do what he says, we can't invent anything that will get us near Him. And why are we following this path? Where does it lead? Towards Himself, His heaven, His grace—however you want to individualize Him. 'Heaven' means near to Him. In the Qur'an of the Holy Prophet, who I agree is the most perfect of all humankind, there is the testimony of the shortest distance between man and God: this consists in two bows: the Prophet bows in submission to God; then God bows to the Prophet in mercy.

He explained that God had only one desire: "to get us into His mercy." Only Islam brought this about in a rational and efficient manner, for in Islam, as opposed to other religions, reason was supreme. (I had never, until I read brilliant Islamic hermeneutic scholarship such as that of Seyyed Hossein Nasr[28] [discredited with the present regime for his close ties with the Shah], thought of Islam as a pre-eminently rational religion. It is strange how Islam has seemed to be almost the victim of a conspiracy that would create the sense—even subconsciously—that it was, of all the major religions, the most primitive, barbaric, and unlyrical.) As this serious Irish Muslim spoke there was the sense he was a teacher, upholding the sacredness of his Tradition, lecturing to a benighted audience. There was a tremendous strength and conviction in his presentation of Islam—behind the words there was a total commitment; he

---

[28] See especially *Ideals and realities of Islam* (London: George Allen & Unwin, 1966).

80

would never be persuaded by parent, friend, or Western intellectual that he had perhaps misjudged the West. He had lived among the infidels; he knew that corruption of the system; and now he had vowed to purify himself of all the wretchedness that he had been exposed to in living in an unGodly civilization, utterly dislocated from the original sources of spiritual vitality.

There was only one goal now: God. God was the real destination—even beyond Paradise. In between God and one's self resided all the Prophets and the Imams. The greater *jihad* (the war against one's baser self) did not have any "ceasefires," whereas the lesser *jihad*, for example the war against Iraq, would come to an end. In man was a "rebel against God" and desires that represented a will opposed to God's laws was a will that would have to be conquered. Studying here in Qum among the other, mostly Iranian, Muslim students and teachers, Mohammed Salaman Tawheedi of Dublin origin found that his heart responded with love to the knowledge of the scriptures, to the all-encompassing system of law and belief that emerged from those scriptures. I asked him the difference between the love felt by someone who gives himself to dancing and the love he experienced in studying and practising Islam. He defined love as "a power which emits from a pure heart towards some infinite source of goodness, purity, and light." This love came about in the inner relationship of the soul and God; any activity that did not address itself to this relationship could not, in the highest sense of the word, love, be properly called love.

As much as I respected his commitment and the integrity of his religion I still experienced a more than slight reaction to the West; not that he should be uncritical of the West; not that he should even desist from attributing much of his misery (and the misery of many millions of others) to the prevailing conditioning and culture of the West. No, what concerned me was the violence of his rejection of anything to do with his origins; he could not see—however modest it might be—the positive (at least potentially so) aspects of Western society. And I felt that psychologically, however justified his critique might be in terms of the ideology he now embraced, he was transferring some of his own lack of wholeness and inner harmony (i.e. his own negativity) to a more abstract enemy: Western way of life. He was not a disinterested Muslim and the faults of the West became the means of ventilating some of his still existing rage, a rage borne not just of frustration of his spiritual heart, but borne of a personality that had not yet perfected itself, had not yet evolved out of his own limitations.

I remember one moment when we were eating lunch together, seeing that some subtle level of his consciousness still yearned to identify with his origins. This was not conscious; perhaps I should say that his *un-*

conscious rebelled against the abrupt and decisive shift in his whole metaphysical and emotional allegiance, and that he would never entirely escape—at least if individuality counted something in the development of the soul, if collective, racial memories signified anything—from his Western roots, that indeed, God himself had placed him in the West in order to learn and master things that could not be learned and mastered anywhere else. But he had uprooted himself and was convinced in the deepest part of his being that he had only done what was necessary, what God willed. The West was hopelessly lost spiritually, was a land of darkness, a land of evil. Only when Islamic troops occupied the West would there be any opportunity for salvation. For me I had wished that his surrender and espousal of Islam could have tempered his antipathy for his origins, for that very antipathy was subjectively and not just objectively based. He had to make the West out as evil in order to legitimize to his unconscious his decision to become a Muslim. On some subtle level he suffered the consequences of abjuring his Western origins, although for the time being it might be a spiritual transfusion that he had experienced in annihilating the currents of individuality and identity that he had involuntarily derived from the geography of his birth, the psychology of his tribal roots. He struck me as quite an exceptional human being, a strongly individualistic personality despite his disavowal of the importance of the ego. No, I almost questioned him about the reaction I felt within his psyche, but I felt that might even be too dangerous; he needed this fresh and universal identification; clearly he had derived powerful rewards from Islam; he could, in four years of studying, read Arabic, speak fluent Farsi, and live happily without returning to Europe. And it was not likely, he said, that he would return to Ireland for quite some time; he might never go back.

His Islamic faith had brought us together; his Islamic faith had integrated and consecrated his own life; his Islamic faith had given him a final and unswervable purpose; and yet his Islamic faith had also delimited the form of communication we could have, because somewhere I sensed some level of affinity between us that could never be experienced, let alone articulated, because the orientation of Islam did not align itself with the exploration of individual feelings, of open-ended communication, of the personal unknown. One's duties, one's attitudes, one's orientation—especially in the case of a Westerner who had severed himself from his indigenous past—defined the boundaries of conversation and experience; we were not permitted to find out where we happened to be in the universe, free of all dogmatic ideas, free of all conceptions of absolutes. I yearned in a moment to see him suddenly free of Islam—not because of anything unworthy or even inappropriate in his bond to being a Muslim—but because something about his own conflict and inner tension when he was still but an individual, remained unresolved; his role as an actor in the drama had not consummated itself. Some powerful current of meaning and feeling related to his own uniqueness remained unanswered, and in ambivalence, an ambivalence, however, that could not now be understood and discovered in its real significance. While on the one hand I could rejoice in the undeniable happiness he had achieved in embracing Islam, in the dignity with which he now lived his life, still, on another level I grieved at what I intuitively knew to be some sort of amputation of the specific configuration of his selfhood, a selfhood that could only master its fate in environs that were Western.

Nevertheless there were, at least in moments, feelings of appreciation that passed between us, and although he could not probably find any sort of doctrinal or legitimate intellectual reason for this appreciation, it was obvious that under different circumstances we could have been close friends. There was something noble, proud, distinguished about his soul, his bearing, his intellect. The arbitrary manner, the dismissal of Western values, the assumed superiority of Islam to anything else: all this could not prevent him from revealing a power and attractiveness that was distinctly individual, and not the consequence of his Islamic purifications.

I met his American wife (they had met in Tehran only two years ago where he was teaching Islam) briefly and we said goodbye, his last words being an entreaty "not to write too critically about me." I detected in that remark an obvious gesture of humour, but also—and this struck me as significant—a Western mannerism, a supplication, however facetious in tone, that reflected his still individualized orientation, for the remark had nothing to do with Islam, and was uttered in perhaps the most unguarded and spontaneous fashion of anything that he had thus far said. He was vulnerable in that moment; he was transcending his doctrinaire outlook; he was human.

Interview with a Prominent Critic of the Regime, a Member of the Majlis

I had wanted to speak to a government official who did not take the radical line of most of those whom I had met in Iran on this visit. I had previously corresponded with Dr. Mehdi Bazargan, the first prime minister of the Provisional Government formed under the supervision of Imam Khomeini in February 1979. Bazargan was considered a moderate, but his allegiance to Islam was unarguable. He had been a staunch foe of the Shah, had been imprisoned and tortured, and was with the Imam when Khomeini lived in his villa in France after being expelled from Iraq under pressure from the Shah. Bazargan had responded favourably to an open letter I had written to Khomeini in June of 1981, in which I expressed my deep concerns about the executions.[29] There he had confirmed my doubts about the wisdom of attributing all the ills of the present government to the United States, about the wisdom of absolute measures of retaliation against the deceived Mujahaddin, now referred to contemptuously as the Munafeqin, the "hypocrites." Bazargan was a devout Muslim, close to the Imam, but he adopted an attitude of mildness and restraint when it came to militant sloganeering, militant hatred of America, militant determination to imprison all those who criticized the policies, the actions, the rhetoric of the *'ulama*-dominated government and the revolutionary courts.

I had hoped to meet with Bazargan, but instead was given the opportunity to speak with Ebrahim Yazdi, the former foreign minister in the Bazargan government, and the Imam's representative in the United States while Khomeini was in exile. Yazdi had formerly been a prominent pathologist at the University of Texas and an articulate opponent of the Shah. Now he was under constant attack from the more radical and conservative elements in the country, especially in the Majlis where Ayatollah Khalkhali had tried to get a motion of censure in order to oust him from any sort of power. He was a kind of martyr to a more liberal and democratic vision of Iran—and of Islam; my two hour discussion—held in the presence of six or seven other Muslims and journalists—provided me with the most persuasive and characteristic criticism of the regime—from the point of view of someone who still supported the revolution. Yazdi's remarks made the interview with Bazargan unnecessary, for he spoke for a whole sector of intelligent and cultured Iranians (and Muslims) who were disturbed by the demagogic, strident, irrational personality of the revolution—as it expressed itself in the refusal to permit open discussion, open debate about matters pertaining to the running of the government, and matters affecting the treatment of both the mild and the violent critics of the revolution. If men like Yazdi were finally silenced the one hope of moderating the revolution would be lost. To listen to Yazdi was to listen to the voice of an eminently reasonable, just, and intelligent man. It was, however, a voice that did not carry the spirituality of the revolution; it was a voice

---

[29] See Appendix for the letter to Khomeini and the response of Bazargan. For a contrast to Bazargan's response and as perhaps the most eloquent apology for the punitive actions of the revolutionary courts, see the letter of Ali Quli Qarai which follows that of Bazargan.

84

that had not heard the deepest and most absolute note of the revolution; no, for the purposes of hearing the song of the revolution, Dr. Ebrahim Yazdi was tone deaf. But in the next breath to say that he was therefore deceived or prejudiced in his disquisition on the faults and problems of the regime would be incorrect. Indeed, if one listened to the content of his argument one would have to become a convinced liberal or moderate; one would have to acknowledge that something highly irrational, reckless, and intemperate was taking over the country, and that Yazdi's most vocal opponents eschewed reason or compromise, were driven to enact a radical form of Islam that would decimate the last vestiges of intelligent, democratic discourse, that would bring about a society more closed than the society of the Shah.

But Yazdi still supported the revolution—a revolution that he had fought for. He claimed absolute allegiance to Islam and was, in his estimation, only trying to see things the way they were, not to impose some idea that avoided objectivity at any cost (and this seemed to be a valid interpretation of the revolution at one level: one had to, in a certain sense, believe that 2 plus 2 was 5—if such a belief was the functional equivalent of truth in so far as it strengthened the revolution and unified the people in their belief in Islam. Yazdi was one of those who insisted that 2 plus 2 was 4 and not 5. However, in saying 2 plus 2 was 5 it could be possible, within the complexity of God's Script, that one came closer towards another, more universal truth). For the present time a more absolutist, authoritarian, and black-and-white view of reality served the revolution, served the cause of Islam. Dr. Yazdi was not one of those persons blessed to understand the necessity of absolute irrationality in the service of radical transformation. In such transformation it may be that debate is merely a waste of precious energy, that the important thing is to believe and act according to those principles and procedures that seem to most unify and consolidate the spirituality of the revolution. Throughout my conversation with Yazdi I was aware of his undoubted sincerity, but also the sterility of his heart—at least in the sense of his ability to manifest the poetic feeling that characterized so many of the soldiers and Revolutionary Guards at the war front, the students at Qum. This revolution was, for those who were given the knowingness that it was being guided by Truth, an intimation of Paradise; for those not able to participate in this graced belief, the revolution represented an advanced state of Hell. Ebrahim Yazdi was in a small minority of people who were in between. It was hard to imagine their ever gaining any kind of influence, especially now under the exigencies of war.

The interview which follows will reveal some of the philosophical concerns—perhaps metaphysical biases—of the author, but the central point about the interview (at least the part of it that is quoted here) centers on the status of Imam Khomeini, for although I had yet to meet the Imam at this point in my visit, I did sense that without his presence, without his leadership, the revolution would not have happened, nor would it have lasted as long as it has. The majority—or, at least, the most virulent and prominent majority—of the Iranian people expressed a love for Ayatollah Khomeini that was categorically different from any expression of affection or loyalty that characterized any group of people for a political leader (the Imam, I was told, was the Commander-in-Chief of the Armed Forces and received reports from the war front each day and made his recommendations to the generals and to the commanders of the Revolutionary Guards) in this century and even in all the history I had read. Only the Prophet seemed—at least in my reading of the facts—to have accomplished the following that the Imam had now, and it was this extraordinary devotion for the Imam which prompted me to inquire about his spiritual status, for of course I had read about his profound understanding of Islamic mysticism, that he had even taught courses in mysticism, and his writings[30] on the subject of mysticism were classical in their delineation of the difference between the Absolute and the Relative, in their delineation of the state of beatitude and wholeness achieved by the mystic (usually referred to as a Sufi). And while I was aware of the danger of assuming that Muslims placed Imam Khomeini on a different plane of reality than themselves, a plane of reality that presupposed a different ontological mode of being —a state of enlightened Self-awareness—nevertheless the psychological atmosphere, the presumed idea of his enlightenment seemed to dominate the consciousness of the people, seemed indeed to be at the very heart of the revolution. I had heard about Dr. Yazdi's criticism of the revolution—or criticism of the radicalizing of the revolution—and I wondered whether support or criticism of the revolution and the will of the prevailing powers of authority came from some either recognized or unacknowledged idea of the fallibility, the personal limitations of the Imam, who for all intents and purposes, did act as the supreme guide of the revolution, the oracle, the diviner of what lay hidden in the Script. At the same time I thought to open my conversation by assuming that part of his restraint in endorsing everything that was happening in Iran was due in part to his realization that there was an expression of individuation that, corrupted as it might be, expressed itself creatively within Western civilization. I had anticipated that part of his more controlled criticism of the West had come about because his con-

---

[30] See Hamid Algar's excellent translation of Khomeini's speeches and writings: *Islam and Revolution: Writings and Declarations of Imam Khomeini* (Berkeley: Mizan Press, 1981).

86

tacts in the West had made him respectful of at least some of the pluralistic, variegated modes of self-expression that were a dominant characteristic of a civilization that had essentially 'liberated' itself from a dependence upon a unified, mythologically-shaped vision of the universe. But for Yazdi the question did not produce any productive discussion and I soon moved on to my curiosity about the state of consciousness—or state of esteem in which he was held by the people, and especially himself (Yazdi)—of the Imam, for clearly right from the start I sensed the absence of that strange yet innocent manna (or mania) of the revolution that was available only to those who knew in their hearts that all the martyrs were alive, that Allah Himself was orchestrating this revolution.

R.C.:   Dr. Yazdi, do you feel this revolution has anything to learn from Western civilization? In other words, do you feel that the way in which the ideology of Islam has been expressed in this revolution, its unmitigated hostility towards the West, is necessary to preserve its embryonic integrity? That, at some point, it will begin to acknowledge that the house of Goethe will never be the house of the Prophet? That these are essential divergencies of universal meaning that, ultimately, are irreconcilable? Is this antipathy towards the West a strategically necessary response, and to what extent do you feel that it could, at some point, become something that could act as a curse upon this revolution?

E.Y.:   It depends upon how you define Western civilization...

R.C.:   I define—at least in the context of my question—Western civilization as that complex of history and experience that has, at least in its more modern phases, freed the individuality of man in the realm of his own subjectivity, freed him to express himself outside of a mythology that necessarily puts limits upon his freedom of expression. Do you think this 'freedom' of the self to act according to individual rather than universally revealed values is simply an aberration, something that leads to the pathology of the soul? Granted, there has been a corruption of the individual because of the breakdown of tradition and the unfettered indulgence of sensual appetite, but is there something valid in the Faustian emphasis on experience for one's self as opposed to submission to an acknowledged power greater than oneself: i.e. God?

E.Y.:   When one talks about man expressing himself, then we have to first define the nature of man. Because we know one of the biggest problems of Western culture—I differentiate between Western civilization and Western culture—is mental pollution, the alienation of man from his own true nature. As long as you have not solved the problem of the alienation of man in Western culture, or, as you say, Western civilization, then the problem of 'self-expression' will not be solved. Because what you call self-expression is a by-product of that civilization. One is under the influence of the environment in a Western society. That influence is a form of artificial conditioning of tastes and attitudes that alienates man from his real self. Therefore when you speak about his "self-expression," what is it that he or she is expressing? Is one expressing the true nature of the human being, or is one expressing the alienated and alienating conditioning that the environment has imposed on one?

R.C.: In other words what you are saying is that it is not part of God's plan for man to think of his existence as problematical. Emphasis on the unknowability, on the ambiguity of existence is just the outcome of his alienation from himself and God; it does not have an ontologically valid purpose, say, as expressed for instance in the philosophy of existentialism. You are saying that all forms of self-expression in the West which essentially do not address themselves to the nature of man in an absolute sense—and his consequent obligation to obey the laws of God—are in fact a product of the alienation of man from his true nature?

E.Y.: Particularly, massive progress in communication continuously places man under the influence of rapacious consumerist propaganda; this enticement, this coercion of and influence upon his mind creates mental pollution. There is talk of soil pollution, water pollution, air pollution but one never hears anything about mental pollution. The West criticizes us because in an Islamic society we want to condition man to think this way or that way. But in the West you are continuously conditioning man's attitudes and sense of reality; perhaps less directly, but the impact is there.

R.C.: Unconsciously.

E.Y.: Unconsciously. And this form of conditioning (generated by uncontrollable consumerist manipulation) is more cheating and deceiving than the conditioning you accuse us of. Your wife thinks that it is *she* who is going to buy the Tide, or this and that. But actually she is not. Her desire is created by something outside herself. You are consuming so many products, and you think and believe that it is *you* who is doing the choosing, the buying, making a decision; but that is not the real *you*. So where is that free expression?

R.C. *(Sensing that this topic has been exhausted, anxious to stimulate a more controversial conversation.)*: Has God provided within the script of Western civilization any other ultimate solution than the Christian one? Or, to make it simpler: you are a Muslim. Do you feel that Islam is inevitable once the West wakes up to its alienation, when the pain of this alienation presumably becomes too great? Will the West turn to Islam, or do you feel there is a different ontological dimension that operates in the Western sphere of experience, an ontological dimension that reinforces the sense of multiplicity, of differentiation of the ego, the sense of the self as a unique event in the universe whose sanctity would in some sense be denied in that sphere of experience whose ontology only recognizes the Oneness of existence, and the need for man to define himself according to an a priori order? *(At this point I knew we couldn't go any further with this topic unless Dr. Yazdi truly grasped the meaning of my line of questioning, the significance of which was, at least in my estimation, crucial to a final assessment of the revolution and its relationship to Western civilization.)*

E.Y.:   The West is coming. They are coming. And I am very optimistic because God, in the Holy Qur'an is saying that "O you, mankind, you are denying, or you are resistant, you resent the message of God. But you eventually will come to God's terms. But in a very long way, in a very long way."

R.C.:   The resistance then is purely perverse—it is the evil within man rebelling against what is known innately to be true? There is no final—or even relative—value in man's resistance of mythology?

E.Y.:   Why does he resist? Because man wants to test, man wants to do things by himself. When a man wants to be a human being, wants to go through maturation, wants to experience everything—he is heedless of restraints. Western society is going through these experiences, and they are going to learn that this freedom is not real freedom; they are going to learn it the hard way. They are seeking that point of freedom, what they call freedom of expression, but this is not what it means actually *to be.* Western society has many social ills, and they are experimenting with this and that, but I don't have any doubt that eventually they will come to recognize that the only answer to their ills is that which delivers to each man his true nature and the true nature of God. We call this Islam.

R.C. *(At this point I moved the conversation to an altogether different topic: the perceived spiritual status of Imam Khomeini. Familiar as I was with the literature on Sufism, and having read the mystical writings of Imam Khomeini, I had assumed there was a general consensus as to the established state of 'Self-realization' on the part of the Imam—but I was interested in how explicitly this was acknowledged and how such a state was operationally defined. My speculations were, as will be seen, met with considerable opposition. I did, however, wish to touch the most sensitive nerve of the revolution and, perhaps, even to provocatively draw out a reaction from Yazdi, that he might see the basis of his conditional support for the revolution.):*   My second question: do you accept the idea that the Imam is capable of violating the laws of the universe? *(In Islamic and other mystical writing, there is a fundamental agreement that the permanent state of liberation from the ego brings with it a spontaneous lawfulness; which is to say that the overcoming of narrow selfhood removes the primary source of resistance within the individual to the intention of God's intelligence, and therefore all the actions of the 'realized' individual are in accordance with those laws which support the positive and creative development of all creatures. An individual who has achieved this wholeness of consciousness cannot—even if he should try to—break the laws of Being, because his very individuality is now determined by the laws which uphold the unfolding of the universe, the awakening of consciousness.)*

E.Y.:   The what?

R.C.:   Do you believe the Imam is without error, that he has achieved a state of selfhood such that all his actions are supportive to what is good and beneficial for the universe? To what extent would you qualify his status? Has he reached some level of personal functioning that, in its character, differs from the mode of functioning of yourself or myself?

E.Y.:   Of course; we are all different from each other. These differences are natural.

R.C.:   But...

E.Y.:   The decisions we are making are directly related to our understanding of the ideology of Islam. To the extent of our deep understanding of social problems and social ills, to the extent of our understanding of human nature—this will determine the validity of our actions. The more knowledgeable you are in these areas, and the more you are prepared to analyze and synthesize, the more creative and appropriate you will be in answering the problems. Of course if you compare the Imam with me you could say he is at a higher level; he understands the depths of Islam better than I do; and the nature of Iranians, the nature of man in general better than I do...

R.C.:   But he is not one with God? I don't mean one with God in the Absolute sense...*(This turned out to be an unfortunate wording, but it did, nevertheless, trigger off a candid and doctrinal rebuttal that answered my question indirectly.)*

E.Y.:   In Islam we don't believe that.

R.C.:   But has he extinguished that within him which separates him absolutely from God?

E.Y.:   I don't understand. What are you separating from God?

(At this point it became obvious that Dr. Yazdi had no understanding—at least intuitively—of the mystical experience; he was stuck rather absolutely within a frame of reference which did not yield up any sort of feeling that could guide him towards the truth that I was seeking to have revealed. He seemed dumb to the tendencies within the movement of our conversation which inexorably was leading to some sort of climax of meaning. The concept of transcendence and wholeness of the Self did not creatively constitute part of his experience, or his understanding. He quite simply

*was cut off from this knowledge and this intuition, which immediately
began to explain to me his difficulty with the divinely irrational nature of
the revolution. Without this capacity to absorb and to appreciate the
mystical power of what was happening in Iran, and the source of that
power (which, judging from my observations, was attributed to the integrity
of the Imam) one would be, no matter how much one believed in Islam
(which Dr. Yazdi did), frustrated, baffled, and, ultimately, disillusioned
with what was happening. But just as I was about to clarify my question, the
blind Lebanese professor, who had become irritated by the complexities
and, perhaps in his estimation, irrelevancies of my questions, interjected
with his own comment. I had experienced how the movement of my inter-
rogation had unsettled him somewhere, that he was being driven towards a
region within himself that reacted strongly to the immediacy of mystery
and the sense of the intellectual unknown. He was not, of course, conscious
of this, and this is purely an intuitive judgement of my own: it may in
fact not be true; however I felt that in some sort of mysterious way the
content and feeling of the dialogue—and particularly this issue about the
state of consciousness of the Imam—had touched the very place in which
Dr. A. was connected up with the blindness that Allah had given him to
bear from birth. The tension created by my line of questions threatened
to break out in some peremptory dismissal of the significance of continuing
on the topic at hand. But for myself it seemed I was stirring up that kind
of stress that would, if released into words, clear the air. Thus I welcomed
the interposing of the professor.)*

Dr. A.:   Excuse me. You are asking a theological question.

R.C.:   It's a very political question actually. It is a political question
in a very profound sense.

E.Y.:   If you say that the Imam has reached to the state that we call
ma'sumin[31] and that he has come to say that *ana al-haqq*[32] this is not . . .

R.C. *(My concern at this moment is to keep from getting into precise,
formulated Shi'a theological categories; rather I wish to elicit from Dr.
Yazdi a more generalized idea of the Imam's state of consciousness—or
at least how his personhood is perceived by others as occupying a different
order of closeness to God.):*   Well, obviously many Iranians, many
Muslims—and even most Muslims at this conference—in whatever way
they may express it, look upon Imam Khomeini as a human being who has

---

[31] "*Ma'sumin*: those possessing the quality of *'ismat* [divinely bestowed freedom from
error and sin]; i.e., the Prophet, Fatima [daughter of the Prophet], and the Twelve
Imams." (From Algar, op. cit. pp. 156 and 162.)

[32] Yazdi quotes the Arabic words attributed to Mansur al-Hallaj: "I am the Truth"
(meaning, I am God, one with Him)—for which he was burned at the stake.

transcended that particular kind of fallibility that characterizes the existence of most of the rest of us.

E.Y.:   No they do not.

R.C.:   This is an impression—whether this conception is articulated or not—that is undeniably true, a tacitly shared assumption that forms one of the cornerstones of the revolution.

E.Y.:   I cannot speak on their behalf, but I can talk about my own ideas and I believe you are mistaken about this matter.

R.C.:   Most Muslims, most Iranians see the Imam as just someone who is more learned and pious than they are, but not someone who has achieved some form of grace or purified perception?

Dr. A.:   May I speak? This is most certainly a theological issue.

R.C.:   It is not theological; it is a political question. *(Of course it is theological in its content, but its implications are profoundly political since if a leader of a country is thought to receive his instructions from heaven, or from a source that makes his decisions perfectly appropriate, then it follows that however much this notion is understood theologically, it—the idea of the Imam's status with God relative to other men—will continue to exert the most far-reaching influence on the thinking and behaviour of the people. As far as I was concerned this perception of the Imam as a God-realized human being was the critical factor in the mystique of the revolution. To insist the question was merely "theological" was to avoid entering into the deepest secret of the revolution, the very heart of the power and inspiration that actuated the revolution.)*

E.Y.:   Excuse me, but the Imam has not said anything to confirm your idea. Indeed he has made it clear he is an ordinary, simple human being.

Dr. A.:   The question is theological because in Islam the two are together. But I think it is important to discuss because many Americans and Canadians make this mistake, because the term Imam is used for Imam Khomeini. They think to themselves: "Okay, so what's the difference between him [Khomeini] and the Imam." Now we believe, actually Imam Khomeini himself believes, there is a great difference. *(I understood this point, just as Meister Eckhart or any Christian mystic would not consider himself within the same model of perfection of Christ; this did not however prevent the Christian mystic from finding his own inner 'Christness,' his own inner pure consciousness which was identified with "the kingdom of heaven within you." Khomeini I knew to be of a different category of 'realization' than the Imams or the Prophet because he—Imam Khomeini—had, to use an expression I have come across in Islam,* built himself, *that is to say, what he was was the result of his own efforts to reach a state of permanent harmony with God. It was Islam that had destroyed his ego-separateness, which had unified him with Allah.)*

Dr. A. (continuing):   We believe that the Imams like the Prophets, are protected by God from error. I don't like the term "infallible." *(I decided he was correct: "infallible" had the wrong connotation; it was too absolute.)* This is the meaning of the Arabic word *ma'sum.* The implication of your contention is that Imam Khomeini is a *ma'sum.* And as he is the representative of the Twelfth Imam, who is in the world but hidden from you, whose return we all wait for—his [Khomeini's] decisions are closer, because of his learning and piety, and more consciousness of spirituality,—his decisions are closer to the truth than are mine, but he is like me, subject to error. He is not a *ma'sum.*

R.C.:   Fine. Then I am to understand from your analysis that he is not a realized Sufi, that he is not someone who has achieved a form of enlightenment.

E.Y.:   I would say he is not a realized Sufi. This is what I have been saying. He has never made any such claims; he has never said he speaks *al-Haqq.*

R.C. *(Obstinately, unable to let this crucial controversy die away, still attempting to have Dr. Yazdi understand my question from a more intuitive level. If he dropped his Islamic constructs he might see that all the evidence—at least that based upon the dynamics of Khomeini's leadership and his relationship to the people, and his formidable decision-making skills—points towards a psychological perception, albeit an unexpressed one, that coincides with my own formulation of his [Khomeini's] more universalized consciousness.):*   No, but a realized Sufi does not announce his status, yet his actions reflect a different mode of being, a mode of being that is without selfishness, that is without—and spontaneously so—reference to his own limited ego. From my own point of view it matters little whether the people actually recognized this fact of the Imam from a theological standpoint; the fact is that the Imam's status is reflected in the consciousness of the people; it is a premise of the first order. Imam Khomeini has been accorded a categorically different status than anyone else in Iran and this is not accounted for just by his charisma or his undaunted courage throughout the many years of persecution under the Shah. Whether admitted or not, the assumption is there and if Allah Himself announced through a vision of the Prophet to each Muslim that Imam Khomeini was an undefiled instrument of His purpose, there would be little difference in fact from the way in which the Imam is currently seen by the people, by these same Muslims. No human being in the world (at least no human being connected to political destiny) receives this unqualified adulation and reverence. It is a spontaneous flow of emotion that seems correlated with that achievement of the spirit which is at the basis of the perfectibility of mankind. It is like Jesus among the multitudes, only in this case the Imam is not proclaiming he is the Messiah. Surely the people acknowledge in their hearts that the Imam has extinguished something that leaves him undarkened by the ignorance that characterizes the rest of us; surely the people do in fact experience the Imam as a source of light, a source of purified wisdom and unbounded consciousness. He has overcome his separateness; he exists in a relationship—at least on a primary level—of oneness with God.

Dr. A.:   Robin, you know, where the Imam is, all of us are supposed to be, but no one of us could say he would be like the Twelfth Imam or . . .

R.C. *(Sensing the need to buttress up my reasons for persisting with this argument.)*:   This is something which I have addressed to various individuals and groups in Iran: the students who took over the American Embassy, various Muslim scholars, members of the Revolutionary Guards, and most all of the responses I have obtained accord—however informally and imprecisely—with the general principle that I have been proposing in this discussion. Yes, they do, in some sense, believe that he has removed the stain of sin from himself in a way that has allowed him to achieve a kind of perpetual grace. This is acknowledged. Now it may be dangerous to pursue this idea to its logical (or illogical) limits, but it seems most pertinent to understanding how one set of people are essentially uncritical about the general direction of the revolution, while another set of people remain highly skeptical, or downright opposed, to the dominant pattern of the revolution.

E.Y.:   No. You have to look at it two ways: one is the way in which the people judge him, and the way in which he himself presents himself. *(The implication of Yazdi's comment seems pretty obvious: Khomeini allows the people to sustain the idea of his purity and sinless action, but meanwhile he makes it clear to others that this is a fiction. This seems hardly consistent with the uncompromising integrity of Imam Khomeini. He has made it clear that he regards himself as acting as the supreme leader in the absence of the Twelfth Imam. Somewhere here there is a contradiction, a contradiction, however, only for Dr. A. and for Dr. Yazdi, who remain unconvinced of my thesis, my metaphysical—and political— conclusions. But I felt inspired to prolong this dialectic in order to perhaps uncover the real reasons for the increasing isolation of Dr. Yazdi and others (for example, Dr. Bazargan) from the heart of the revolution. It should be noted, however, that once off this topic, Dr. Yazdi spoke convincingly and persuasively about matters related to extremism and moderation in the course of the revolution. But here again there was not much* barakah, *although most of his points were irrefutable.)*

R.C.:   The only reason I asked the question is because I know that you have a more sophisticated and complex view of this revolution than many of its more enthusiastic adherents and I was wondering perhaps,

whether some of your difficulties in consenting to what are currently
some of the more controversial practices—such as the executions—
arose because of your concern with the uncritical attitude of so many
others—especially towards the Imam. I am trying to get at this issue
not primarily in a political way but through an understanding that goes
deep into the unconscious of the people, the place where the archetypes
of religion touch and cling to the soul. The mystique of Imam Khomeini
is perhaps the most fascinating and powerful aspect of this revolution; I
wish only to account for that mystique since it goes beyond the relative
boundaries of ecstatic confidence that other peoples of the world reserve
for their leaders. Imam Khomeini is quietly and noisily perceived and
treated in an extraordinary way: without some reference to the idea of
the perfection of man, which is a constant theme of Islam and even of
many of the speeches of Imam Khomeini,[33] one cannot explain this
phenomenon. If Imam Khomeini has not achieved the purpose of
Islam[34] how can any devout Muslim expect to. This is, is it not, the
victory of the greater *jihad*?

But let me move to a third question: do you feel—whatever he is—
there is any danger in the way people look to the Imam?

E.Y.:   No, I don't think so. You see I have to look at this from a
certain perspective. Whenever any society—a revolution, or a social
movement—is based upon religion, and the religion becomes the ideology of that society, then it has to do with human nature, because it is
certain that religion is a part of human nature. Religious feeling,
religious sensibility is a part of the human being, like the sense of duty is
a part of the human being. So this religious sensation is deeply rooted in
human nature and it expresses itself, and is different in its nature, than
all other ideologies. And whenever you are dealing with a movement
which is based upon religious sensation, religious understanding, religious belief, then this experience goes much deeper down into the soul
than does revolutionary experience based upon another ideology.

R.C.:   Of course. In fact, religion in its highest sense *(assuming that
religion is to do with ultimate truth and ultimate reality)* is understood as
objective sensitivity to life. Religious sensitivity should purify and make
more innocent one's perception of the world. This is, at least, how
I understand religion in its more elevated and mystical sense.

E.Y.:   No, no. I am talking about religious sense as it expresses itself

---

[33] As, for instance, in a speech of April 17, 1980: "But if one trains one's self, *one's
everything will become divine* [emphasis added] and one's divine powers will be victorious."
Council for the Celebrations, p. 10.

[34] Ibid. p. 13: "Human beings are transformable and movable creatures who can elevate
themselves from mere nature to a divine position." (July 2, 1979)

in the human being. But you are talking about the manifestation. If, for example, you get a person in Africa, in America, who has religious understanding, religious belief, but they are not actually reflecting the truth, then one cannot speak of a "sensitivity to reality." This is important; this is how we differentiate between a correct and true religion, and a false and incorrect religion. But look, for example, at Bertrand Russell talking about Marxism, communism, as a religion; he argued that the communists have converted, have replaced religious feeling with a more systematic dogma. And when you examine the phenomenon of communism you see that Marxists have the same attitude towards their charismatic leaders.[35]

R.C.:   You are saying then that the attitude of the Iranians towards their leader has no special merit or distinction from that of other people towards their leaders—within a revolutionary situation. *(This was perhaps to overstate the case of Yazdi, but it pushed my point further and forced him to commit himself to a further elaboration.)*

E.Y.:   It is the same thing but expressed in a different way. Since in the case of Iran it is Islam that is the revolutionary ideology that determines the consciousness of the people, and since Islam is a true religion and the only true religion of the world, it therefore satisfies the religious feeling, the religious sensibility of the individual; moreover it is a rational religion and so it can appeal to the human mind. Nevertheless this need to adore a leader is there, but this adulation is taking place in the healthy context of Islam.

R.C.:   Well, if I were God I would make sure that Ayatollah Khomeini was in that state of consciousness which accorded with the people's perception of him, which says he is nearest to God . . . But let's move on to another question.

E.Y.:   But then it is very natural that people evolve such attitudes, particularly, as I have said, in the case of men who can understand the feelings of the people. The Imam is such a person.

R.C.:   My intuition suggests that if such a state of consciousness exists, it is imperative for the purity of the revolution and the ultimate integrity of Islam that the Imam exists in this elevated and natural state of consciousness that is described in the Sufi texts. But I can also see that in this context I am being greeted with considerable resistance to this idea. It is, however, a concept that is not familiar to the West anyway, *so I would never try to describe it into a Western sensibility* [emphasis added]. But in any case, it was of interest to me.

[35] He may have been thinking of Mao, Ho Chi Minh, or even Castro. I suppose the issue could only be resolved by someone comparing the feelings of the people in these countries during the lifetimes of these leaders with those of the Iranian people.

E.Y.: Of course I have an analysis for this too. If you look at the Qur'an carefully you see that many parts of the Qur'an reveal that the Prophet was commanded to perform *tahajjud*. It means the extra prayers during the night, that this is necessary for the elevation of man's soul, and the Imam is a person who, as far as we know, from the age of thirty has been practising this.[36] In a sense he is a Sufi. And he has these experiences.

R.C.: But my point is that either an individual is liberated or he is not. He is enlightened, or he is in ignorance. Either the impulse of God dominates his awareness, or the impulse of the ego dominates his awareness. And this is not something to be determined by his own mood or attitude. He wears dark, foggy glasses; or he wears golden glasses. It is a matter of being bounded or unbounded on the level of consciousness.

E.Y.: That particular problem needs more discussion because I believe in what William James says about the religious experiences. Because when you go through such practice [the night prayers] for a long time and you divorce yourself from any worldly attractions you reach a stage when you are given a problem you can immediately concentrate and get the answer. It's completely true. See, it's completely different from what I get from your question. So, I look at it this way, in Islamic history we have the tradition in which a great religious leader, a mullah, wants to issue an opinion. He goes and does his prayers and after the prostrations he comes with a clear answer. What does it mean? How do you describe this phenomenon? To me it is like you have a problem, and when there is noise around you, many-sided distractions, you cannot find the answer. But then you go into private, you concentrate.

R.C.: God answers the question for you.

E.Y.: God of course has the answers. God wants something to be done; He needs truth. He says He does these things through the truth. The more knowledgeable you are about the subject and the more you are capable to concentrate on any given answer, the more realistic will be your answers. To me the Imam is such a person, a person who has deep knowledge of religion and he has a long history of this religious inner experience, that I say prepares him to act efficiently, so that when you ask a question or he wanted to give an answer to a question, he has mastered this art of concentration and synthesizing and giving you an

---

[36] One of the prominent ayatollahs who lived with Imam Khomeini confirmed this statistic: for all forty years that he lived with the Imam not once did the Imam fail to perform his supererogatory prayers—at two o'clock in the morning. This means after going to sleep he would wake himself, would rise, wash himself, and then pray. Then again at dawn he would once again perform his regular prayers, meaning that his sleep was interrupted twice. We in the West might call these austerities; whatever we may call them they are supposed to purify the consciousness and heart of the worshipper, and, from what can be gathered, the Imam has been the beneficiary of his own one-pointed devotion.

answer. *(Of course this is a very different description of heightened consciousness than I am interested in discovering in my questioning; for Dr. Yazdi, the state of consciousness of the Imam applies only to the performance of actions, i.e. the content of his actions; it does not apply to a permanent and on-going condition of awareness that is structured in a value of being that is non-resistant to God, and indeed is at one with the being of existence.)*

R.C.: Of course, the real Sufi finds this "answer" comes effortlessly; it is spontaneous and the concentration takes place automatically as it were. It is as if the computation is done for him. He witnesses the action that is performed. This at least is the true understanding of this mode of being that I have been describing. So, let us discuss something else: what do you feel is the reason why you have come under fire and to what extent do you believe that your qualified enthusiasm for this revolution is misunderstood by your opponents, or wilfully ignored? What exactly are the misgivings that you have, as you would express them now, at this point in the revolution? Are you in fact concerned about the direction in which it is going?

E.Y.: Yes, of course.

R.C.: What are those misgivings?

E.Y.: We don't have any revolutionary experience before this revolution so obviously this is our first experience and we are bound to make mistakes, and then when we see these mistakes we get concerned and...

R.C.: Is there a general pattern to these mistakes? Is there a certain direction that the revolution is going in that concerns you?

E.Y.: Yes, yes. This is what we try to express ourselves and why I consider myself and the group with which I am identified as one: we have contributed a great deal to this revolution and to its success. We do revere the Islamic Republic and we stand firm to safeguard the Islamic Republic, and we are not one to leave the country.[37] We are not one to stand for the overthrow of the Islamic Republic.[38] Our criticism, our differences of opinion come because of our love for the revolution and our love and concern for the Islamic Republic. If the prime minister or the president make some mistake I feel I am obliged to tell them and this is not only my view, this is an Islamic view. If you look at the sermons and letters of Hazrat Ali (the First Imam), *Nahj al-Balagha*, you will see that differences of opinion are necessary, that criticism is part of Islam, is even what can safeguard Islam.

---

[37] An obvious reference to the former president, Abolhassan Bani-Sadr who escaped to France in March of 1981.

[38] A reference to the Mujahaddin whose leader Massoud Rajavi has joined forces with Bani-Sadr and called for the overthrow of the Khomeini regime.

Dr. A.:   I had rather hoped that we could ask you some very down to earth questions about the revolution, that this would be very instructive and very interesting.

R.C. *(Sensing the discomfort of Dr. A. and realizing that it was time to ease the tension of the situation I offered to terminate my questions, while at the same time encouraging anyone else to continue in whatever line of questioning he desired, and there was another journalist there from Pakistan.)*:   Well, let me drop my role as interlocutor; I am writing a book about this whole thing and naturally I wish to provoke material for my book. I tend to go about my questing in a relentless sort of fashion. Perhaps this is a good time to give the floor over to someone else.

Dr. A.:   I think, Robin, it will be your responsibility as an objective and sympathetic observer of the revolution not to distort the Islamic understanding of what Imam Khomeini is. It is one of your greatest responsibilities as I see it now, and I think you and I should have a very long talk about it some time when we have time. Also the Faustian principle, which I have lots of ideas about. But this is actually the most dangerous thing that could come out of what you asked: that you may, without wanting it, distort the Islamic understanding of Imam Khomeini.

R.C.:   I am not trying to distort the Islamic understanding; I am merely trying to observe a phenomenological reality, a psychological reality that is paramount to discerning the nature of this revolution. There is some factor in the revolution that makes one think of the time of the Prophet, or—and this is more meaningful to me—Biblical times. The presence of some great Teacher among these people, a Teacher whom they trust with their lives and whom they view as—next to the Prophet and the Imams—a supreme embodiment of Islam: this is a reality that cannot be ignored. Indeed a failure to at least consider this question of purity of self and the religious experience—as applied to Imam Khomeini—will leave one without an adequate basis for comprehending what is going on here in Iran.

Dr. A.:   If you analyze the slogans that we use for Imam Khomeini you will understand what the real picture is of the Imam.

R.C.:   But I don't have to analyze the slogans. I simply have to take the pulse of the people, talk to soldiers and Revolutionary Guards on the battlefield, speak to Islamic theological students. I observe the way in which these various people surrender to the Imam—on the deepest level of their hearts—and the way in which they adore him. What is conveyed is their absolute confidence in the superiority, even perfection of his actions. They see him as a trustee of God, and they attribute to him powers that are not normally available to the rest of us.

Dr. A.:   I think it's much less dangerous to say that it's nearer to the truth that Imam Khomeini is a human being who can make mistakes as well. That's very important. That he doesn't make them is because of the deep piety and deep knowledge; but he can make mistakes. That's very important—that we don't believe that Imam Khomeini is *ma'sum*. We don't believe that. I don't believe Imam Khomeini would. I don't think anyone who is a Muslim would believe that. *(Dr. A. is of course correct in his assertion that Imam Khomeini is not* ma'sum, *which implies the more preordained divinity of consciousness possessed only by the Prophet and the Imams. However, the whole basis of Islam, and most especially the* Tariqah, *the Spiritual Way, in distinction to the* Shari'a, *the Divine Law—the esoteric versus the exoteric dimension of Islam—, points towards a state of pure Being in which the consciousness of the individual expands outwards towards infinity and the ego is harmonized with that unbounded awareness. The sages of India as well as the Sufis have described this state of consciousness as completely natural, as the fulfillment of life, a return to the unmanifest source of all Creation. It is the final destiny of each being in the universe. This is quite a different concept—or we should say, a more generalized concept—from the concept of Prophethood or what the Hindus call 'Avatars'—human beings born with absolutely pure nervous systems, whose existence has been created for a divine purpose. Enlightenment is the achievement of pure consciousness, but out of a previous state of ignorance and sin. The Prophet Mohammad and the Twelve Imams are of course beings whose spiritual status was already perfected at the moment they came out of God. Imam Khomeini was, on the other hand, a human being who had risen above his ego-isolation, his bondage of separateness from Being, and was dwelling in the state of eternal freedom, that is, his primary self had become the Self of the Absolute; his individual self now served the purpose of that Absolute Self. Thus he had become "pure and sinless"—as the Prophet and the Imams had always been. It was this category of enlightenment that I sought to describe and to determine whether Dr. Yazdi understood, and whether he applied it to the Supreme Commander of the Armed Forces in Iran, the* faqih[39] *for present day Iran.)*

---

[39] *Faqih*: "one learned in the principles and ordinances of Islamic law, or more generally, in all aspects of the faith," from Algar, op. cit. p. 150; the supreme authority of Islam in the absence of the Prophet and the Imams. "The Imam [one of the Twelve Imams; the *faqih* of the time] does indeed possess certain spiritual dimensions that are unconnected with his function as ruler. The spiritual status of the Imam is the universal divine viceregency ... pertaining to the whole of creation, by virtue of which all the atoms in the universe humble themselves before the holder of authority. It is one of the essential beliefs of our Shi'a school that no one can attain the spiritual status of the Imams, not even the cherubim or the prophets. In fact, according to the traditions that have been handed down to us, the Most Noble Messenger and the Imams existed before the creation of the world in the form of lights situated beneath the divine throne; they were superior to other men even in the sperm from which they grew and in their physical composition." (Ayatollah Khomeini, "The Form of Islamic Government," in Algar, op. cit. pp. 64-65.)

R.C.: The understanding I have, based upon Islam, is that the normal human being (that is, the human being who has achieved his true inner nature) can no longer violate the laws of God. The true mystic, the true Sufi, the realized Buddhist, the Hindu sage—all proclaim that this is a natural state of life. Thus all religions are completed in the 'normal' man, that is to say the man who, as the Imam says, is the "true and perfect human being."

E.Y.: When you are talking about a man you are talking about man who is subject to error—as Adam was.

R.C.: When I speak of "mistake" or "error" I mean in the sense of causing injury to creation itself, in other words, the expression of a negative force from within one's self. But I believe we have plumbed this topic enough; I am satisfied with the response you have given to me, Dr. Yazdi. There are other journalists here who I am sure have some non-theological questions for you. And I very much respect the comments of Dr. A.

The conversation was then taken over by the Pakistani journalist, and he questioned Dr. Yazdi about his relationship with Bani-Sadr and the alleged sympathetic and compassionate attitude Yazdi expressed to-wards some of the younger members of the Mujahaddin, many of whom were being executed by the Islamic courts. Yazdi expressed his regrets that the revolution had not produced "an open society." During the Shah's regime it was a "closed society"; it was a closed society once again. He disdained the name-calling and false slogans (uttered against himself and the more moderate members of the Majlis). He was certain that the refusal to accept criticism was a dangerous and even anti-Islamic tendency within certain of the leaders of the government. While he agreed that the revolution should be "100% Islamic" he felt that different viewpoints were an essential aspect of the evolution of the Republic. He gave a series of examples that clearly showed how bigoted his opponents were, and how they had wrongly judged him as an enemy of the revolution when in fact, as often as not, he had been more courage-ous and devoted in the times of the struggle against the Shah than some of his critics. About Bani-Sadr he lamented his departure since, Yazdi insisted, this flight from Iran showed how ultimately "egocentric" Bani-Sadr was. He explained that Bani-Sadr's writings revealed he was centered on himself and not on Shi'a Islam, that even Imam Khomeini had privately revealed his own estimation of Bani-Sadr, but that he recommended that Yazdi and others support Bani-Sadr since the people had elected him by an overwhelming majority (76%).

The Mujahaddin (now called the Munafeqin), he said, had been "cheated," "deceived" and had come under improper guidance. He regretted their executions since they were "a great loss for the country." They were "young, very energetic, very devoted" and he wished they could be "rehabilitated." Yazdi felt that the intolerance and the extremist views of the more conservative elements of the revolution hardened these young people and indeed caused the alienation that led to their executions. He said that the opposition to the revolution could be healthy; instead it had become violent because it felt betrayed. He wished the revolution could have taken a different direction so that these young people would not have had to be eliminated. If somehow the regime could have negotiated with the Mujahaddin perhaps this bloodshed could have been prevented.

When confronted with the fact that Imam Khomeini seemed to support the more conservative forces, those who criticized Yazdi and Bazargan, he insisted that the views of the Imam were not proven to be against his (Yazdi's) and that privately he had been encouraged by the Imam to "stand up for [his] own ideas, and to say what [he] thought was right."

Throughout the interview I was aware of the reasonableness of Yazdi and even of the telling arguments he offered up against the position of his critics: for instance, he maintained that there had been little that was constructive in the tirades against himself and Bazargan, that it seemed his critics thought that the problems of the revolution would go away if slogans were used and if he (Yazdi) would silence his criticism and his— sometimes—divergent opinions. However Yazdi, despite his sincerity and his clear-headed view of the revolution, utterly lacked the instinct for this revolution, and the ambience of his own individuality was of a nature quite distinct from the collective feeling that empowered those who were in the vanguard of the revolution, those who moved in the irrational needs, who sensed the advantages, even the necessity, of unifying all points of view under one vision. The revolution had its own logic; that logic was not part of the rational, moderating, accommodating stance of Dr. Yazdi; it was something blind and annihilating. One was possessed by the revolution or one was not possessed. To be sober like Dr. Yazdi was, meant to be in the midst of a war dance, a shamanistic ritual of power and magic, without the ability to move to the right rhythms, and, most importantly, without the ability to derive the benefit and healing inspiration that was the effect of such a celebration of the tribal God (only in this case the God was even beyond his attributes: Islam had ultimately a non-anthropomorphic view of God: he was the Absolute itself[40]), but for the present Allah's grace had to be felt; Yazdi

---

[40] "... we conclude that *Allah* is the name for the Essence of Absolute being." (Ayatollah Khomeini, "He is the Outward and the Inward," ibid. p. 407.)

was not someone who lived in that grace, and it was obvious that nothing could waken in him the secret of that religious passion. He was out of his element, even though rationally his position was unarguably the correct one. But this revolution was born and sustained in the unconscious; one had to have access to a knowledge, an instinct that rivalled the time of the Prophet.

Without such empathy one could not participate in the miracle of this resurgent purity of that Islam that ignored the fourteen centuries of 'progress' and modernization. For Yazdi, no matter how much he conveyed his support for the general goals of the revolution, was unquickened by the spirit of the inner revolution and his eyes were empty of the light that glowed in the eyes of those who were on the battlefront, and even in the faces of millions of the masses. He was not one to ignore the command of the general and charge the invading armies of Iraqis shouting "Allahu Akbar!", needlessly, joyfully offering his life to Allah. (This had happened frequently on the war front: martyrdom was a gift; it was not to be avoided if possible, and although this fanatical "turning in the direction of God" was as often as not militarily unnecessary—and even dangerous—the psychological effect it had on the enemy was dramatic; he was often unnerved by the willingness to be sacrificed (in the charge of battle: nothing passive about this martyrdom), and this weakened him and threw off his own strategy. On the level of the soul the Iranian Revolutionary Guards were always victorious, and the poor Iraqis longed to find some myth to sustain them.) Ebrahim Yazdi was, it seemed, constitutionally unable to summon up the chemistry of self-sacrifice, although it was undeniable the significant role he played in the struggle against the Shah. Here though, under question, he revealed the reason why he was opposed, even despised by certain elements in Iran: the Imam might not issue some blanket condemnation of the 'moderates' but Yazdi's inability to discover the source of sacred power within the revolution meant he did not participate in the continuous sacramental meaning of that revolution. It was an all or nothing proposition, and even though Yazdi supported whole-heartedly the aims of the revolution, even though Yazdi was a devout Muslim, even though he indeed had not been disgraced by the Imam (and was even admonished to stick to his position), still he was instinctively a secularist, or rather a demythologized native; he accepted the tribal beliefs; he could not be transformed by their immediate puritanical frenzy; the mythology was believed, but history had suddenly altered; it was necessary now not only to believe but to intuitively grasp the particular and revivifying power of that mythology as it now enacted itself within this revolution. The revolution, the personality of the Imam, the war with Iraq—all this had to be understood in the heart as being the justification of Islam, as the living proof of Islam. One had to re-experience what Islam was in this context and to identify the circumstances in Iran as the very manifestation of Allah's will, as the very means through which Islam would be regenerated at its source. This was something that came like a dream; it was something like falling in love; it was a vision. Unable to dream, unable to fall in love, and unable to see the Epiphany, Ebrahim Yazdi for all his wisdom and reasonableness was dislocated from the unifying consciousness of the Imam's Islam. There was attenuation where there should have been intensity of feeling; there was blandness and heaviness where there should have been fierce joy and buoyancy. The revolution had not worked its magic inside Dr. Yazdi and one wondered on what basis Allah chose to bless or to ignore his servants. For all this one still had to respect Yazdi; and in his presence one also had to confront the irremediable ambivalence of the revolution.

A Visit with Imam Khomeini

Although there had been talk about seeing the leader of the Islamic Republic, the much hated, much revered Ayatollah Khomeini, I had learned that it was better—with something as portentously important as such a visit—to make the effort and then accept what happened. I had already been through the experience of trying to see "The Imam" in March of 1980, when I made three visits to the gate leading into his villa in North Tehran. Then his house was guarded carefully, with Revolutionary Guards pacing across the roof. But now the security had been multiplied, so that I estimated upwards of 500 persons were responsible for assisting the activities of the Imam and locking him into the tightest security. We were told when we arrived in Tehran that if we did indeed get to see Khomeini we wouldn't know until the last moment. This seemed to fit into the general tradition of 'holy men,' individuals who devised their schedules according to the whim of divine impulse, or according to a totally improvised sense of the nowness of things, of the changeable, fluctuating conditions of the universe. I had visited mystics, sages, Teachers before, and invariably there was the sense of a final spontaneous bias even in the midst of the most rigid and exacting tradition. Whether it is true or not, the impression one gets from being near spiritually advanced (enlightened) individuals is that they resist the linear, the space/time bounded categories of experience of the rest of us, preferring to adjust their time-table to the exigencies of the moment, to the tug of evolutionary need, to the overwhelming reality of the all-at-onceness of the world. Ayatollah Khomeini was, I gathered from my sources, no different, although he himself followed the most regulated, predictable routine when it came to his Islamic ritual prayers—and all matters pertaining to his religion. But once into activity, he tended to determine his duties by the response he had in a given moment, and there was no sense of preparing some carefully worked-out schedule of events and meetings that might interfere with the responsibility to act according to the immediacy of the moment, to act according to the particular bias of attention that delivered and articulated its meaning in the fact of his experience. I recalled the Buddhist idea of *karma*, that whatever happened to one was the ineluctable consequences of one's past actions, that it was a question of a perfect pattern of cause and effect that determined, for instance, whether one's desire for something was fulfilled. This was very much like the Islamic notion of Allah's will, for constantly in my travels this time and previously in Iran, when wondering whether I could visit with someone (for example the students and the hostages at the American Embassy) I was told, "It will happen, *insha'Allah,*" i.e. God willing. In fact I discovered this kind of happy fatalism was so predominant in the thinking of my Iranian hosts that I simply stopped trying to press for something if I thought the individual was turning over the major responsibility to Allah and not to his continuing efforts. With regard to seeing the Imam it was made clear that this would be entirely up to Allah; therefore, although making it clear that I would be most pleased if Allah chose to bless me by letting me meet with the Imam, I was at the same time reconciled to the weighty forces of religious laissez-faire that tended to be the ultimate—or were perceived as such—determinant of things such as seeing the beloved leader of Iran.

But the night of February 8 it was announced that those invited to the conference would be addressed by Imam Khomeini at his residence in North Tehran. As soon as I heard the confirmation of what had been tentatively scheduled for any one day during the several weeks when the conference was in session, I immediately sensed the significance of this event for myself, for finally I would have the chance to measure the worth of this man directly; he would be held up to the scrutiny of my critical spiritual sensibilities, and the tendentious discussion I had had with the Lebanese professor and Ebrahim Yazdi would begin to mean something quite different, for although one cannot judge the inner state of consciousness of an individual, one can at least decide if there are some signs of a personal performance that would lend some credence to the notion of having achieved a state of 'liberation' from the narrow boundaries of the ego. There was just too much vengeance, blood, and doctrinal absolutism for me to finally assent to the idea that Khomeini was an 'enlightened' being, for although most reputed saints have emerged from a tradition—that is, from an organized, highly structured and antiquitous system of worship and purificatory practices—they are, when they have reached the climax of their devotion, detached from 'politics,' from heavy involvement in the surface appearance of life, from the rigid ideological warfare and clashing of opinions that dominate the more worldly individual. Khomeini's embrace—unconditionally—of harsh Islamic justice, for instance the stoning of an adulterer, the severing of the hand of a thief, and his violent denunciations of the United States and the Soviet Union—his attribution of all problems to the conspiracies of imperialism—all this seemed a little too one-sided and belief-ridden to be the representations of a human being who dwelled in the equanimity and putative bliss of the Absolute, the state of permanent freedom from the primacy of egohood. And then there were the portraits on *Time* magazine, the many depictions of the Imam, especially during the hostage crisis and even after the fall of the Shah: all these suggested a morbid seriousness, a humourless severity, and an apparent absence of gentleness, playfulness, or—and this is most important—compassion. The manifest characteristic of the human personality that had achieved some unity with pure consciousness was the radiant reality of love, the love that was simply the fact of that harmony, the fact of that non-separateness from and absolute cooperation with the laws of the universe that worked for the happiness of each creature. This had been the measure of all the great saints, whether Saint Francis, the Buddha, Lao-Tse, or even the Sufis I had read. Imam Khomeini was a symbol in the West of the most obdurate atavistic pride and implacable hatred. And even some Westerners with whom I had talked who had met Khomeini commented on his charisma, but in the same breath remarked at the total absence of humour or warmth in his demeanour.

Now I had the opportunity to judge for myself.

A Lecture by Ayatollah Khomeini

Once on our way by bus to the Jamaran residence (the hall where Khomeini was to speak was connected to his house) there was the buzzing excitation that indicated something powerful was about to happen. For myself I knew that I could trust my intuition enough to determine whether Ayatollah Khomeini was essentially good, essentially bad, or an admixture. I also sensed that something dramatic was to happen to me, as if the psyche has a presentiment of that which will radically affect one's perceptions, one's experiences. I tend to believe that something within Creation knows what is about to happen, or rather that, given the tendencies of a given situation, some form of the reality that is imminent (but unknowable to the individual) begins to participate in the moment of experience even before the important event has happened. In other words there is the absence of time, the present holds the meaning of the future, especially the immediate future that is to profoundly influence one's experience of reality. If something re-markable is to happen to one, the fact of that reality will still be contained in the reality of experience leading up to the experience which has yet to happen. I knew that whatever would happen in the hall where Khomeini would speak, it would be tumultuous and consequential; how could it be otherwise in a situation in which one individual human being embodied and dictated the intention and the reality of a revolution? The ambivalence, the ambiguity that I had experienced in regard to the person of Khomeini was about to be resolved: I would know the essence of his motivation, the essence of the claims of his countrymen as to his spiritual greatness. The actual event of his speaking followed inevitably from the sequence of steps that started with the bus ride to North Tehran through the various checkpoints, and finally the entrance into the hall. Since it was guaranteed that we would see the Imam, the bus ride contained the reality of that meeting, and therefore the potency of this reality flowed into the present experience of riding towards our destina-tion. In a sense I felt that all of my speculations, hunches, concepts of the revolution would dissolve in the face-to-face encounter with the leader of that revolution. I was not disappointed.

There were at least five or six checkpoints at which we were frisked for any weapons or objects that might be used to threaten the life of the beloved (and hated) leader of Iran and the Islamic Revolution. Nothing —no pencils, no cameras, no objects of any kind—were permitted to be taken past the first checkpoint. As we walked briskly through what seemed a labyrinth of alleys there was the sense of the eagerness with which each invited individual was insuring a suitable view of the speaker—in other words, I was aware that many of us were walking quickly to obtain the best seats. And while we walked I couldn't help but notice the brightness, the alertness, the liveliness in the air itself; this was a very different part of Tehran; it had a humming energy, a vitality, a special kind of consciousness. Was this due to the actual reality of this person called Ayatollah Khomeini, or was it due to the attitude that characterized the people's estimation of Khomeini? I felt at the time it could be both, since again I determined that something was indeed objectively different about the space we were entering. This was the center of the opposite of apathy and lassitude that I had found on the streets of Tehran; here in the lanes leading up to the lecture hall in the early morning—it was about eight o'clock—hundreds of Revolutionary Guards, ordinary citizens, and clergymen were all part of the corridor of guardians and staff who orbited around the sun of Khomeini. I could see that they relished their work, that this was where (as well as in the midst of battle) the revolution manifested its living force. Indeed I thought that we were approaching the very source of the revolution, so harmonized did the climate of feeling seem in conjunction with the principles, the mythological realities of the revolution.

Now the reader should realize at this point in my story that I was well aware of all those things attributed to the regime, and especially the authority of the Imam: the brutal torture, the thousands of executions, the raping of women prisoners, the resuscitation of SAVAK; the abolishment of music, dance, and any offending aesthetic or recreational activities that are accepted as normal in the modern world; the killing of young children, the shooting of high school girls, censorship of the press, the cruel campaign of murder and desecration of the Baha'i community, the refusal to permit Amnesty International to enter Iran, —in short the systematic and violent overthrow of all semblance of democracy, the instituting of a system of rule that compared unfavourably with the Shah even at his worst. I had heard all these things; I had even heard these things from people whose integrity and credibility I could not doubt. Iran was in a state of vicious madness and the source of that evil repression was none other than the person whom I was to see perform and later meet. Before the shifting towards a concerted campaign against all 'opponents' of the regime (which had caused this increased hostility against him), Ayatollah Khomeini had been the object of extreme hatred in the United States for being linked intimately with the seizing of the innocent American diplomats. Then there were still many forces in Iran who supported Khomeini; now, however, in the wake of the executions and persecution of opponents of the regime the hatred of Khomeini has been entrenched even in the hearts of many who had fought against the Shah, Iranians who had even served in the provisional government, who had, in fact, been loyal to Khomeini up until the last six months. Now I was to see in the flesh the personage whose will had dominated Iran, whose policies (although attributed to God) had caused so much disruption in Iran and had drawn so much negativity from the West.

I secured a seat at the front of the hall; Khomeini's chair, draped with a white sheet, was situated on a stage above us at least fifteen feet from floor level. A white-bearded mullah surveyed us as we entered the hall, and adjusted the microphone, waiting patiently for the sign that the Imam would be coming through the closed door to the right of the stage

108

upon which he would give his lecture. The hall was redolent with whispered expectation, and from time to time certain Muslims would shout a slogan or a passage from the Qur'an and would then be joined by the hundreds of other Muslims and Revolutionary Guards who were in attendance. No smoking was allowed inside the hall and the reverence that was predominant in the attitude of all those waiting for the Imam's entrance made this scene one in which the usual smells and ambience of Iran were significantly altered. Even as I looked up at the stage at the place where Khomeini had given hundreds of speeches my eyes registered the physical calm, the physical purity, the physical freshness that hovered, or rather collected in a block of solid, translucent energy that seemed in such contrast to the hotel we had been in, to in fact every other environment I had been in in two trips to Iran. Even the mosques did not radiate this quality, this wholeness of energy. Could the Imam after all be an enlightened human being, a true Sufi—or perhaps even more? All signs indicated that something was used to happening in this hall that transcended anything in Iran that happened outside the hall—the only feeling that seemed at all familiar with this feeling was the war front and then when I had walked through Beheshte Zahra Cemetery. I could only account for this by assuming that perhaps martyrdom was real, that the sudden and sanctified splitting of the soul from the body, carrying that soul up into heaven because of the intention of the martyr, has created an energy that was holy, an energy that was blessed by Allah himself. Whatever was the case the atmosphere where Khomeini's chair sat was radiant and alive. Harmony, not hatred, dominated here.

While we waited for the Imam, a parade of Lebanese Palestinian children whose parents had been killed in Israeli bombing attacks (and who had been adopted by the Iranian government at the behest of Khomeini) marched into the hall singing in Arabic various songs about the revolution. They stood in front of us just below the stage, looking slightly more bewildered than the hundreds of Iranian students from the Islamic high schools that had marched and shouted for us. They had been invited to listen to the Imam, and in their yachting-like uniforms (blue caps, white dress) they patiently stood, while their teachers organized their chanting and their positioning. Each day, apparently, Khomeini met with individuals and groups associated with the running of the revolution. He was especially interested in those children whose parents had been killed in refugee camps by strafing Israeli jets. They constituted the oppressed, the people who suffered innocently at the hands of the aggressors; they were thus specially suited to the categories of moral judgement of Islam and the revolution. Only another manifestation of evil could have created these orphans; the Palestinians were the victims of American imperialism, since it was American weapons that had drawn the blood of the fathers and mothers of these children. Everything was separated into good and evil; each struggle in the world fell into the categorization of the oppressed fighting against the oppressors. These Lebanese children were symbols of that struggle, were symbols for the moral distinctions necessary to uphold the revolution and maintain its absolutist basis. Without the reality of evil, one cannot posit the existence of its opposite: good. The Iranians themselves might not be qualified to call themselves pure, but their Islamic motivation was pure, and the enemy certainly was evil. How could it be that it was anything but God that would oppose evil; since evil existed, what countered it was good. The Iranians had been taught to think in this way by their leader; nothing, not the distinctions of Ebrahim Yazdi, nor the resistance of the Mujahaddin could deter those supporters of the "Line of the Imam" from sticking to these black and white categories of judgement, for only in this way could the allegory of good versus evil be enacted.

We were there for about forty-five minutes before there were signs that the Imam was about to make his entrance. The signal was clear; several other turbaned *'ulama* emerged from the door and indicated to the mullah who was waiting on stage that the chieftain, priest, holy man, commander, and Imam was on his way. At the appearance of Khomeini in the doorway everyone jumped to his feet and began shouting, "Khomeini!" "Khomeini!" "Khomeini!" in the most vibrant, athletic, rejoicing, militant tribute that I had ever witnessed for another human being. Everyone seemed completely taken over by the spontaneous surge of love and adulation, and yet there was the proclaiming with every cell of their heart the absolute confidence that what and who they were honouring was worthy of such honour in the eyes of Allah. Indeed I would say that the explosion of ecstasy and power that greeted the Imam was itself not so much a simple reflex based upon a fixed idea of the Imam; it was rather the natural and exuberant hymn of praise, of celebration that was demanded by the very majesty and overpowering charisma of this man. For once the door opened for him I experienced a hurricane of energy surge through the door, and in his brown robes, his black-turbaned head, his white beard he stirred every molecule in the building and riveted the attention in a way that made everything else disappear. He was a flowing mass of light that penetrated into the consciousness of each person in the hall. He destroyed all images that one tried to hold before one in sizing him up. He was so dominant in his presence that I found myself organized in my sensations by that which took me far beyond my own concepts, my own way of processing experience.

I had expected—no matter what the apparent stature of the man—to find myself scrutinizing his face, exploring his motivation, wondering about his real nature. Khomeini's power, grace, and absolute domination destroyed all my modes of evaluation and I was left to simply experience the energy and feeling that radiated from his presence on the stage. A hurricane he was, yet immediately one could see there was a point of absolute stillness inside that hurricane; while fierce and commanding, he was yet serene and receptive. Something was immovable inside him, yet that immovability moved the whole country of Iran. This was no ordinary human being; in fact even of all the so-called saints I had met—the Dalai Lama, Buddhist monks, Hindu sages—none possessed quite the electrifying presence of Khomeini. For those who could see (and feel) there could be no question about his integrity, nor about the claim, however muted by people like Yazdi, by his people that he had gone beyond the normal (or abnormal) selfhood of the human being and had taken residence in something absolute. This absoluteness was declared in the air, it was declared in the movement of his body, it was declared in the motion of his hands, it was declared in the fire of his personality, it was declared in the stillness of his consciousness. There was no mystery about why he was so loved by millions of Iranians and Muslims throughout the world and he demonstrated, to this observer at least, the empirical foundation for the notion of higher states of consciousness. Yes, the severity, the humourlessness, the absolutist judgement was apparent; yet, given the circumstances within which he was placed, there was the affirmation of appropriateness in his every gesture and aspect. This was the most extraordinary person I had seen.

At first he did not speak; another religious leader addressed the audience, Khomeini sitting in a kind of immaculate silence and perfect equilibrium. He was motionless; he was detached; he was in an ocean of peacefulness; and yet something was in pure motion; something was dynamically involved; something was ready to wage constant war. He dwarfed all those people whom I had met in Iran; he dominated the stage even while the other mullah spoke. All eyes were on Khomeini, and there was not the slightest trace of egotism, of self-consciousness, even, if I can say it, of inner dialogue or random thinking. His whole being focused relentlessly yet spontaneously on the point of concentration that aesthetically and spiritually fitted into the dramatic scene we were witnessing. Despite the fierce intention, the absolute sense of uncompromising rectitude, there was yet the sense of something perfectly effortless and smooth that dictated the manifest movements of his hands, the sound of his throat clearing, the focus of his attention. Here hundreds of patriots and Muslims had shouted his greatness, had sworn their love, their absolute adulation; yet while receiving all this he remained within himself, he remained unmoved; he remained in the dignity of some imperturbable inner state that was beyond the boundaries of a causation that I was familiar with.

The reader may wince at the extravagance of my description of this man; he must know, however, that despite everything that I had heard, despite the contradictory evidence I had received before (the seeming violence of the rhetoric, the lack of creative playfulness and so on), the actual and immediate impression of what Imam Khomeini was had nothing to do with some sort of idea or concept. The experience was too overpowering for that. Imagine for a moment the pushing of the body of oneself out of one's mother's womb, or the moment when one might awaken to the fact that one was being created inside a foetal body, or the moment when one was conscious of dying, or the moment when one first discovered the power of eros: these experiences have as their basis a primary determinant outside of the frame of reference of the individual; what is dominant is the intrinsic nature of the reality which is giving birth to the experience. Such is what happened on the morning of Wednesday, February 9th, 1982 in North Tehran. The subjectivity of the experience seemed to be objectified by something that was at the very basis of my consciousness; I transcended the mode of experience that normally determined what sensations, thoughts, feelings constellated into my awareness of self. Khomeini was that powerful; Khomeini was that strong; Khomeini was that egoless and invincible. In a moment I saw all the impulses of the revolution, the whole history of the over-throw of the Shah, the rhythms of martyrdom, the bygone Islamic civili-zation that had temporarily overshadowed the West: all of this was contained in the presence of this man. He was the source of the revival of Islam, he was the source of the revolution, he was the source of whatever power this revolution and Islam represented to the world. Without him I am certain the monarchy would still be in place and Islam would be effectively eliminated as a factor in the political destiny of the Middle East. Once seeing Khomeini I questioned whether even the revolution in Iran would survive in its vitality and coherence for it seemed pretty obvious that all inspiration was derived from Khomeini's leadership. Khomeini was the revolution. Those given the awareness or feeling to know what he represented (the wholeness of life biased through Islam) could not help but be filled with the fervour of Islam, the blessed confidence of martyrdom, the determination to spread Islam to the world. He uplifted and transformed; this was done not through some projected idea of his charisma; it was done by the actual material of life; it was accomplished through the intention of that which had created this whole drama. No, Khomeini was at the center of this Islamic eruption; Khomeini was the fountainhead of the spiritual power that flowed into the hearts of Muslims throughout the Middle East—at least those Muslims who instinctively were close to the heart of Islam.

He did not smile once; his face was implacably set in the resolution of his will; God demanded everything from him; he had given his life to serving God. There was nothing to laugh at, to be amused at, to wonder about; his course had been set and he was in the determined consequences of that course: to bring Islam into the prominence which its divine genesis had portended. He lived for Islam; he had become the instrument of Islam; he had no purpose but the enactment of Islam. His individuality seemed merged with the universality of his higher purpose. I detected no mental entropy, no inner reactions to his environment; no, there was only the inevitable pattern of duty that placed him into the servitude of Allah. Of course neither science nor psychology could verify these observations; they entirely escaped the instruments, the diagnosis of experiential reality; nevertheless one might suspect that his brain waves would yield readings of hemispheric coherence not typical of those of us still in the normal grip of conflict, ambivalence, and insecurity. Physiologically, octogenarian that he was, there was the impression of soundness, of efficiency, of non-wasted energy and performance. Everything he did—from the motion of his hands to the opening of his mouth to the sound of his words—was under the aegis of one ordering intelligence. He was totally non-divided; he gave the sense of someone who had not only mastered himself but was himself now the servant of another master, and one can only assume that he had either hallucinated himself into the experience of submitting to God, or that indeed he had achieved that permanent grace that was the subject of my controversial discussion with Ebrahim Yazdi and the Lebanese professor. Here he was, perhaps the most hated man of post-Hitler civilization, yet one saw him as being utterly undemagogic; one saw him as—at the very least—an Old Testament prophet, an Islamic Moses come to drive Pharaoh from his lands (Pharaohism being expressed in all those values and activities that ignored the reality and pre-eminence of Allah).

Despite the hatred (and I thought of all the millions of people who had gone through so many days of their lives during the hostage crisis filled with negative thoughts about "The Ayatollah"—how the most powerful hostility had focused itself on him) he yet appeared untouched by this destructive energy. He had been strong enough to survive it; he had been perhaps strong enough to be chosen to release it; now he was hated even more for thousands, perhaps millions, of his countrymen—not to mention Saddam Hussein and the monarchs of the region—now turned against him. I intuited that the very hatred directed against him had in fact strengthened the revolution, had in fact made him that much more powerful; he did not live for the approval of others; he did not live to be a hero; he did not live for any personal satisfaction; he lived for the truth he experienced in the laws of Islam, in the revelations of the Prophet, in the happiness and immortality that could be achieved through Islam.

All this will seem preposterous to most of those who read this book, and yet the clarity with which these impressions asserted themselves made them self-evident and as truthful as the awakening from a dream. Khomeini was for real, and the projection of the personal, or I should say, impersonal presence of Khomeini diminished the impression of any other political leader I had seen. He might be the enemy of pluralistic values; he might be the enemy of individualist freedom; he might be the enemy of democratic government; he might be the enemy of the metaphysics of variable subjectivity (i.e. the universe of the individual); but one could not deny that, despite his severe countenance and the rigid and inflexible values and laws for which he stood, he was, for all that, the most towering force of wholeness and integrity; he was a microcosm of Truth as it passed through Islam. He was not someone with whom one could discuss the meaning of individual choice, or the sensuous beauty of ballet, but he was yet the most formidable human being on the stage of international politics, and he seemed, at least from my vantage point, to be easily a contemporary of Christ himself; not that Khomeini would ever compare himself with Christ—but he radiated that same uncompromising integrity and one-pointed intention. How was it that a human being who had not tasted the variety of human experience, how was it that a human being who denied the experimental riches of personal freedom, how was it that such a person could contain, could embody so much of the order of the universe itself? Well, for those readers who find the apologetics of stoning to death adulterers a trifle disconcerting—or the execution of homosexuals—the description and interpretation I have given may seem the most inflated form of self-distorting perception. Nevertheless I wish to make it clear that one must—at least for purposes of drawing some conclusions about this revolution and the adamantine love in which Khomeini is held by over half of his countrymen— separate the ideological statements of Khomeini from the spontaneous measure of the man's stature as a human being. His stature is not so much derived from his words, nor his authority, but from the living expression of his being, from the very way in which the universe reacts to the organized form of his personality. For all his extremist rhetoric, for all his bitterness towards the United States, for all his cursing of the West, he still transcends the content of his words, the content of his writings; what is primary is the elemental grace that floods into one's heart with the slightest intention to open oneself to the naturalness of one's experience. A film or theatre director, if he were to view the

114

performance of Ayatollah Khomeini would say this was the one actor who could play the role of a Messiah—or the Twelfth Imam, so magnificent was his stage presence, so absolute was the sense of his confidence, so unalterable was his will.

And yet I must go further: Imam Khomeini broke into my heart and my brain with a current of emotion that I can only describe as extreme positivity, what I prefer to call 'love.' Yes, despite his call for Islamic executions (and in his very speech that day he called for a pardoning of thousands of prisoners who were amenable to change of allegiance[41]), his unwavering sternness of mien, his invulnerability to individual feeling, he was charged with a love that actually seemed to purify my heart, to fill it with a bliss that I had not known before. Even while he just sat there—before he spoke, while one of the mullahs gave the predictable tirade against the superpowers, the predictable paean to Islam—I found myself gazing upon his face (and the light that surrounded him) and at the same time being filled up with that energy that I associated with the most vital kind of creativity and power. He was a generator of the energy and feeling that overwhelms the heart and cleanses the—if I may say it—soul. I had wanted to retain my disinterestedness, my critical detachment when seeing the Imam. I had known myself to be not capable of being dominated by another human being; I had taken a certain amount of satisfaction in knowing that my inner integrity could not be disturbed by some experience outside of myself. Yet here I was losing the boundaries of my own individuality; here I was discovering feelings and refined sensations that had been unknown to me. Here I was being filled up by a mad Muslim holy man, the individual who was thought least likely perhaps in the whole world to be capable of conferring upon a Western journalist the sense of divine happiness, divine clarity of awareness. But this was my experience; Imam Khomeini was experienced to be that singular reality which could expand my consciousness, purify my heart, clarify my brain, and leave in his wake the sense of an undiminishable grace, a grace that somewhere I still carry with me, however overshadowed it might be by present preoccupations.

Feeling the energy of Beheshte Zahra Cemetery had drawn out pure emotion from me; here in the presence of the fierce embodiment of militant Islam I had received the flowering of my own individuality, the vision of bright integrity that reached up towards heaven itself. There were no metaphors for the sense of reality that swept over me, and it can only be carved in the memory of the universe that what I saw that day,

---

[41] On April 1, 1982, in observance of the Third Anniversary of the proclaiming of the Islamic Republic, the Iranian government released 4,939 political and criminal prisoners and reduced the sentences of 7,087 others.—Ed.

what I experienced in my heart—the meaning that articulated itself spontaneously and irrevocably in my soul—was the single most important fact of this revolution, but more still, the single most important fact about existence itself. A human being could after all achieve a greatness that proclaimed contact with a Creator. Imam Ruhullah Al-Musavi Al-Khomeini might be declared insane, a monster, a killer, an enemy of freedom and light; he was nevertheless a supreme testimony to the power of man to achieve a perfect integrity, and within that integrity, the most awesome kind of personal beauty and grace. Since Khomeini was indeed a man of God, since Khomeini did embody the truth of Islam, since indeed Khomeini deserved to be loved with Shi'a martyrdom passion, it behooved us on the outside to try to understand this revolution and to see why it might be possible that God would visit such a reality upon us. The reality I have described here is the reality that is at the very center of the future of the Middle East. I believe that until someone can recognize the truth of what I have written here, he or she cannot comprehend the design of destiny, nor the forces that now shape the events of the Middle East. The face of Jerry Falwell in comparison to the face of Ayatollah Khomeini is for me the difference between the pudgy Bible salesman and John the Baptist.

Of course since there is no consensus about the nature of God, or in fact whether he even exists, therefore there is little chance that there can be any sort of significant agreement about whether he is found manifesting in the consciousness of a human being, the one creature in this world whose nervous system would seem capable (because of its self-conscious reflectivity) of conveying or embodying the finest expression of intelligence. If God is anything He is Intelligence. The accounts of Christian mystics, the saints of the East, and of course the Sufis (not to mention the prophets) make it quite clear what the evidence of a God-shaken, God-possessed human being is: the actions of such an individual are taken over by an intelligence that seems to be computing the activities of the larger world; the specific and localized ego of such an individual no longer determines or controls the actions which flow from his or her individuality. That individuality has been universalized, and the physical, mental, and emotional character of such an individual must necessarily reflect the universal reality now embodied in his or her consciousness. Did Imam Khomeini fit this description, these criteria?

So much did he conform to these standards that even if one did not have any religious frame of reference, or any kind of touchstone for the mystical, the transcendental, one would still witness a torrential energy, an unshakable stillness, and an indefatigable love and compassion. Yes there was the austere, unrelenting point of concentration in his countenance, but even if ignorant of its cause, one still sensed the oughtness of

116

this expression: i.e. its configuration, its character was being determined by Necessity. True, if one has achieved a state of equilibrium with the Divine such that one's resistance to the force of God's intelligence no longer exists (the false ego has been annihilated) then the method through which such a state has been achieved will be reflected in the face, in the personality of the individual. Ayatollah Khomeini's march towards the realization of his own unbounded nature, the awakening of himself to pure consciousness, to the Absolute, had not been through effortless pleasure, through some simple and natural technique of transcendence; no, it had been achieved through the most indomitable, titanic will, through the most exacting and unswerving devotion to the rules and ceremonies of Islam. One experienced, in looking up at him, how Khomeini had as if from the first breath he drew as an infant, been one-pointedly living his life for the highest purpose and within the most universal tradition. Like the famous saints of India, he had, right from the beginning, sought enlightenment, giving up all the idle pleasures of youth to concentrate his intention upon the goal of all human life, the fully realized Self. His individuality was still there, and that individuality because of its conditional and contingent nature, could not be made of the Absolute; however his individuality was now held inside that absolute, now had its purpose in serving that absolute, and my impression was that I had never seen such an uncompromising expression of the Absolute.

Khomeini is apparently familiar with the concept of Allah as the Absolute. I quote from four separate lectures (emphases added):

The names of God are . . . signs of His Sacred Essence; and it is only His names that are knowable to man. The Essence Itself is something that lies totally beyond the reach of man, and even the Seal of the Prophets, the most knowledgeable and noble of men, was unable to attain knowledge of the Essence. *The Sacred Essence is unknown to all but Itself.*[42]

Once light or being is absolute and undifferentiated, it must include all perfections within itself, since the loss of a single perfection entails individuation. If there is even a single point of deficiency in the Divine Essence, it will mean that a point of being is absent; being will no longer be absolute, and becoming deficient, it will also become contingent and no longer necessary, for necessary being is absolute perfection and beauty. Therefore, when we regard the matter using the imperfect method of rational proof, we conclude that *Allah is the name for the Essence of absolute being, Which is the source of all manifestations.* It contains all the names and all the attributes and is absolute perfection, perfection without individuation.[43]

---

[42] Algar, op. cit. p. 367.
[43] Ibid. p. 407.

...that goal for the sake of which all the prophets came: *to lead man forth from this world, out of the darkness, and to convey him to the realm of absolute light.* The prophets wanted to immerse man in that absolute light, to merge the drop with the ocean...It is for this purpose that all the prophets were sent. All true knowledge and objective reality belong exclusively to that light; we are all non-beings, and our origin is that light. All the prophets were sent to deliver us from the darkness and *convey us to the absolute light*, freeing us from both the veils of darkness and those of light.[44]

Some will even succeed, while still in this world, in reaching a stage that is now beyond our imagination—that of non-being, of being effaced in God.[45]

If Khomeini, who is viewed as the exemplar of Islam, as the most realized of all Muslims living in the world, as the shadow of the Twelfth Imam—if such a person as he has not reached that "absolute light" where one is "effaced in God" how can we believe the Imam when he promises that Islam and the Prophets existed for this very goal? The Imam may, for obvious reasons, draw people's attention away from the notion of his own successful inner *jihad*, but the very fact that he allows his portrait and his own reputation to stand as being the supreme expression of this revolution is a tacit admission that he has in fact achieved this state in which he, as a drop, has merged into the Absolute (Allah), the ocean. The clue to the sternness, the sense of implacable will and hardness in his face is the fact that the means to this goal have come about through a perpetual *jihad*, which is "inconceivable unless a person turns his back on his own desires and the world."[46] Khomeini has defined "the world" in the context of this analysis as "the aggregate of man's aspirations that effectively constitute his world, not the external world of nature with the sun and the moon, which are manifestations of God. It is the world in this narrow, individual sense that prevents man from drawing near to the realm of sanctity and perfection."[47]

We agree that coming close to and eventually reaching God must be, if there is such a thing as God, the highest pursuit of man, since this logically is what God seeks for man, this logically, because it ends in deathlessness and bliss, is what man seeks for himself. Khomeini in one of his speeches relates a tradition of the Prophet:

When anyone leaves his home, migrating to God and His Messenger, and is then overtaken by death, it is incumbent on God to reward him.[48]

44 Ibid. p. 396.

45 Ibid. p. 385.

46 Ibid. pp. 386-387.

47 Ibid. p. 388.

48 Ibid. p. 382.

118

However, it is obvious that in order to reach this goal much has to be sacrificed. The goal is the completion of man for the source of "all true knowledge" dwells there, and "objective reality belongs exclusively to that light"; "our origin is that light." God, it would seem, rewards us with the summit of His love only if we prove we are willing to forego so many of the experiences that He has made available to man on this earth. And this is the source of an earlier denunciation of Khomeini's puritanism as "a joyless and morbid devotion to a God who demands constant sacrifice."[49] Khomeini has interpreted the will of God through the Qur'an, through the principles of justice of the Prophet and the Imams; there is no suggestion that one could achieve the climax of Being through some path or system of devotion that did not demand "constant sacrifice." Now whether it is true that God ultimately has created this universe solely to have man transcend it, and much of man's earthly pleasures to ensnare him, to tempt him into sin, is a question presumably only answerable by God. In my own intuition about this matter I believe there may be ways towards God (the Absolute, the Divine Essence) which may be more compatible with the desires of man, which may not demand such control and discipline. One thing is obvious, however: Imam Ruhullah Al-Musavi Al-Khomeini has achieved his goal, since although he still strived for the perfecting of his own country and the establishment of the primacy of Islam throughout the Middle East (and of course the world) he was entirely detached from all inner anxiety, inner turmoil, inner strife.[50] The profound discipline and austerity of his whole life might reflect itself in the adamantine features of his character and even his face, but the magnificence of the fullness that had overtaken his whole being left no doubt about the reward, nor the reality that now was his. From this writer's perspective Imam Khomeini radiated everything promised in the scriptures of Islam, and that which he radiated was what was absolute in this universe. It was the source of the universe—biased as I have said, through the idiom of Islam—that directed the course of the revolution; it was the source of the universe that determined the adoration of the people; it was the source of the universe that directed the resurgence of Islam. However much we in the

---

[49] Farhang, op. cit.

[50] "The man who is thus contented in himself certainly continues to act in the world, but his behaviour has become natural behaviour. It is no longer motivated by selfish desires, nor is its effectiveness disturbed by any shortcomings that might arise from dullness on his part. This comes about because he has fulfilled the purpose of all possible desires and all possible actions in his life. He now engages himself in actions motivated not by selfish individuality but by cosmic purpose. Through him works the divine intelligence, for he has become a fitting instrument to carry out the divine plan in the world. Such a life is a natural life." (Maharishi Mahesh Yogi, *Bhagavad-Gita: A New Translation and Commentary* (Harmondsworth: Penguin, 1969), p. 209.)

West might decry Khomeini, however much Khomeini's countrymen—many in exile—might condemn, and attempt to destroy this revolution, and however much even persons such as Ebrahim Yazdi might issue their very qualified approval of what was happening in Iran, the primary impulse was being directed by something absolute, as that Absolute passed through the person and consciousness of Ayatollah Khomeini. All his writings, his speeches, and now this performance (as I said, one didn't even have to listen to the content of this present talk) pointed towards the confluence of the successful outer *jihad* and the successful inner *jihad*. Imam Khomeini was the embodiment of that fusion (the establishment of an Islamic Republic, the conquering of external enemies, the victory of Islam in other parts of the world—and the establishment of that inner condition of integration and union which was the victory of the higher self over the lower self, and the mergence of the individuality into God); this revolution was the enactment of that fusion. To doubt Khomeini's state of consciousness, or his understanding of and devotion to Islam was to entirely miss the essence of this revolution and the future of Islam in the Middle East. I, who could not surrender my own intuition of the more cooperative, intrinsically supporting nature of the universe towards the completion and fulfillment of itself within the microcosm of man (and thus the final and essential justification for the primary impulse of Western civilization with its emphasis on and over-glorification of the individual and the uniqueness of the personality), could not become a Muslim, could not join in the sweeping, bitter castigations of Western values and metaphysics, and could not even recommend that all of humanity submit to the rigours of Islam. Nevertheless I had to admit that the figure of the man before me in this hall was the figure of a man who enjoyed the total blessings of God, and because he had given up so much, because he had lived his life in absolute devotion to God, his stature seemed to participate in a glorious power, beauty, and dignity that I knew might quite well be denied the individual who achieved—if this were indeed possible—the same goal through means not as demanding and austere. I knew that Khomeini was confronting all the evil in the world, and through Islam something was taking place that would forever alter the direction of the Script: Imam Khomeini was the counterpoint to brutal secularism, indulgent hedonism, and obsessive egoism, traits that dominated the West. Whether one believed in Islam, however, or whether one agreed with Imam Khomeini's revolution or its policies, or whether one indeed even believed in God, one would have been impervious and crude indeed if one were unable to receive some of the overflowing love, strength, purity, and grace that was the very essence of the man of eighty-one years who began now to speak to us effortlessly, without the slightest harshness of voice, with an almost melodic tone, with all the stillness and vibrancy of the universe itself breathing itself through his being. All the paradoxes I have described were there: the harshness, the serenity; the austerity of expression, the richness of compassion; the absolute rigidity of will yet an apparent infinite flexibility of suggested power; total concentration yet complete detachment. It grieved me to know that this secret—recognizing the nearness to or distance from God of another human being—was denied to virtually all politicians of the world, not to mention the Western media. I was either hopelessly insane—or so were all the mystics, saints, sages, and prophets—for the experience here overwhelmingly declared the supreme integrity of life, of man, and of Imam Khomeini. Naturally it was also part of God's design to enable man to reject the more extravagant aspects of my description of Khomeini, to even come to the conclusion that I had come under the influence of something evil (as the Nazis did under Hitler, or as the followers at Jonestown did under Reverend James Jones); however my own confidence in the organized, teleological tendencies of life to acquaint me with the design of what is true, or congruent with Plato's idea of The Good, emphatically declared the spectacle that I had witnessed this day was a spectacle of holiness and truth of the very highest order. And as Khomeini spoke I simply listened to the rhythms, the sounds apart from the meaning of the words. There was not one point at which I experienced any diminution of the intensity of his consciousness, the fullness of his heart; his influence upon my own nervous system continued throughout the time that he was sitting on the stage, and throughout that time I felt that I had received the very highest gift that could be conferred upon me, given my own particular development as a human being. Many a reader will wince at this account and may well dismiss this book, since it is clear that I have lost all my objectivity, an objectivity that was more intact up until the meeting with Khomeini. But for me, the analysis I have given of my experience is the most objective and objectifying part of this book. The final subjective experience: the encounter with what is absolute—this, and only this can give to the realm of subjectivity its objective reality. I would never become a Muslim; I would never consider all Western culture, philosophy, art, and values to be antithetical to life—as these Muslims did. I would even find myself unable to adopt the stance of hostility towards everything non-Islamic in the world. But I would forever honour Ayatollah Khomeini as an absolutely pure and remarkable human being, a human being who exalted the vision of man's worth and man's destiny, a human being who demonstrated the glory of God as He manifested through the tradition of Islam. And this was the most important message that was given to my soul in Iran: Ayatollah Khomeini is hated, reviled, ridiculed in the West; it was much like the

Pharisees persecuting Jesus, mocking his words. Ayatollah Khomeini would survive this constant execration, and his Islamic Revolution, whether it spread to other countries or not, would be triumphant. Those unable or unwilling to accept the design of fate in Iran—with its uncompromising allegiance to pure Islam—would have to suffer—either in exile, if one were an Iranian, or in the West, if one were opposed to mythological absolutism. One thinks of Moses, Mohammad, Christ, Buddha, or Confucius: would any of these beings compromise with the forces of secularism or materialist atheism? It was just not part of the mythic response to deny the supremacy of that religious structure, and the obedience to that structure was the only absolute. How would Henry Kissinger fathom the author of the Sermon on the Mount or the author of the Bhagavad-Gita? Kissinger was perhaps the exemplar of the tradition of demythification, the tradition of statecraft built upon *Realpolitik*; such a demythologizing of the cosmos and the realm of political affairs was what had invited the rebirth of myth, the rebirth of scriptural, transcendental politics. The Islamic Revolution in Iran under the leadership of Ayatollah Khomeini announced to the world that God still liked the myths He had sent down to man in order that man might know his origin and his final destination. I was a witness to this fact on Wednesday, February 9, 1982.

The Specific Influence of the Imam on the Consciousness of the Author

The powerful concentration of compassion, vitality, and, yes, bliss that radiated from Imam Khomeini kept this writer bathed in a purifying energy and feeling that expressed itself in the most profound sense of vulnerability and gratitude. I felt I was being given more of the ocean of existence and within the form of that ocean (as flowing through the Imam) was the clarity of the divine; it was in these thirty minutes that the Imam was on stage that I experienced all the cells in my mind and in my heart bursting with healing love and appreciation. I was being given everything that perhaps could be given to someone, just because it was only through another human being that God himself could concentrate his intention, his presence, his most perfect meaning. I felt even that my whole life was being clarified, that knowledge about my own destiny, my own unused power and integrity was awakening, that I would henceforth be a better, deeper, and more expanded human being. The feelings that surged through me had a strangely objectifying influence; this was

122

not sentimental gushings; it was as if the Imam's wholeness was able to move towards everything in Creation in rivers of tenderness and meaning that opened up, refined, and glorified the heart. The Imam was—not out of any intention, but just because of his pure state of being— creating me in the image of what some day I might become, and the sense of something divine and absolute playing through me from the reality of the Imam was the most sublime experience of my life. I remember listening to Handel's *Messiah* when the Hallelujah chorus played, how that seemed as purely sublime an experience as I had had, given the circumstance of finding that music expressing the highest and most exalting emotion which one was capable of. I thought of the moments of extreme love and surrender to another person. I thought of the moments when I as a father have touched the essence of my daughter's soul. I thought of the moments when I had triumphed in some athletic contest. I thought of the moments when I had received the benefits of prayer and the audiences I had had with some well-regarded saints. But this experience for its sheer power and purifying fires of feeling and meaning, coming at this point in my life, was the most beautiful experience I could imagine receiving from even God Himself.

When Imam Khomeini left the stage and the audience was filing out of the door, I just stood and watched the place where Khomeini had been sitting: it was radiant with the energy that was now inside my heart. The glow was still present and I simply moved in the waves of this aftermath of shining power. Inside I still felt the most perfect and purifying tears of my life. V. S. Naipaul could see the absurdity of a mythology that resisted the rational, resisted the blessings of modern, secular civilization. He could even write brilliantly within his bias, perhaps more brilliantly than any mythologically-seized writer. Still his heart would not respond to the most innocent impulses which made Christ declare, "Except ye be converted, and become as little children, ye shall not enter into the kingdom of heaven." Naipaul would be denied entrance into heaven because he is anaesthetized to that feeling of life that through the Imam had so charged my whole being. He would not see the particular order in the air, the absence of negativity and deadness, the presence of total harmony and purity. For me these facts were apparent on a physical level of perception. For Naipaul they would be mere imagination. The degree to which a human being acts in accordance with the laws of Creation determines the degree of harmony and happiness that emanates from him—or so was the experience of the writer. But one had to be touched by that which takes away one's doubts about what Wallace Stevens calls the "deft beneficence" of the "actual"; Naipaul and Mike Wallace of CBS (who first interviewed Khomeini after the seizing of the hostages) had not touched that deft beneficence; that beneficence was deft enough to escape detection by many intelligent human beings. Just who was chosen to be touched by it remained—and would remain—a secret only to That which had created all this. Somehow one had to be shown what God was, and then the most advanced knowledge was how to recognize his presence when he appeared—and when he disappeared. God was, according to the mystics, absolutely present everywhere, but within the dance of relativity he was present in varying and approximating degrees depending upon the amount of him that was able to manifest through a particular object or being, or environment. A fully realized man like the Imam could radiate God in perhaps his most potent and most intelligently articulated form. Even the Qur'an itself was one of those symbols of God's mystery, for many persons could read it and come to the conclusion that its poetry was surpassable, that its message was redundant, that its organization was disturbingly non-linear, and yet, if God so chose (or if one were willing to surrender to its Arabic cadences, its inner nature) one could find its power revealed. "The highest share is reserved for the one to whom it was revealed: 'The only person who truly knows the Qur'an is he who was addressed by it.'"[51] Khomeini was like the Qur'an; and the recitation of the scriptures and verses of his heart was being performed spontaneously and continuously by Allah. Obviously only selected creatures in this world were capable of knowing the Qur'an was divinely inspired; only selected creatures in this world were capable of knowing there was such a thing as God; only selected creatures in this world were blessed enough to know the integrity and the power that was embodied in this Islamic teacher, *Time* magazine's 1979 Man of the Year (*Time* of course giving this tribute as it would have given Hitler Man of the Year award at the point that he had established his Nazi rule in Germany just before the war).

One still, when leaving this impression, has to face the contradictions, the ambivalences of the revolution and the knowledge that there were many good, intelligent, and creative human beings on this earth who would, with all sincerity, oppose Imam Khomeini and his Islamic mandate. But this did not take away the fact that the reality of the Imam's person eloquently spoke of a final order, a final consummation that made the opponents of Islam and himself much less eloquent and complete in their arguments, since they were opposing that which had been blessed by the Absolute itself, that which had created this universe —and, I hasten to add, the hate that now dominated the hearts of millions of people. I looked at the space previously occupied by the Imam and saw the invisible reality of this universe.

[51] Ayatollah Khomeini, in Algar, op. cit. p. 415.

124

Since the remains of a human being (after he or she has left a room) who is pure and filled with the wholeness of life give light and energy to the atmosphere, it was relatively easy to find myself just lingering with what had happened to me and having my attention fall on the stage and the white sheet in the chair above me. Before this experience of seeing Imam Khomeini I rather thought that I would find the flaw of the revolution, because somewhere Khomeini himself would reveal some form of narrowness, some form of restriction, some form of limitation. However, despite the rigorous, adamant mould in which his face was cast, despite the firm, unyielding adherence to the absolute dogma of Islam, there was the benediction of Being, the benediction of the fullness of life; I was receiving what is called in the East *darshan*, the sacred energy and power that is given off by a saint, by a realized human being, only in this case, because of the tumultuous meaning of the revolution (the first time perhaps since the Prophet Mohammad himself that a sage, a mystic had brought about violent political change which led to revolution and war—and quite possibly a whole change in the design of international politics), because of the international consequences of the activities of Imam Khomeini there was an additional power and purpose in the presence of this man. The guru or the saint most often does not disturb the secular order; the monk, the mystic has his followers, but their activities represent an apolitical process of purification and change; here, however, although beyond the grip of what was changing and relative (i.e. being established in the purity of Being) Ayatollah Khomeini was leading a revolution that touched the lives of everyone, a revolution that went smack into the world of *Realpolitik*, the United Nations, the CIA, and the manoeuvrings of Moscow: until this point the only challenge to the West and capitalism had come from the doctrine of socialism, from the atheistic Marxist-Leninist theories (and revolutions); now religious conservatism, indeed the very essence of "the opiate of the people," had awakened people to the power of myth, of religious truth. The fact that Khomeini stood at the center of all this, the fact that he was the reason for all this, and the fact that his consciousness moved in the articulated unfolding of the intention of Allah, meant that his spiritual grace and power was that much more potent, that much more 'cosmic' in its significance; here was a Muslim holy man turning the world upside-down, demonstrating that religion can and does play a vital role in the outcome of world events. It was even a religious position to denounce the religiosity of this revolution, since such a condemnation was itself a statement that God himself did not want to be mixed up with the most important affairs of the world, or else, of course, that God did not exist. Only Allah could vindicate the revolution, and this could only happen by having the

Iranian nation continue to defy the predictions of secularized oracles, who no doubt wondered about the threat of the Soviet Union, or thought in terms of a democratic socialist successor to Khomeini. Naturally if my observations and biases are correct the Islamic Revolution of Iran would be triumphant in the most absolute sense: Iran would remain under the domination of Shi'a Islam, a whole nation would subscribe to the values, to the principles of a major religious system, and doing so, challenge the arrogance of Western humanistic ideology, as well as the levelling doctrine of scientific, dialectical materialism.

It was one thing to stand in the presence of a saint, a recognized Master or Guru; I had already done this on a number of occasions. It is quite another thing to stand in the presence of a religious personality who manifested the qualities of a saint, an ancient sage, but who at the same time was the apex of a whole transformation in the configuration of world politics. Khomeini's revolution would forever alter the dialectics of world conflict; the superpowers would continue their ideological warfare, but one country would remain unattached to and autonomous of the world giants, and would create a fresh dimension to the debate about the 'free' world and the totalitarian world. Science and progress had driven God from the stage of world events; now it seemed that God wished to return; it was through the person and consciousness of Ayatollah Ruhullah Khomeini that this unexpected and mystifying process was taking place, a process that could only be understood in the utter calm at the center of the Islamic storm: Khomeini's consciousness, which manifested as the Absolute as it, unimpeded and unresisted, passed through his nervous system.

After five minutes, apart from the presence of those Revolutionary Guards who were presently living on the premises of the Imam's sacred territory, I was the only member of the audience who remained in the hall; the rest of the delegates to the conference had gone back to their buses. It was the grace of the situation that had even allowed me to pause there for such a long time and to ignore the obvious momentum of the departing crowd, the obvious directive to return to the buses and leave this place of power and light. But standing in my own appreciation, or rather, standing in the protecting beneficence of Imam Khomeini's spiritual remains, I was as if invisible until such time as my fulfillment was complete. It so happened that the Revolutionary Guards noticed me throughout the speech of the Imam, and noticed the effect this experience had—and was continuing to have—as I stood in the almost empty hall and just gazed effortlessly, still with the lovely burning bliss in my heart. My translator, Mohammad Abbaszadeh, conferred with the Revolutionary Guards and it became a source of some satisfaction

126

for them to see a Westerner moved in the brilliance of their leader's hallowed presence. I could see that they too understood and felt the absolute fact of Khomeini's real nature, that that nature had been sanctified by God, that this fact was at the source of the revolution; clearly Ebrahim Yazdi could not feel this fact, and thus his problems with the more irrational manifestations of the revolution. The faces of the Revolutionary Guards glowed with the joy and rapture of having seen their beloved leader, and yet to find that someone (a non-Muslim) could participate in that love, this was a moment of vindication for the revolution, for Islam, for everything that was happening in Iran. They expressed a desire to interview me, and I walked over to the wall and leaned there while they asked me—not, it so happened, about their Imam, but about the revolution. Well, there was a returning surge of pure feeling that welled up in my eyes and began again to cleanse my heart, and I found that, quite innocently (this was the purest emotion I had experienced since walking through Beheshte Zahra Cemetery two years before), that emotion took over my whole being, and my inarticulate reply was the most eloquent response I could give to the question. They could see what was still holding me, and they silently shared that sacred consensual validation of their leader. Finally, after these organic, I can even say objectifying, tears had stilled somewhat I began to give expression to my thoughts, all in terms of the experience I had just had.

The river of feeling was still moving through my heart, but it seemed possible to give expression to the idea of how my experience this day had revealed the sources of inspiration of the revolution. The inside of the revolution was now inside me, and although it was not in the destiny of things that I had been born in Iran, to become a Muslim fighting in the revolution (there were other revolutions, non-Islamic in their character, which were perhaps, on a smaller scale, as necessary as this revolution: God, it seems, expresses different tendencies in different places; even the passion of the individual had some meaning in the script; Islam was not the only way God fulfilled himself through man), I joined this revolution on the level of my heart, in so far as I knew its origin was pure, and that therefore it needed my modest prayers. The complex issue was to discern where God perhaps was not about to support the universalizing of the revolution, but I was pretty certain I could experience the sanctity of this revolution, the sanctity of Islam, and the sanctity of Imam Khomeini, without however altering my sense of the very different destiny in store for the Western world. And there were still challenges for these Iranian warriors; their inner *jihad* was not complete; therefore their vision was still subject to some distortions; they still, even in repeating the words of their Imam, could greatly oversimplify the forces of truth that sought articulation in the world, and particularly in the sphere of nationhood. They were, at least the great majority of them, probably incapable of the mercy, compassion, or wisdom that would enable them to understand how someone could be sincere and even highly developed and still resist this revolution. The revolution was for some; it was for Iran; it may have even been for the Middle East itself; this did not mean, however, that anyone who might oppose the revolution, or resist the Islamization of the world, was evil. As far as I was concerned even God himself might not lend absolute support to the attempt to make his Creation completely Islamic. One thing was certain, though, it was through Islam and only Islam that he was reviving the power of one of his mythologies, subtly undermining the growing assumption that secularism (Western and Eastern) had banished him from the stage of world events. This was the great dilemma for the sensitive observer of this revolution: to realize that it was a purifying miracle, a necessary miracle, a decisive force for the spiritual regeneration of mankind. The Islamic Revolution in Iran would show that it was not subject to the cause and effect paradigm of modern international politics, where the sense of the divine was absolutely absent, where the notion of God was irrelevant to the analysis of events. Islam—through the Imam and this revolution—was the simplest and most adamant challenge to this idea, and its very intransigence, its refusal to play the game of politics according to the rules of Machiavelli was an important statement about the reservoirs of meaning and truth that had slipped from the consciousness of man. The Islamic Revolution in Iran was the most efficient and powerful means to bring about this recognition, this confrontation, this awakening. Even the rise of conservative religion in America was itself part of the tendency in Creation at this time, although one did feel that the evangelical expression of Christianity was not sufficiently archetypal or richly mythological to be comparable to what was happening in Iran, and the difference in leadership between Jerry Falwell and Imam Khomeini demonstrated God's own opinion of that difference—and its significance.

What was important for many Westerners was to realize that yes, this revolution was not acceptable as a model for society in Europe or in North America; no, the individual in the West had become just too sophisticated, too knowing of the inexhaustible creative particularisms of subjective experience, of individual expression. Islam could have, perhaps, at the time of Mohammad, conquered the whole world; now, however, things had gone too far through the demythologizing of mankind; there was some truth that had to come out from that demythologizing, from that self-sufficiency, from that fetish of the ego. But whatever that truth was, it had not found its integrated system of argument that would amount to an answer to this revolution; in a primitive but fundamental sense, this revolution, under the beautifully realized leadership of Ayatollah Ruhullah Khomeini was the purest uprising of the spirit in the world today. The criteria one had to adopt were of course different from those used to assess, say, the Nicaraguan Revolution, the Cuban Revolution; nevertheless the demonstration that there was a non-material reality at the basis of existence needed to be proclaimed; Islam and this revolution was the means to demonstrate this truth, and all those born within the range where its influence was likely to predominate were themselves chosen to come to grips with its mythological power.

None of these things were of course repeated to the Revolutionary Guards. To declare there are many truths, that there are other ways to God besides through Islam, that Islam is a universal truth but not a truth that would universalize its spiritual hegemony throughout the whole world is not the appropriate or useful truth to plead to someone who must see Islam as *the only* truth. For a Muslim, and especially a Muslim in Iran, to spend his energy and thinking on the idea that truth is pluralistic, that his religion is relative to other things, that he should adopt a moderate attitude with respect to spreading the truth of Islam—this is to dilute the necessary power of his motivation and therefore the energy necessary to accomplish the goal for which Islam was given to the world. That goal was the knowledge of surrender to that which had created this universe, that goal was the movement, the evolution of the self towards a greater harmony with the universe, that goal was the achievement—in its highest sense—that was now embodied in the Imam himself: the eternalizing of the individual through the expansion of the ego into the Absolute. One must, if one is to move efficiently towards such a goal, not doubt the supreme efficacy of the system of worship, purification, and action revealed by one religion. Even Allah has willed it this way; on the other side, after one has touched the benediction of God, then one can intuitively recognize that there must be many ways to what is Absolute, as many ways as God has manifested in choosing his prophets, for each religion diverges at some point from every other religion; Islam was certainly no exception, but it was of some significance that God was choosing this religion through which to remind all men of the pre-eminent significance of the spiritual dimension of life; the Islamic Revolution happened because of the stature of Imam Khomeini. There was no other recognized leader of another major religion—even the Pope—who could match the intensity, nor the magnitude of holiness that radiated from the Imam.

What I did utter to the Revolutionary Guards was recorded, and I consider my statements to be the most spontaneously expansive and satisfying remarks I have ever been allowed to make after witnessing a spectacle of extreme aesthetic brilliance. One could have just watched Rudolph Nureyev dance Swan Lake, one could have just watched a superbly coached North Carolina basketball team win the NCAA championship, one could have fallen in love with the most beautiful woman or man, one could have ascended to the top of Everest, or one could have heard Bach's Mass in B Minor while sitting in Westminster Abbey—but none of these experiences would have equalled what happened to me this day, for to be truly open to receive the grace of Ayatollah Khomeini was to receive the reflection of God Himself as He could only concentrate Himself through the nervous system of a human being. I received that grace and all the attendant meanings that danced through my mind. My life was clarified—not through being imaged by Islam and not even by the intention of Khomeini himself—but through the fact that in something Absolute passing through—perpetually—the consciousness and personality of Imam Khomeini God Himself could instruct me in the lessons I still had to learn. Those instructions inscribed themselves inside my heart, and I emerged from my encounter with Imam Khomeini even more individuated and integrated than I had been before coming to Iran. The truth of Khomeini —his state of consciousness, the magnificence of his personal integrity— went even beyond Islam; it was affecting Creation on the level of the actual molecules of life itself, and all of Creation was being healed, but especially those persons fortunate to be open to receive what he was. Somehow this day had been prepared for me by all my previous experiences, but most especially by my association with the spiritual and intuitive side of life. Carl Jung, were he alive today, would have been one of the few prominent Western intellectuals to have recognized and applauded the role and the integrity of Ayatollah Khomeini, for Jung knew the sickness that had descended into man's soul when modern man tried to cut himself off from the myths of the past. Jung would have seen this revolution as the attempt of the collective unconscious to assert some form of equilibrium after having been so unbalanced by the rationalizing of man's soul, by the exorcism of God from the universe.

Having made my comments, inspired as they were, the Revolutionary Guards offered to let me meet the Imam personally; now it may strike the reader as preposterous but after being filled up by the Imam, having in fact received the ocean of love and power that I had, to see him personally seemed superfluous; I had been given (or so I felt) all that which God would have wished for me to receive; to meet the Imam personally was to ask the Imam to focus on me personally; I knew his time was too precious for that; I knew that whatever questions I had about the revolution and his role in it had been answered. It thus seemed almost unnatural to ask for a personal audience with the Imam. Nevertheless I could see with what eagerness this offer had been made and I realized that even though it might be just a formality, and even though I would not think of pressing my individuality upon the Imam, it would nevertheless add to my credibility in the West, and it would enable me to see whether there was anything different to the Imam when he was in a personal encounter with someone. I therefore agreed to the tentative meeting, which was eagerly sought by my translator and guide, Mohammad Abbaszadeh.

We were ushered through a gate into the pathway leading up to the house of the Imam. We waited there for some thirty minutes and then were invited to wait in a room within the house itself. Taking off our shoes we were asked to sit down, where tea was served to us (in Iran tea is served constantly), where various mullahs sat, also waiting for an audience. Now here the atmosphere was again exhilarating, vibrating with freshness and purity; compared to the hotel it was as if one were breathing into the exhaust pipe of a car and then breathing the air on a Himalayan mountain, so much did the consciousness of Khomeini make a difference, so much did the reverence and perpetually charged ambience affect the environment. There was one crudely insensitive mullah who continued to draw the exhaust fumes into his lungs; apparently even in the house of the Imam, there was permission to persist with one's addictions. But even the polluting effect of the cigarette smoke was not sufficient to take away the dominant reality of the consciousness inside this house. I closed my eyes and just experienced the serenity in the air, and then after about fifteen minutes (and there were some incredulous looks by the various mullahs who wondered how an obviously Western and non-Islamic journalist had been permitted inside the residence of the Imam: most Western journalists had not even been allowed inside Iran for the past fourteen months; to be awaiting a personal meeting with the Imam, well that was past all reason—and I felt the miraculous fact of my situation) we were told, hastily, that the Imam had suddenly changed his schedule and was going into the hall once again to address a new audience of devotees, high school students and some of the poor from South Tehran; this would mean that we couldn't be received in his own private room, that we would (the interpreter and I) have to intercept him on his way into the hall. We rushed to the passageway which joined the house with the hall, and were told almost immediately upon reaching our position, below the passageway, on the ground, that the Imam was on his way. Khomeini came through the doors of his house and again there was the whirlwind of divine energy, the swirling power of love and solemnity that carried its intention within a total sense of universality. He approached me, was told by Mohammad my name and where I was from, and his hand

reached down as both my hands went up to receive him. I held his hand
for a few moments and he sent the thunderbolts of his immovable power
into my eyes. It was as I had imagined it would be: there was nothing to
say in those ten to fifteen seconds when in silence I received once again
this unbounded ocean of supreme purposefulness. He was what he was
inside the hall, only this time the universe was closer, but it was as if
seeing the face of Jehovah in a moment when Jehovah took the form of
the mask of the human being. There was no wish, nor intention to
disturb the wholeness of this moment of union with him, and my
individuality seemed to form in a kind of non-anxious and harmonizing
expansiveness that could bring about no needs. I had been filled before
he touched my hand (or rather as I grasped his hand with both my
hands); I was reminded of the sense of eternal replenishment that was
the reality of himself as he was nearest to me. My trip to Iran seemed to
have completed itself; I could have gone home after the Imam had left
the hall; now, having seen him close up, I experienced that the answers
had come in the form of a steady revelation. The Imam never really
personalized himself, and even all those who loved him and who were
with him never expected him to personalize himself; he was universal
and impersonal, and because of this he was capable of infinite compassion and devotion to all those who chose to follow the path of Islam.
Even during the lecture I noticed his son, Ahmad, would turn in the
direction of his father (he was seated just to the right of Khomeini) and
gaze upon his father with the sense of knowledge that Khomeini was no
longer his father; Khomeini was his Teacher; Khomeini was the source
of living wisdom; Khomeini was the embodiment of Islam. Ahmad
studied him as if to see the confirmation of this idea of the Imam's
consistent appropriateness. He, Ahmad, had gained, from the dispas-
sionate equilibrium of his father, his own beautiful serenity, and by
watching his father closely he registered the impulses of intelligence that
served to show Ahmad the proper movements of the universe as they
might embody themselves (and did) within a human being. It was the
disciple looking up at his Master—the Master's closest disciple. His
father had transcended the status of father; he was the father to the
whole nation of Iran and to devout Muslims everywhere. It was, then,
this impersonal reality of Khomeini that gave to him the expression of
supreme devotion to God and to Islam.

Mohammad kissed fervently the hand of the Imam as he passed on
from me to extend his hand down (his left hand) to Mohammad. It was a
beautiful hand, a hand that, however aged, still retained the vitality of
life, and was no doubt covered with the impressions of the lips of
thousands of Iranians. To kiss this hand was for a Muslim to receive a
special kind of grace, and Mohammad told me eagerly afterwards that

132

his own hand (he held it open to me) "would never touch anything evil or impure for the rest of my life." And when I returned to the hotel many of the Muslims were amazed that I had seen the Imam personally, and they wanted to see my hand, to express their envy and their assurance that my hand was now considered holy!

We walked down through the alleys leading to a street where a taxi would take us back to the hotel; I felt the conspiracy of time and space trying to gradually diminish my experience, but with just the slightest turning of my attention I was able to hold the full meaning and intensity of it—at least as it now translated itself into my present circumstances. I felt how so much tension had gone out of me, the tension brought about by the apparent contradictions and excesses of the revolution. I knew that I had discovered and experienced the great secret of the revolution; I knew that somehow I would try to communicate that secret in my book on Iran. That secret has been told; it is the truth about this revolution, but it is equally obvious that many people will assume I have exaggerated or that I have been deluded; others may even feel that I have betrayed the cause of freedom and democracy by writing as I have. (I have friends who now are in adamant opposition to the regime, having been close to individuals who have been executed or discredited or persecuted by the present regime.) But I insist that this is the reality that everyone must at least consider; it may be rejected, but still the argument must be made, and I have made it here. And I readily confess that all my subsequent experiences in Iran carried with them the vision of the integrity of the leader of the revolution, and therefore I found a touchstone to measure and determine the meaning of various events to which I was exposed. While I was in the presence of the Imam I had a yearning that all politicians of note take the time to visit Imam Khomeini. I still have that yearning. Imam Khomeini is the most charismatic political leader of the twentieth century—and he is much more besides. He is one of a handful of individuals I have met who have left me transformed. He is there in Iran supporting one of the precious pillars of God: Islam and the supreme truth of surrender to God.

Freedom of Knowledge and Inquiry in an Islamic Society

After seeing Imam Khomeini I returned to the more relative and fallible expressions of the revolution. For instance, the evening of the day that we visited the Imam, various members of the Ministry of Culture came

to address us on the topic of the role of the university in an Islamic
republic, and the role of the artist. The Islamizing of the university,
which had been alluded to in a previous lecture by someone in the
Ministry of Education, was now discussed in some detail. Naturally, as
someone who has been raised to respect the disinterested inquiry free of
ideological biases, I suspected the attempt to make the curriculum
totally Islamic would compromise in the most serious sense any underlying idea of objective, open-ended exploration of the universe.[52] However one must realize that, according to Islam, the major questions
about the origin, the nature, and the purpose of this universe have
already been settled—as has man's role within this known and divinely
revealed universe. Therefore knowledge means simply the extension of
man's skills, the development of further means to improve man's condition, and the discovery of how education can lead man to a more
intimate connection with the Creator. The notion of a philosophy
student asking the ultimate questions: "Who am I?" "Does God exist?"
"Is anything certainly true?" "Are there ethical absolutes?" "Can the
unjust man be happy?"—no longer exists, or such questions exist, but
they are answered absolutely, without recourse to mere logic or empirical verification. God himself (who, we must assume, is the authority on
this universe) has already spoken through the prophets; therefore his
universe is knowable and is understood within very absolute laws. As I
listened to the sincere but humourless (they were deadly serious)
members of the ministry discuss their program for Islamizing the
universities I wondered if perhaps—at least in some circumstance—it
might be more innocent and ultimately more creative—to arrange for
some suspension of a priori belief; at least this way the student would
have to exert more effort, and would have to accept more of the
unknown, before having his quest satisfied. If there are reasonable
doubts about what the nature of this universe is (whether, for instance, it
is purposeful or indifferent), is this not part of the process of man's
education, to come to terms with the fact that God (at least for some) has
deliberately sown seeds of doubt and mystery, and that therefore there is
a special kind of joy and satisfaction in realizing, in facing all the
evidence of the universe's, not to mention God's, unknowableness?
Jacques Monod's brilliant argument for a universe determined by
chance and not necessity[53] is part of the aesthetic richness of the
universe—and the Creator—for here one faces the evidence that a
strong case can be made for the random and non-theistic view of the

[52] See pp. 69-75 for discussion of this topic.

[53] Jacques Monod, *Chance and Necessity*, trans. Austryn Wainhouse (New York: Vintage,
1972).

134

universe. Was the basis of such compelling and elegant arguments merely the work of the devil—assuming that God exists? No matter, I had to find out how this Islamic republic would bring about the total restructuring of the universities. At the same time I wondered whether, just as a matter of principle, there might not be thousands of teachers and professors whose integrity would be compromised were they to give their assent to the educational process in which the cosmology of Islam was the dominant fact, the one fact from which everything else proceeded.

But the steps towards the establishment of the universities within the Islamic mould were based upon, according to the ministry, the idea that all knowledge was to lead man towards God, that all knowledge was to lead man towards perfection. The universities would henceforth be linked to society, would act as institutions devoted to enriching man's spirit and imbuing everyone with the values of Islam. And the syllabus would be worked out "according to the wishes of the Imam." Anyone who was against Islam was automatically suspect as being an agent of those political parties that were working for the destruction of the regime, and therefore these people would have to be eliminated from the universities. Did they recognize that perhaps an individual could not accept the cosmology of Islam without this meaning that he was hostile to the regime? But this was too difficult a question to answer. The fact was that belief in Islam was a sign of God's pleasure; doubt of Islam was a sign of the opposite. The very basis of one's security and fulfillment in Iran was in direct proportion to one's faith in Islam, and now this would extend to the universities themselves. The tradition in the West, where the great majority of academics are non-religious and hardly pious, would now be challenged by this mythologized tradition in Iran, where faith in God and extreme piety were considered as prerequisites for knowing anything worthwhile about the universe. Of course this mythology and its many impressive apologists (not the least of whom being the Imam himself) was more archetypally authentic than Bob Jones University where the faculty took an oath of allegiance to the principles of fundamentalist Christianity. I suppose one, if secularist in orientation, doesn't make the distinction between pure mythology and particularized, narrow mythology—as the example of Iran and Bob Jones University perhaps suggests; nevertheless this is a distinction that counts. Islam had not had its reformation, had not had its internal feuding that had broken it into schisms which could never be healed. On the contrary Islam, despite the differences between Shi'a and Sunni, was united under the inspiration of this revolution and here, in the only country in the world, religion was forming the basis of all academic life.

Knowledge—and the university—was to heighten man's relationship with God and "to serve the people." Knowledge was to bring about a "spiritual relationship among all the people . . . to serve humanity . . . and to enrich the culture of the people with Islam." Islam, then, was considered to be intrinsic to life itself, and therefore if the universe really did work according to the truths of the Qur'an—and God said it did!—then to base the process of education upon this reality was to harmonize this process with God himself, and to eventually enlist the divine to regulate and define the whole unfoldment of knowledge of the Absolute. Allah, or the Absolute, was at the end of every field of knowledge, from mathematics and physics, to literature and art.

The Concept of the Artist in an Islamic Society

We were asked to submit questions on paper to the speakers. I asked the question whether the artist in an Islamic society could possibly create pure art if he was, as a premise of his circumstance, required to create that which was purely Islamic. Was Creation itself Islamic? Could anyone who was without religious beliefs describe Creation as inherently and manifestly Islamic? How could it be certified that a given work of art was outside the definition of art that glorified Allah? Would this mean that Michelangelo's sculpture was blasphemous because it showed the human form as nude? Was not the artist—at least the artist understood in his most unfettered and dangerously alive sense—subject only to the condition of his own imagination? Was the impulse of the artist simply the expression of an imagination that sought only to confirm the Islamic universe?

(I suppose my Western conditioning had made me see the artist in terms of someone like Picasso, or Hemingway, or Stravinsky, artists most unlikely to approach their art ideologically. If there was a God and art was one of the means that he kept his Creation fresh it seemed that little art of the twentieth century would lead one to the conclusion that God asked people to come towards Islam.) But I realized at the same time, that if God were pleased in fact that Iran had become Islamic, then it followed that some great art that was truly in the tradition of the great Islamic art of the past, would flower in present day Iran and that religious art would once again be revived. Eventually I might even think that it was necessary for Iran to produce art that, however Islamically acceptable, would have to partake in the universality of beauty that is of course the final criterion of any greatness aesthetically.

But as my question was translated I did sense a shock momentarily, as

136

the question did pose somewhat of a challenge to the very devout and hard-working (and quite eloquent) speakers from the Culture Ministry. The concept went like this: the spirit of the artist should be in agreement with Islam. Art should not become "a substitute for God." It cannot take the place of God. Art should not seduce people away from God, and it must not become something that is seen, or is capable of being seen, as something other than what will draw human beings towards God. The notion of the ego of the artist, the cult of the individualistic artist was in violation of the purpose of art, was in violation indeed to the very nature of the artistic process. What was necessary was for the artist to offer his work to God, that his work was what inspired people to give honour to God.

Certainly this was the case with the great religious art of the past; but was God, in his modern phase, capable of acting upon man to produce masterpieces in the great tradition of the Gothic cathedrals, the Byzantine icons, the Buddhist temples, and, indeed, the decorative mosques? Perhaps, but the hostility to images would seem to restrict the role and activity of the Islamic artist. In any event we would see whether God deemed it necessary to display the sensibility of the imagination through this revolution. Thus far I had not seen that aesthetic sensibility amounted for much in the Islamic Republic, but I would not discount that possibility in the future. For myself, to produce this art was itself a test of the ultimate integrity and validity of the revolution, even if at present it was not one of the priorities.

A Visit to South Tehran

One of my most helpful guides and translators was Asghar Manoussi, who insisted on having me visit South Tehran where the scandalous poverty was legendary, and from where many of the recruits for the Revolutionary Guards were drawn. Although I had visited a family living in one of the mud houses (one room) in my previous trip it was felt that without this experience of the abject poverty I would not understand how this revolution was for the masses, for the oppressed. The hosts who had arranged for the conference in Iran had, according to Asghar, avoided having the delegates come to South Tehran because still, despite the work of the revolution, there were hundreds of thousands of Iranians in the grip of the poverty they had known under the Shah, and they were thus still susceptible to the blandishments of the Mujahaddin who confronted them with the fact that the government was ignoring their plight, and would continue to exploit them. We walked down into the rows of mud huts and there encountered an Iraqi father who had been kicked out of Baghdad because of his Iranian ancestry and suspected sympathies with Khomeini. He turned out to be a devout Muslim, despite his somewhat scruffy, unkempt appearance (and I say this outside of the fact of his tattered clothes and the grinding impoverishment of his circumstances) and depressed spirit. He insisted that Imam Khomeini was "the sun of the world," that the Imam "was like God," that this revolution was "Allah's revolution." I asked him why it was that Allah had made him poor; he explained that though poor he was physically, he was inwardly spiritually rich, and that the revolution would eventually change even his material situation. His life, he insisted, was now invigorated by the revolution and his inner happiness and his love for the Imam compensated him for his poverty, and indeed made him feel he was more fortunate than someone who was more wealthy than he. He lived in the hut with his family, a wife and seven children. The children spoke Arabic and Farsi and seemed quite reconciled to their surroundings. All my attempts to draw out some dissenting viewpoint—or to discern some source of conflict about the revolution— were not fulfilled. Somehow, despite the horrendous conditions of their situation they were imbued with the revolution and were much happier to be in Iran, along with the more than 60,000 other Iraqis who were expelled for similar reasons. Their belief in the revolution would make it hard, it seemed, for the Mujahaddin to gain converts, so spiritualized was their vision of this world—however primitive and child-like that faith in the ultimate beneficence of this revolution might be.

A Visit with the Family
of a Famous Martyr of the Revolution

Asghar insisted that I meet the family of the martyr whose name was given to the street that Asghar lives on. The martyr was Abdullah Mesgar, a young Ph.D. in Economics, whose bravery, whose Islamic piety, whose charismatic personality made him "the candle of our neighbourhood" according to Asghar. This man evoked the highest praise from Asghar and from all the young people who lived in this part of South Tehran. It was said that he was utterly selfless and spent the whole night in prayers to Allah.

Even as a ten-year-old boy, according to his brother and father, Abdullah thought of nothing but God, was said to speak to God. He was altogether a legend in Iran and his involvement with the revolution began when he was but a high school student. He had followed the activities and direction of Imam Khomeini many years before the revolution actually broke out in its full fury. He had accompanied Imam Khomeini when the Imam arrived by plane in Tehran after his exile in Iraq and in France. Abdullah had also been active as one of the supreme commanders of Sepah, the Revolutionary Guards; before the coming to power of Imam Khomeini, during the rule of the Shah, SAVAK had come to the house of Abdullah and seized him and later tortured him so that when he came out of jail he had to have major operations on his stomach. As a leader of Sepah he had gone to Kurdistan where the Marxist groups (or the rebel Kurds) had beaten him nearly to death in an effort to convert him away from his allegiance to Khomeini. He had survived even this, having to succumb to yet another operation, and after recovering he went to the battlefront where the war with Iraq had been going on for fifteen days. The night before an Iraqi tank had attacked his position (he was apparently in his prayers at that moment) and killed him, he had phoned his mother to say, "I am going to Karbala. See you there." Karbala of course being the place of martyrdom of the supreme martyr Imam Hussein, the grandson of Mohammad. For all martyrs Karbala symbolizes the consecration of martyrdom. Abdullah lived (at least in the minds of his family and thousands of Iranians) as a pure example of the perfect soldier of Islam. He had been an exceptional student, a loyal friend, a devout Muslim, a courageous warrior. As I heard both his brother, father, and Asghar talk about his exploits I tried to determine to what extent the legend had been created out of a desire to immortalize someone, and to what extent it had actually come out of the natural and deserving status that Abdullah deserved. The room where our discussion took place was a room that had been the bedroom of Abdullah. The room was now considered to be a place of power and it was kept as a sort of shrine, with photographs of Abdullah, and many of his belongings permanently in place. Sitting in this room, hearing of Abdullah, and seeing the extent to which Abdullah had left a mark upon all these people it became obvious to me that he had in fact earned his reputation, that he was one of those heroes of a revolution, of a cause, which give to that revolution and cause so much of its inspiration. It was an individual such as Abdullah who proved the power of martyrdom, who proved the sacredness of the revolution and Islam, for from his life others derived all the power and determination necessary to further the goals of that revolution. Abdullah's spirit was now stronger in death than it had even been in life and this made one wonder whether in fact the martyr does give an added power to his cause when he dies, that a martyr's blood redeems those who live and fight for that same cause. Could martyrdom be the essential element in the success of the war with Iraq? My contact with the family of Abdullah made me believe this was a truth.

It was stories or realities like this one that made the revolution, that formed the mythic power of the revolution, that confirmed absolutely the authority, the promises of Imam Khomeini. Abdullah embodied the ideals for which others should live, and when someone achieved these ideals, as apparently Abdullah had, then the effects on the living were undeniable and undiminishable. Abdullah's power continued to grow over time and the very events in present day Iran simply supported the consolidation of Abdullah's mystique. One Abdullah was enough to give hope and inspiration to thousands of young Iranian soldiers and Revolutionary Guards, and the opposition just did not have access to the grace, or the mythology to effectively produce their own martyrs—at least martyrs who so easily, who so naturally established their reputations and formed the magnetic power that would unify and strengthen the revolution. Was Allah on the side of Abdullah in such an absolute manner that all that which opposed him was considered absolutely evil? Certainly as I found out the details of Abdullah from his family I sensed that some sacred force was assisting the legend, thus suggesting indeed that the concept of martyrdom and the ideals for which Abdullah had died exalted him in the hierarchy of souls that had left their earthly bodies. To look forward to being a martyr for Khomeini and Islam was a fortune to be devoutly wished for; no other young person in the world today was given such a heady, mythologically powerful set of symbols and context in which to live and to die. This again was absolutely vital for observers of this revolution to realize: that the dead gave power to the living; that the dead were still—and would be eternally—soldiers of Islam.

A Confrontation with an American Muslim Woman

After visiting the home of Abdullah and the parents of Asghar (the latter were sweet, humble, and filled with hospitality: the illiterate father composed poetry on the spot and the mother adorned in her chador provided the perfect example of the beautifully devoted Muslim woman, whose life revolved around the figure of Imam Khomeini) we were invited to a dinner at the home of a young Iranian student who had lived in the United States and who was hosting a number of the North American Muslims, including three American Muslim women.

When I was just finishing my dessert one of the women, a girl from New York who now lived in Washington and whom I had seen on a number of occasions during the time I was in Iran, spoke to me. (She had seemed somewhat unnatural in her black chador, as if she was resisting the cultural tendencies of our birthplace, as if she was in some sense ignoring her responsibilities.)

This girl who now lived in Washington asked me what my impressions were of the revolution. Now the question seemed innocent enough, but in her tone I detected some belligerence, some suspiciousness, some tendentious pressuring. I gave an answer which indicated my essentially positive view but qualified this with a rather complex assessment of the continuing need to extend and evolve within the revolution so that the revolution became both an outer and inner revolution (i.e. the outer *jihad* and the inner *jihad*). She then asked what I had been doing that day. Again I answered without any defensiveness, trying to undermine her anxiety, her apparent doubts about my motivation, for now as she looked at me, as she listened to my answers she showed that she had made up her mind about me, and, whatever that judgement might be, the implication was that I was up to something no good, that there was some flaw in my presentation, that I was somehow fooling people, or was a hypocrite in some way.

Well, after giving my answers to several more questions she suddenly point-blank asked me why I wasn't a Muslim if I saw the revolution in the terms that I described (and while in Iran I tended to describe the revolution in terms that would facilitate the information I sought in my interviews). I tried to explain that although I believed in God, that although I saw the significance and validity of Islam, it was not in the interests of my credibility as a Western journalist to become a Muslim, that one ultimately did not have to become a Muslim to do service for God. Admittedly this was partially disingenuous as an argument; after all, she was a Westerner; she had become a Muslim; I, on the other hand, intuitively felt that I was not supposed to make such a commitment. I admired Islam; I admired the primary impulse of this revolution; and I knew that I appreciated Khomeini as much as almost any Muslim; but religion for me consisted of the acts of my life and the desire to make the greatest difference in my own life and in the lives of others. Without some knowledge as to the very decisive reasons for my not becoming a Muslim (and I had studied under an authentic teacher, who had profoundly enriched my inner life, who had given me a discipline that would bring me close to the essence of the religious experience: it was this relationship that made it unnecessary to seek for the same rewards through Islam)—without this knowledge she had some basis for remaining suspicious. She had read much of what I had written on Islam before;

she had to acknowledge that I had understood the revolution, that indeed I seemed to have an inside track on what were the real issues at stake in Islam. Yet I was not a Muslim; she had given up her non-Muslim, American freedom to become a Muslim, and therefore risked extreme censure and opprobrium from probably most of her friends, her parents, and certainly the majority of her countrymen. Now here she was confronting one of the members of her tribe (non-Islamic tribe) who, while enjoying the contact with Islam, while meeting with Imam Khomeini (which I later learned greatly irked her: a non-Muslim had gained permission to see the Imam, while she, a Muslim, had been denied permission: where was justice here?), nevertheless retained the privileges of selfhood that she was forced to surrender in order to conform to the laws of Islam.

There was something contemptuous, chastising, and anxious in her manner of speaking as she pressed for the real reasons for my reluctance to come into the Islamic fold. I felt how she had made a tremendous sacrifice of personal freedom and even prestige by becoming a Muslim; I saw also how it might just be that she had become a Muslim for not entirely spiritual reasons. Certainly she was absolutely sincere as a Muslim, and certainly she would perform the necessary rites of Islam; and yet there was an ambivalence inside her that she could not resolve; somewhere her unconscious rebelled against the decision she had made since the particular problems and challenges she faced as a human being (who was born into a non-Islamic culture) were not, at least to my vision, being dealt with creatively within her commitment to Islam. She seemed to me much like a young North American who had joined some cult, for the spirit of Islam did not naturally breathe itself through her being; she was the least natural Muslim I had ever met, although she was clearly intelligent and full of a willingness to give herself to her new faith. Somewhere the archetypes collided; even in her personal manner she did not evince those qualities that would enable her to smoothly and spontaneously harmonize herself with Islam—Shi'a Islam. The archetype of being a Westerner, of being an American from the East Coast, of being a person who reflected her culture, the bias of the collective psychology of her country and all its styles of expression—this archetypal pattern was so ingrained within her psyche that I could see no evidence that Islam had transformed her into its own archetype. The other Muslims I had met seemed much more purely attuned to the idiom of Islam; they did not have to fight against tendencies that seemed foreign to Islam.

Now I am not sure how conscious all this was, and perhaps I have my own unconscious biases; for one, this woman seemed too feisty, aggressive, and ungraceful in her outward expression; she did not seem womanly and confident enough to make her insecurity secondary to her commitment to Islam. Somewhere with the other Muslims I had met (mostly from the Middle East) there seemed a quite remarkable blend of personality and mythology, but with this young American Muslim there was a discordance; her commitment to Islam had not come about on the wave of a religious experience; that she was now religious in intent I do not deny, but that she had gained that serenity and grace that would allow her to make the difficult adjustment to Islam in her own country, this I very much doubted. She was in the White Anglo-Saxon Protestant genus and the Islamic genus just could not efface or transmute that cultural chromosomal pattern. Not that I would be surprised if I met her some day and discovered she had learned the art of surrender, the art of expressing herself within Islam naturally, but for now there was this irritation within her, the repression of her unconscious ambivalence, and the failure to master the art of yielding and receptiveness that are part of every religion, as well as part of the distinctiveness of womanhood.

I, as someone who carried my non-Islamic status without any hindrances in Islamic Iran, appeared to her unconscious (her submerged, richly ancient consciousness) as someone who was gaining the benefit of Islam without making the formal sacrifice that would entitle me to some of those benefits (benefits = friendship and respect of Muslims, the insights into Islam and the Revolution, the meeting with the Imam). She was thus projecting her own repressed doubts about what she had done, trying desperately to gain some confession or admission from me that would expose me in front of the other Muslims (who, throughout this altercation, supported me, intuitively aware as they were—these were all males—of the stress that was behind her arguments, her accusations) and take away the influence and the mystique that I seemed to have acquired without effort.

Even in her chador I sensed something unnatural; she just looked like an attractive American girl who was covering herself with a black gown and veil; she was not meant to be covered—at least until she had grown into herself such as to become part of the consciousness of Islam that seemed so much more rooted in the soil of the Middle East, and especially here in Iran (although I had thought from time to time of the pre-Islamic civilization of Iran, of Cyrus the Great, of Zoroastrian culture—how this civilization perhaps made it more difficult for an American to absorb Islam in totality than for an Arab). No, she was not ready for Islam; she would do better by returning to her previous situation and adopting the garb and the ritual of her native culture, however profane and unstructured that might be. And the real evidence for my perception was the fact that I did not see any of the marks of

Islam on her; she seemed to me untouched by her faith and her experience with Islam. All her prayers, her fasting, her reading of the Qur'an, her good works, had not awakened the spirit of Islam within her; she was not moving in the motions of someone who has found their authentically pure absolute for living.

Now this might sound outrageously arrogant of the writer to make such an analysis, and no doubt others would view the circumstances differently; in any event her strident manner, her aggressiveness in pursuing her argument about my hypocrisy reached the point where I began to experience that it was a religious duty to point out to her the strain of her contention, and the unattractive style within which she was presenting her own self. I even broached the issue of her non-Islamic awareness, how she was perverting the spirit of Islam by arguing from such an ego-bound position, for it was finally the incitement of her ego that was driving her into this confrontation. At one point I became quite abrupt with her and upbraided her on choosing such a non-Islamic mode to argue for Islam. There was nothing left of Islam once her anger and frustration were aroused, and it was a kind of poetic justice I thought for me, a non-Muslim, to demonstrate the lack of spiritual motivation that was responsible for the conflict between us. This just pushed her further into her tension, and having given up all possibility of resources of intelligence and reasonableness, she simply made herself look like a fool, although she would later prey (quite justifiably, mind you) upon several Iranian Muslims (including Asghar Manoussi) and condemn them for not supporting her, for not being true to Islam.

But it was the perfect encounter: I had always felt that God had created his various mythologies according to a particular circumstance, a particular culture, a particular ethos; however universal each religion might be there was the necessity finally of discovering how to fulfill one's own cultural destiny without a violent rejection of all the currents of individuating difference that characterized that culture. For this woman to become a Muslim—given her own personality, her own level of growth and development as an American woman—appeared to be unnatural, and whatever benefits Islam would give to her, eventually God would have his way, and she would find that although Islam might give her the inner experience she craved she would not have to wear her Muslimhood with such ostentation and pride. Carl Jung makes a particularly telling point when he discusses the practice of many Westerners who adopt the ways of yoga, a point not entirely irrelevant to our analysis of the American Muslim:

There could be no greater mistake than for a Westerner to take up the direct practice of Chinese yoga for that would merely strengthen his will and consciousness against the unconscious and bring about the very effect to be avoided.

144

The neurosis would then simply be intensified. It cannot be emphasised enough that we are not Orientals, and that we have an entirely different point of departure in these matters.[54]

This is not to deny the spiritual efficacy of Islam for the American or European citizen; Islam is universal; however its genesis was not part of a tradition that fitted in perfectly with the Western consciousness, and indeed it seemed to answer so perfectly to the region in which it found its Prophet. Perhaps what is universal does not imply also the need to find out what particular geography and culture seems most readily responsive to that universality. But since God has taken the trouble to manifest himself in such diverse ways (comparing the great world religions) it can be ascertained that he chooses one system rather than another for a particular group of people, a particular region of the world, because that system is especially adapted to the specific cultural, ethnic, and psychological makeup of those people—else why not just one religion? For the lady with whom I was arguing about Islam it seemed she had too suddenly and wantonly jettisoned her Western consciousness, although I was quite prepared to see the influence of Islam working on her in a more beneficial way when we next met. In the mean time she became the least surrendered Muslim that I had met, the least intuitive, the most non-Islamic in her personal expression.

It is a credit to Islam and the Muslims present, however, that every one of them recognized the particular psychological stress that the woman was under, and how she was arguing from a position of ego-laden passion, whereas I seemed, at least by contrast, somewhat disinterested. Various Muslims present attempted to support my position and to steer her out of the narrow boxed-in position she was taking. But it was a dramatic moment that I should not wished to have missed, since it demonstrated one of my own firm beliefs: that one must be loyal to the origins of one's birth, that God has chosen for us to be born in a particular place because that is the place where we can articulate the pattern of our individuality best. This is not to say that one should not attempt yoga, Eastern meditation, Zen Buddhism, or even Islam, but it does mean that what one gains from those disciplines and religions must integrate itself into one's present surroundings. One cannot uproot oneself in this respect with impunity. The Irish Muslim, although much more established in the cultural milieu of Islam than the American Muslim woman, nevertheless had something yet to face, if his soul was to reach some joyful consummation, and this would bear upon his Western origins. On the other hand it seemed that for someone to live in

---

[54] *The Secret of the Golden Flower; a Chinese Book of Life,* trans. R. Wilhelm. Foreword by C. G. Jung (London: Routledge and Kegan Paul, 1962.)

Iran and not to be a Muslim—at least at this stage in the drama—was equally incongruous as for the American woman to become a Muslim.[55]

Certainly one hoped that everyone would develop some sort of understanding of the terrible hubris of ego obsession, of spiritual voidness that dominated the West; Islam, while it might not be doctrinally embraced, nevertheless could profoundly alter the thinking of the West and make the West aware of the perils of abandoning altogether the richness of myth, the concept of life as an allegory, the notion of the divine. The alternative to Christianity and formal Judaism had not made man happier, nor had it any inherent beauty or compelling power that would make it competitive with the present efflorescence of Islam—at least in terms of an intensity and purposefulness. But my American friend would have to discover her way to some of this truth; in the mean time I was grateful to test out the empirical evidence for some of my own hypotheses about conversion to alien religions; Islam was not alien to any man, but in the most ideal scenario for religious regeneration, one would have hoped that God would have provided the resources and the myth (after all one did not think that Judaeo-Christian belief was made obsolete by the ascendancy of Islam) necessary to re-inspire man in his quest for answers to ultimate questions. Perhaps one might even have to become Muslim for some time in order to come to know the roots of one's own birth-given myth; certainly many of those individuals who had gone through the 1960's in North America had discovered in their connection with Eastern philosophy and meditation the essence of what their own culture was, and that such philosophy and inward prayer had enriched their appreciation for the myths endemic to their civilization.

The tension between the American Muslim and myself was a creative tension in so far as I felt I was provoking the right kind of confrontation that was meaningful for a discussion of values and the proper place of religion. I had a profound respect for Islam, and while I honoured the piety, the surrender, the purified idealism of so many Iranians who were deeply engaged in their struggle to bring about an Islamic state, I nevertheless was sensitive when I felt an outsider tried to pick up that myth and mould it to fit his own individuated cultural predispositions, or rather when that myth was used to invalidate the basic spirit of his or her culture and civilization. In the case of the American woman I felt

[55] Of course there might be quite a number of Iranians whose association with the West, with individualism, pluralism, and secular sophistication, would make it aesthetically possible for them to abjure their Islamic countrymen and to defiantly assert their own right of choice and individual life style. But they would probably end up leaving Iran eventually as the prevailing mood and consciousness would be too antagonistic to their own established habits and disposition. For the majority of Iranians, however, Islam was what God had chosen for them.

146

that this violation had been committed; I honoured her for her choosing to become a Muslim, but I waited for the sign of approval from God which would indicate that she had chosen something that was natural and necessary. Of course I could have been absolutely wrong about this, but the fact that the Muslims present were so easily moved to support my objections to the charges being brought against me by the American Muslim seemed to verify that even Islam was trying to awaken the American lady to some knowledge that would allow her to begin to enjoy the benefit of her courageous and bold commitment to Islam.

A Visit to Evin Prison and the Place of Executions

Evin Prison had been a notorious institution under the Shah: torture and executions were standard fare; now, however, ironically enough, Evin Prison had become an even greater symbol of injustice, cruelty, and criminality, for it was here that supposedly four thousand Iranians had been executed in the past six months; it was here that torture was practised as a matter of routine; it was here that school children were locked up in cells together; that fourteen prisoners shared a cell made for only two prisoners. At least these were the rumours.

My experience tended to suggest that the opponents of the regime greatly exaggerated the claims of brutality and aborted justice. Indeed I would say that for the most part (there had in fact been cases in which forms of mild torture had been inflicted, but an investigation ordered by the Imam had virtually eliminated this practice, and those who practised these abuses were not at the forefront of the revolution, and did not understand the necessity for absolute scrupulousness with regard to the treatment of prisoners—as required by Islam) these charges were false. While I cannot be certain that many incidents of extreme barbarity and vengeance were in fact carried out against the young enemies of the regime, I can at the same time attest to the fact that the whole prevailing atmosphere at the prison was decidedly contrary to the picture depicted by Western journalists and Iranian dissidents living in exile.

In the first place the mood of the prison was not one of violence, repression, or anger (which is the dominant impression of any prison in North America). Here, although there were security points and armed guards patrolling the yards, there was a sense of peace, of warmth, of discipline—like a religious reform school. The tension, the building-up of frustration, the sense of cold, isolated brutality was entirely absent. And this was because the Imam had made it an absolute to turn the prison into an educational institution, where Islam and the Revolution would dominate. Those in charge of the prison (and the governor of the prison was himself held under the Shah for fourteen years, to be released at the successful conclusion of the revolutionary phase when Imam Khomeini returned to Iran) were friendly with the prisoners, were confident they were treating their captives benignly, were without resentment or sense of revenge, and were (and this is most important) devoutly Islamic. Whether it is known or not, prisons in our society are places of the most concentrated negativity and violence; the very air is charged with the most savage, murderous feelings, and it is quite likely that the consciousness generated inside a prison contributes to the tension within the society, for here human beings are held against their will, here they live in a climate of fear and violence, here they are told they are subhuman, here they become hardened and bitter, here they lose their souls. At Evin Prison, on the other hand, although there were more than five thousand prisoners, the sense—wherever one went—was of the supreme confidence of the authorities that the prisoners could be reformed, that their loyalty to the subversive organizations in Iran could be undermined. In the attempt to bring about such change within the prisoner, teachers of Islamic ideology were assigned to various sections of the prison, and these teachers were, by and large, liked by the prisoners. The reader will not believe it, but the mass conversion of the prisoners from their allegiance to the Mujahaddin (and hatred of the regime) appeared utterly genuine; I spoke with hundreds of prisoners and even structured my questions (and in private assured them of absolute confidentiality of response, explaining I was a journalist, and that their remarks would remain anonymous) so that they might be tempted to be as candid as possible. As far as I could determine the vast majority of those who had been accused of bombings and insurrection—and even murder—had experienced a total change of thinking and feeling about the revolution and now turned against those who they felt had deceived them, without rancour, and without even a sense of sympathy. I walked and mixed with prisoners in various sections of the prison; while there were a few prisoners who maintained a critical view of the revolution, most everyone I talked to insisted they were happy where they were, that they did not view their incarceration as punitive, and that they were glad they were receiving ideological training in Islam; and they swore their allegiance to Khomeini. I waited for the signs of contrived, forced conversion, the evidence of a purely political and opportunistic decision, but these individuals (mostly young boys and men between fifteen and twenty-five) had made their peace with the revolution and showed no falseness in their enthusiasm. Some of them assured me they were happy they had been recruited by the Mujahaddin,

148

because in the intensity of their exposure to Islam they had become much more loyal and devoted than they would have been had they not been exposed to Islam in this context. And Imam Khomeini had announced during the very speech that I witnessed that he wanted at least 1700 prisoners to be pardoned in celebration of the Third Anniversary of the revolution. Certainly many of these prisoners with whom I spoke would be selected for forgiveness. And even under the laws of Islam, a murderer can be forgiven if the family of the victim decides to show clemency, or if it can be determined that he has undergone a change of heart and genuinely seeks to avail himself of the laws of Islam.

And throughout my visit in Evin Prison I was struck by the casualness —no weapons inside the prison, the governor sitting with the prisoners, the lack of formal regulations, the sense of improvisation—and friendliness of everyone. Am I deceived? Well, I suppose one has to visit this prison to determine whether what I am saying is false, or the result of the most subtle and brilliant propaganda manipulation; but my experience was convincing; the rumours about brutality were simply the means used by the Mujahaddin to discredit the regime in the eyes of the foreign press. No doubt in the past there had been many abuses, many miscarriages of justice; but if anyone were to delve into Islamic justice and see the faces of those who assumed responsibility for the sentencing and treatment of the prisoners he or she would realize that it was not merely a matter of pride that the laws of Islam were followed exactly and thoroughly in every case, but a matter of the most fervent love. I can say quite unequivocally that the objection to the Islamic courts has to be based on the objection to Islam; there is no room for sadism or a purely personal form of revenge; Islam removes the element of personality or individual subjectivity. The law has been derived from God; it must be carried out in the spirit of servitude to God. Now this may in given instances be a terrible thing measured by Western jurisprudent standards; but to simply accuse the Iranian authorities of brutality and immoral judgement à la Nazi or Gulag style is not only inaccurate, it is entirely without foundation in fact.

Now of course the sense of justice we see illustrated by Christ with the woman taken in adultery is foreign to the Islamic courts:

Jesus went unto the mount of Olives. And early in the morning he came again into the temple, and all the people came unto him; and he sat down, and taught them. And the scribes and Pharisees brought unto him a woman taken in adultery; and when they had set her in the midst, they say unto him, Master, this woman was taken in adultery, in the very act. Now Moses in the law commanded us, that such should be stoned; but what sayest thou? This they said, tempting him, that they might have to accuse him. But Jesus stooped down, and with his finger wrote on the ground, as though he heard them not. So when they continued asking him, he lifted up himself, and said unto them, He that is without sin among you, let him first cast a stone at her. And again he stooped down, and wrote on the ground. And they which heard it, being convinced by their own conscience, went out one by one, beginning at the eldest, even unto the last: and Jesus was left alone, and the woman standing in the midst. When Jesus had lifted up himself, and saw none but the woman, he said unto her, Woman, where are those thine accusers? hath no man condemned thee? She said, No man, Lord. And Jesus said unto her, Neither do I condemn thee: go, and sin no more.[56]

I had even posed this question to Ayatollah Khalkhali in an interview at the hotel; Khalkhali, and later an Islamic judge, simply talked about the laws of God as absolute and that Islamic justice was absolutely merciful in every respect. The emphasis of the story according to them was Jesus' attempt to avoid the trap being laid for him by his accusors; his response to the woman was more to extricate himself and shame the Pharisees than to respond to the particular crime of the woman. In any case, this kind of mercy (except when Khomeini decides as he had just done to pardon thousands of prisoners, although I would wonder whether adulterers would escape their punishment, so heinous a sin did Allah and Mohammad make of it—not to mention Moses) was not part of the ethos of Islam, although the comments of Ayatollah Khomeini on the requisite qualities of an Islamic judge bear some attention:

There are two essential qualities in the believer: he executes justice whenever necessary, with the utmost force and decisiveness and without exhibiting the least trace of feeling; and he displays the utmost love and solicitude whenever they are called for.[57]

St. Paul says, "The letter killeth but the spirit giveth life." It is my understanding that the very implacability of Islamic justice is a certain expression of the absoluteness of Islam; Islamic justice makes no compromises, and there is no possibility of mitigating a sentence or punishment on the basis of the context of the moment; for instance, the highest form of judgement, we would have to believe, if the system of justice is based upon God's laws, would be if God himself spoke out and passed judgement on the situation. Believing as I do in the multiplicity and complexity of Creation I cannot imagine God treating individuals the same; He would consider the particular configuration of the person's motivation, background, and level of consciousness: the violence or absoluteness of punishment surely would have to reflect the absoluteness of God himself, which is why it could be, if applied non-contextually,

---

[56] St. John 8:1-11

[57] Algar, op. cit. pp. 89-90.

150

extremely harsh. Jesus' response to the adulteress was not applicable in the context of Islam; everything depended (the particular character of God as it manifested through Islam) on the very inflexibility and severity of its injunctions, its system of retribution; in Islam everything was consistent, and the primary importance of total submission to God did not entail taking it upon oneself to determine where God's laws (as revealed to Mohammad) could be breached or tampered with through some kind of intuitive (as in the case of Christ) justice. Islam posited the existence of good and evil; what was declared wrong in Islam represented the expression of that which was evil in man; therefore it (evil) must be punished with utmost severity; only in this way could a society purify itself of crime and vice.

And I suppose that I was concerned by the fact that an Islamic judge, and a Muslim who applies the code of Islamic jurisprudence, based upon the Qur'an and the *shari'a*, the latter drawn not just from the Qur'an but from the examples of the Prophet during his own lifetime—both in terms of practice and in terms of pronouncements—do not creatively deal with the existential fact of the singularity of the moment, the singularity of the person who is being brought before justice, the infinite diversity of motive and intention that resulted in the prosecution of the accused. Is God really against all his laws being broken—under any circumstance? No, for then the liberated individual would see that God's creation ran according to Buddhist law, according to Taoist law, according to Hindu law, according to Judaic law, according to Christian law, or, perhaps, according to Islamic law. Obviously it is one universe yet the proscriptions vary—as do the recommended punishments. How can this be? Only by positing the idea that Creation (and therefore God's laws) is based upon the impulses of intelligence that declare whether life has intrinsically been violated, not whether a particular law institutionalized within that society has been violated. Was the universe injured by the breaking of that law? Could it not be possible that a law would be broken in order to fulfill the law of evolutionary, aesthetic impulse? I believe so, and the testimony of those who have succeeded in transcending legal law and contacting organic law are variations on St. Paul's exhortation: "Love and do what you will."

But of course not everyone can go the route of the saint, and therefore, in the absence of perfect intuitional judgement, and in the interests of preserving order, laws must be applied universally and without recourse to particularism or context. Nevertheless, to the extent that the Islamic judges in Iran today were unaware of the very approximate justice they were in fact carrying out (measured, as I have argued, by the relationship between actual impulse and legislated law) they might be creating a condition of inflexibility of awareness that would eliminate the possibility of an individual human being rising above mere law and commanding the laws of the universe itself. The Sermon on the Mount differs considerably from the Ten Commandments. Both declarations are thought to have come from God. Is God capricious? Hardly, but his Creation is so vast, the circumstances of man so complex, that a diversified expression of religious law has to be manifested through various prophets, thus implying that the highest stage of justice is that situation in which the judge is able to receive the impulses of God directly, and thus to pronounce judgement upon the sinner, the criminal, as God spontaneously reacts in the given moment when that judgement is called for.

The Islamic judges and prosecutors that I met and talked with seemed absolutely sincere, totally in command of their field, and willing to listen to reasons; they were, however, without that movement of mercy that comes in the intuition of the more non-legalistic, i.e. impulse-centred, facts of reality, and I wondered whether they might at some point place themselves in the position of being Pharisaical if someone (such as Christ) began to suspect that the laws of Islam might perhaps be inimical—at least in certain instances—to the full vision of God, justice, and truth, as witnessed in the lives of the saints, sages, and mystics. And of course this was the real danger of Islam (or rather the practitioners of Islam): they would have to yoke themselves to the shibboleths of Islam, but they would have to anticipate that this obedience, this absolute adherence to Islamic law as it literally and exoterically expressed itself in the *shari'a*, eventually would enable them (as it had through the Imam, even though he rigidly embraced Islam in its more overt meaning) to go beyond Islam and come into that understanding that is described in the *Bhagavad-Gita*:

But a jivan-mukta, a man of cosmic consciousness, finds himself at the ultimate fulfilment of all the duties prescribed for Him. He knows Reality with such great fullness that he becomes established in That, in the state of absolute bliss-consciousness. This is how, having gained the final aim of the whole Vedic way of life, such a man rises above the field of Vedic injunctions about right and wrong and also above the need for Vedic rituals; he rises above the need of the Vedic guidance.[58]

The more positive side of Western individualism, the demythologizing of man, has been to emphasize that more spontaneous, impulsive, and contextual morality that demonstrates that in certain instances, the laws—Islamic, Christian, Judaic, Vedic—can be broken, in order that some more individualistic meaning can be expressed, a meaning that

[58] Maharishi Mahesh Yogi, op. cit. p. 132.

152

affirms the undogmatic nature of a dramatist's intention, for God surely is more of a dramatist—or at least he is equally a dramatist—than he is a law-giver, a legalistic punisher. Else why Creation? Why even set up Creation so that the rules can be transgressed? But all this is much too complicated in dealing with the issue at hand, which was Islamic justice as it has operated during the revolution. The dominant impression at Evin Prison, despite my fears about the Pharisaical possibilities, was of the spirit of the revolution working to transform the prison, working to transform the prisoners, and the evidence of Islam was no less obvious than it had been in the hospitals for the wounded, nor at the *jihad* construction site, nor at the war front. Given that this was a prison it surely was the most idealistically run prison on the earth, whatever excesses had been, and perhaps from time to time still were, committed in the name of Allah. The Iranians had committed themselves to the idea that they were carrying out the justice that God would have them carry out; taking such a risk (that is, assuming there was a God, that indeed Islam was the revealed word of God) meant discovering whether God in fact approved of the methods and the attitudes that prevailed here, as elsewhere in Iran. My conclusion was that the sincerity was undeniable, the purity of intention to fulfill Islamic justice was manifest, and the feeling of the essential rightness (in the context of this situation of an Islamic revolution) was declared in my heart. The Iranians looked at justice in terms of both worlds; the physical and the spiritual world. God had legislated through the Prophet Mohammad the punishments for various crimes; this Islamic republic would carry out those commandments, eschewing any sort of compromise with modernism, with Western jurisprudence. To attack the actions of the Revolutionary Courts was to attack Islam, which was to attack God; what was happening therefore in Evin Prison was the will of God. Such motivation on the part of the legal authorities in Iran was hard to dismiss as mere brutality, except, for instance, if you are convinced that: either God does not exist; myths are formed from superstitious fears and infantile fantasies; or, God updates himself and is becoming more merciful and liberal of late and therefore would not prescribe stoning for an adult married woman who was charged with adultery. Thus Imam Khomeini, in a spirited defence of Islamic law, especially as it concerns the drinking of alcoholic beverages, declares:

Many forms of corruption that have appeared in society derive from alcohol. The collisions that take place on our roads, and the murders and suicides [Khomeini is writing in 1970, nine years before the revolution], are very often caused by the consumption of alcohol.... But still, some say, it is quite unobjectionable for someone to drink alcohol (after all, they do it in the West); so let alcohol be bought and sold freely.

But when Islam wishes to prevent the consumption of alcohol—one of the major evils—stipulating that the drinker should receive eighty lashes, or sexual vice, decreeing that the fornicator be given one hundred lashes (and the married man or woman be stoned), then they start wailing and lamenting: "What a harsh law that is, reflecting the harshness of the Arabs!" They are not aware that these penal provisions of Islam are intended to keep great nations from being destroyed by corruption. Sexual vice has now reached such proportions that it is destroying entire generations, corrupting our youth, and causing them to neglect all forms of work. They are all rushing to enjoy the various forms of vice that have become so freely available and so enthusiastically promoted. Why should it be regarded as harsh if Islam stipulates that an offender should be publicly flogged in order to protect the younger generation from corruption?[59]

Khomeini, Muslims, and many orthodox religious people believe that the laws of God (as embodied in religion) are to prevent man from contaminating society, that there are sacred energies within man that are dissipated by sexual licence, by the consumption of alcohol, by self-indulgence of all kinds. They believe that the actual strength and integrity of a whole society is weakened when these energies are not controlled, when the spirit of man is violated by his appetites. These laws preserve the inner order and purity of the society, thus making it strong and healthy, and capable of rising to God. This idea is behind everything that is currently happening in the Islamic courts. Now the fact that the major offence is collaboration with the Mujahaddin whom the Iranians claim have murdered over seven hundred innocent Iranians in the past two years, still does not alter the basic premise of Islamic justice: man is to be ruled by God; Islam is the perfect system of justice; those who seek to destroy the Islamic Republic are at best deceived, at worst, victims of their own evil. The fact that many of the Mujahaddin are idealistic revolutionaries who would have given (and did give) their lives for the revolution against the Shah now, in the present context of Iran, counts for little, if nothing at all. They are punished with the same severity as the notorious agents of SAVAK. And Islamic justice cannot really make such distinctions. In any event nothing would shame the Iranians into changing the conditions inside Evin Prison. They believe these conditions are excellent and that Amnesty International, which has been prohibited from inspecting the prisons (the Iranians will not let AI enter Iran and carry out their investigation of human rights unless AI condemns the killings of the hundreds of innocent Iranians at the hands of those people who AI seeks to defend—the Mujahaddin), has no mandate from Allah and, however idealistically motivated, is still basically a secularized authority, without that divine vision that would make its

<hr>

[59] Algar, op. cit. pp. 33-34.

findings or its recommendations, or its denunciations, valid. They insisted that no one under the age of sixteen had been executed, that each case was considered carefully, that clemency of the most extreme order had been demonstrated, and that the stories of brutality were lies used by their opponents to tarnish the reputation of the Islamic Republic.

One prisoner told me that he wished "they would take my family to this *holy place*."(!) He insisted that there was freedom of expression in the prison and each Friday evening there was a debate of ideas where those who still argued against the regime could bring forth their ideology and be listened to by all prisoners who wished to attend. Then there would be an exchange of views and, according to the report of this prisoner, the Mujahaddin lost most of the debates; it seemed that those who supported the revolution in its present direction were much too eloquent and knowledgeable (they invoked Allah and Islam of course) for the subversives, for the minority of subversives, that is, who had not already committed apostasy against the Mujahaddin. I even met one young person, twenty-one, with a family, who had been involved in a bombing that had killed five Revolutionary Guards; because of his willingness to be reformed, because of his commitment to Islam (as a result of his exposure in the prison to the ideology of Islam) he was to be pardoned and looked forward to returning to his family. This was not some kind of forced admission of sins; this was the authentic movement of his heart, and he was quite obviously deeply involved in the revolution and wishing to redeem himself on the battlefront.

Again, like everything else about this regime, the understanding and evaluation of the prison depended upon one's sympathy for Islam, depended upon one's ability to intuit whether this revolution resonated with impulses that were natural to the universe. From my point of view, despite the strong doubts I had before entering into the prison, it was clear that here the revolution was progressing; here, instead of thousands of resentful prisoners, there was the recruiting of good Muslims. These individuals like the Iraqi prisoners of war, were becoming soldiers of Islam and they would, instead of draining the country of its will and spirit, be strengthening the country and turning into much more devout supporters of the regime than had they not become involved in the assassinations and bombings, had they not been convinced initially that the revolution had betrayed the people, as the Mujahaddin insisted.

Each cell had its own television set which pumped the regular (and special) Islamic programs; there was also a library where all I could see were books on Islam (what else was necessary to read at this time?!), where many of the prisoners congregated and had more private tutorials from their Islamic teacher, a Revolutionary Guard whose presence suggested piety and fearlessness. The prisoners loved him. At the end of my visit the prisoners—perhaps four hundred that were finishing their prayers in the mosque inside the prison—shouted, "Long live Khomeini!" and "Allahu Akbar" and "Death to Rajavi!" (the leader of the Muja-haddin now having fled Iran and living in France). There was no real argument to be made against what was happening in the prison; a pure mythology, a perfected religion (if one suggests that Buddhism, Hindu-ism, Christianity, Judaism, are perfected religions, that is to say, they have established themselves in a richness of doctrine and ritual that make them much more than that now hated word "cults") was deter-mining the activities everywhere in Iran and within this prison the Iranians had every reason to make it a showpiece of Islamic justice. Measured by this criterion—is it purely Islamic—I declared it a success and was quite overwhelmed by the achievement of the Iranians in creating an institution that was so opposite to its reputation in the West. The religious instinct: this was what was required to understand and appreciate what the Iranians were doing. Even at Evin Prison.

On the Hideous Executions in Iran

The West has recoiled in horror at the (estimates vary; Iranians will tell you the figure is about 1500; hostile critics of the regime will claim 8,000) executions that have taken place in Iran. Since the revolution succeeded, the Iranians claim 1600 persons have died at the hands of assassins, at the hands of now outlawed political groups such as the Mujahaddin. In the past two years, they say seven hundred persons have been murdered including hundreds of religious leaders and government officials. What-ever are the real facts it is clear that these individuals who seek to intimidate people by killing the leaders of Iran would be dealt with harshly in whatever country they carried out their deeds. In Chile, in Argentina, in El Salvador, in Guatemala thousands of people have disappeared, have been tortured, have been executed by death squads. Although there is protest over these killings and abuse of human rights, the United States government and even the Canadian government virtually overlooks these abuses since they are thought to be the excesses perpetrated by an over-zealous guarding of democracy, a revulsion of the monolith of communism. Torture, death squads are in violation of Islam, but the executions do take place and one does feel pain in contemplating some of the human beings who have been dealt with in a manner that makes no attempt to find a mitigating circumstance or qualification—whether it is a famous poet, writer, Baha'i, or youthful idealist of the left. However the Western reader should understand the context within which these executions take place. Those that administer this lethal punishment are chosen because of their Islamic faith, the purity of their devotion to the Imam, and their willingness to perform this act knowing that they too are judged in that moment of carrying out the laws of God. The executions are not welcomed but they are performed as a ceremony of purification and the third letter, previously alluded to, in the appendix makes the best case for them I can think of from the Islamic point of view.

I remember, while in Evin Prison, seeing a video tape of the trial of six high school girls (16 and 17 years old), where the girls defiantly hurled abuse at their accusors and where they demonstrated their hatred for the regime. While I watched their actions I felt in my heart these creatures are innocent; they are too young to know what they are doing; they truly believe the regime is repressive; they believe they are making a sacrifice that will help their country. I grieved in the contemplation that perhaps as the tape came to an end I would discover they had been executed and this I knew would be a sin against God. The report of the governor of the prison was that they had been released after the trial but he was somewhat nebulous about the details; apparently some of them had been re-arrested and were now awaiting another trial in the prison. I knew that with all the executions, some would have been innocent, and I could not judge how many deserved to be executed. Executions in my view should—if they have to take place at all—be reserved for hardened criminals, people who have turned into subhuman instruments of greed and perversion. But Islam had its laws and when seventy-two government officials had been assassinated in one explosion there would have to be reprisals just to make it clear the government would not tolerate this attempt to destroy the Islamic Republic. Many of those assassins blew themselves up in their various attempts on the lives of prominent mullahs (these were the figures most detested by the Mujahaddin for it was with them that the power of the revolution and its dominant character lay), and there could be no question about the bravery, the determination, nor the idealism of some of those who had been executed. But the revolution had to survive; as far as the Iranians were concerned survival meant swift punishment to those who were resisting the will of Khomeini, and thus the will of Allah.

One would not have to go very far to find someone as distressed and tortured about the regime as someone else was inspired and ecstatic. Thus the "Heaven and Hell" of present day Iran. One outspoken critic gave a moving diatribe against everything the revolution stood for. The man was absolutely sincere: during the time of the Shah and the American influence he said things were profitable, pleasant, and lively; Iran was flourishing; there was stability; people could talk freely (except, he noted, about communism and Khomeini) and people were content. With the advent of the revolution, he said, people became crazy; the price of cheese quadrupled; mothers had to wait in line twice a day for three hours for food; the standard of living had declined; all freedom of the press had been curtailed; innocent people had been arrested and executed; the war with Iraq was a deliberate attempt to feed the revolutionary ardour and distract people from the real material problems of the society; television, entertainment had become one-sidedly religious: all enjoyment had fled from Iran; the people were filled with fear; Ayatollah Khomeini was worshipped as God; the government had encouraged hatred of countries like the United States, whom this businessman insisted had helped Iran into the twentieth century; there was a terrible distortion of truth: everything had to be explained according to Islam—and it was not the real Islam, it was fanatical, backward Islam which opposed progress just on principle; and finally he confided that his life had been turned into a hell, that to live in Iran today was to live in constant terror, frustration, and misery. As he spoke one had to conclude that, according to his own consciousness and value system (and he was a pleasant, courteous, and reasonable man, an Iranian who had been imbued with the Western spirit, a modern man of the world who had lost the love of his mythology, a man who was in genuine torment), his case against the regime was valid. I asked him (we had met secretly, out of earshot of those Revolutionary Guards who, he insisted, were out to get him, who were bent upon finding enemies of the regime, who lived just for the money they received, who were mercenary and cold-blooded)—I asked him about his wife and children, assuming as I did that at least his family would be sympathetic to his indictment of the regime, to the vicissitudes of his present economic, psychological circumstance. "Oh," he said, "my wife is just as crazy as the rest of them; she just watches Khomeini and has become a fanatical Muslim; she doesn't care about money or any of the things she used to. But my children—at least the eldest—he knows a thing or two, and when they force him to pray he just goes through the motions; he knows his father is right."

And this was present day Iran, where within a single family there were total and irreconcilable differences, yet in which a family continued to stay together. For one, Iran was hell; for the other, it was the coming of Paradise. One hated Khomeini; the other adored him in a sort of constant state of beatitude. One lived within the mythology; the other had cast the mythology aside. One looked at life through the eyes of Western freedom and individual comfort; the other, through the eyes of religion and otherworldliness. Both were absolutely sincere. Both passionately argued the rightness of his or her respective position. But the question became: which point of view was being supported by the invisible forces of fate in Iran today? Although I could sympathize with the businessman and see in his eyes his grief and discomfort, I also saw that he had left his own cultural and religious roots, that he was an alien in present day Iran; his imagination just could not absorb or identify with the currents of feeling and meaning that formed the central theme of this revolution. How was it that he was condemned to stay in Iran? He said he had no choice but to remain here, and he fatalistically resigned himself (in non-Muslim fashion) to the miserable conditions of his daily life. There was absolutely no point in trying to see things differently; if his wife could not persuade him, it was unlikely anyone else could, and I was equally certain that he just did not have the right chromosome of sensibility that could allow him to recognize the spirit of the mythic reality of the revolution as authentic and necessary; he was being held in the vision of a reality that was as natural and coherent as he was certain the vision of Islamic Iran was aberrant and chaotic, although the young Revolutionary Guard on the battlefield would simply pity him, or conclude that Allah had determined he was not one of the graced. But this was the tragedy at one level in Iran today; the opponents of the regime felt an abhorrence for what was happening (their indices of evaluation were perfectly valid in the absence of the primacy of myth) that was equivalent to the delirium displayed by those who embraced the revolution. Had God created this split to heighten the pain, to give an edge of the tragic? Islam brooked no compromise; either one felt the impulse of this revolution and accepted all its excesses—and was willing to die for it—, one did not feel that impulse, decried its excesses, and was perhaps willing to die to oppose it. In the absence of the figure of Imam Khomeini I could have understood the possibility of there being an equilibrium morally, but because of the Imam's integrity it was clear that the revolution was necessary, and that those who were unable to leave Iran would have to suffer through his hallucinatory intensity, its absolutist imperative.

On the Treatment of Baha'is

One of the most persistent sources of criticism of the Islamic Revolution in Iran has been allegations of extreme cruelty towards the community of Baha'is. Hundreds of Baha'is are said to have been executed for no other reason than because of their allegiance to a faith that is said to supersede that of Islam. Church property has been destroyed and there appears to be a systematic policy to persecute and eventually eliminate all persons who subscribe to the doctrine of Baha'u'llah, the nineteenth century mystic who is supposed to have initially miraculously survived his execution by orthodox Shi'ite clergy.[60] Having had contact with the Baha'i community here in Canada, and knowing from this contact the absolute sincerity of its members and the positive role the Baha'i church was playing in terms of world unity, I included a condemnatory passage in my open letter to Khomeini[61] regarding the treatment of the Baha'is. I soon found, however, in my contacts with Muslims, and especially Iranian Muslims sympathetic to the revolution, that this issue was not even discussible; the government line was that "no Baha'i who did not have a record of anti-state activity had ever been persecuted" and there did not exist any prejudice against Baha'is that would lead to any transgression of Islamic justice. However, it is also clear that the Iranian Muslims believe the very existence of Baha'ism is itself an artificial, devious product of Russian and British imperialism, that Baha'u'llah was used by the Russians and British in order to weaken Islam, to divide Iran, and to enable Western values, Western customs to inundate the Middle East that much faster, and therefore make Iran susceptible to colonial exploitation.

This is the firm conviction of each Muslim (Iranian) that I have talked to; and the degree to which they are absolutely hostile to the Baha'i faith is such as to make one reluctant to even raise the issue. It sits there in their consciousness at a level where there is the most explosive hatred and contempt, and the reactiveness to the subject of Baha'ism is accountable for the following reasons (apart from the conspiratorial idea of the prophet of Baha'i being a British agent): Baha'i proclaims that Mohammad was not the Seal of the Prophets, for Baha'u'llah's message of the unity of mankind makes Islam and Mohammad relics of the past, makes Islam that which had merely led to Baha'ism; in addition the liberalization (for instance a famous woman Baha'i leader in the

---

[60] It is said that when the smoke of the guns cleared, Baha'u'llah had disappeared; it was determined that the bullets had pierced the ropes around Baha'u'llah; later he was recaptured and executed.

[61] See Appendix.

160

nineteenth century tore off her veil and proclaimed the liberation of women from Islamic customs) of values and laws made Islam appear primitive and backward; Baha'is have their headquarters in Israel and are thought to have collaborated with Israeli agents during the reign of the Shah; Baha'is are also accused of staging demonstrations in support of the Shah during the revolution; Baha'is are (and even the U.S. State Department in its secret memos acknowledges this[62]) found among some of the loyal cabinet and prominent government officials of the Shah, and even one of the most powerful members of the hated SAVAK is reputed to have been a prominent member of the Baha'i community; finally, of the wealthy elite of Iran during the time of the Shah, there was a disproportionate number of Baha'is. Therefore one can understand, however irrational they may be, the feelings of the present regime towards Baha'is: their religion is thought to be a lie; their allegiance, their influence is thought to be directly connected with the destruction of the Islamic Republic of Iran. But, beyond all these factors, the one that stands out is the particular psychological potency of a religion that says in effect, that Islam is obsolete, that the Twelfth Imam has already come, that the present Islamic Revolution (and Imam Khomeini himself) is a perversion of the will of God (for naturally if Baha'u'llah was the final expression of God's plan only a revolution made in the name of Baha'ism—and Baha'is do not believe in violent or revolutionary change—would be historically and spiritually welcome by God). The fact that Baha'is are associated with the echelons of power in the hated Pahlavi dynasty just adds to this outrage, as does the fact of the Zionist connection.

The presumption of the Baha'is in a society in which Islam is triumphantly proclaimed to be the religion of all time, the religion which has universal validity,—the presumption of the Baha'i doctrine which puts to rout all these claims, is a presumption which is bound to invite upon itself persecution. And in the powerful stress within each Muslim I met in Iran about Baha'ism I knew that the Iranians could not react with equanimity or fairness to members of the Baha'i community.

But I believe it is important to recognize some of those factors that have contributed, however mistakenly, to the present persecution of the Baha'is. It is perhaps just too much to ask people who have embraced Islam to have that supreme confidence and wisdom that would allow them to let the Baha'is live in peace, since it is they, the Muslims, who should have compassion upon those who are deluded by Russian or British plots into believing a totally fabricated doctrine of Messianic

---

[62] Documents of the CIA published by the Students, op. cit. p. 33.

succession. The fact that the doctrine of Baha'ism appeals so much to people in the West and therefore cannot be discredited by the Iranians as a plot against Islam, nevertheless does not make much of an impression. For the Iranians, Baha'ism can never participate in the glory of God because it is patently false that God wishes Islam to be superseded by Baha'ism: the Islamic Revolution in Iran is the proof of this.They therefore have to ignore the fact that Baha'ism contains enough grace to give to those who believe in it that piety, that sense of surrender and service that are the signs of a religion that is authentic. No matter, say the Iranian Muslims; Baha'ism will eventually be exposed through the purity of this Islamic Revolution and then the world Baha'is will realize the falseness of their allegiance and abandon Baha'ism. Well, as much as one regrets the attacks upon Baha'is one can only hope that somewhere along the line the Iranian regime will realize the great loss of reputation that is inherent in the course of their revolution as long as this persecution persists, as long as the Iranians cannot prove that such persecution does not exist. This will mean facing and living with the fact of Baha'ism (which will not go away; indeed it has a tradition of martyrdom already and the recent executions have probably done more for the cause, the spirit of Baha'ism than anything). If Baha'ism is to be a viable influence in the Middle East it will survive this persecution and somewhere the revolution (if indeed it has executed innocent people, if indeed God does approve of Baha'ism [within still approving of Islam—and perhaps giving to the latter more mythological resonance, and therefore greater universal power]) will have to pay the price for acting out its aggression upon persons whose only sin was to have belonged to a religion that challenges the pre-eminent truths of Islam.

Departure From Iran

Most noticeable at the Tehran airport were the various wealthy Iranians whose ambience was completely alien to the ambience of the Revolutionary Guards whose members supervised the security checks. Men and women, mothers, lovers, aristocratics all dressed with elegance and style, with—in the case of the women—coloured scarfs substituting for the chadors, worn aesthetically, yet with a kind of underlying protestation. These were the 'beautiful people' of Iran, but some of them genuinely gave that sense of dignity and personal richness that seemed to justify their experience of being completely estranged from the revolution, from its purposes. One young, bearded, leather-jacketed, modish

162

Iranian could not have seemed more incongruous with the Iranian soldier fighting on the battlefield at Susangerd. When I dropped a book of speeches of Imam Khomeini on the floor of the airport bus, he mockingly said: "How dare you drop such a holy book!" (The portrait of Khomeini was visible there on the cover of the book as it fell into the dust.) Other Iranian elite who overheard the comment registered their silent approval and waited for some kind of recognition from myself. I was suitably ambiguous as I thought I might find myself seated with one of these people on the plane. However the seats were arranged such that I did not sit next to any critic of the regime, but it was obvious during the flight—especially at the beginning—that some of these people desired to speak with me, recognizing that I was in fact a Westerner, and possibly a non-Muslim. There was a sort of empathy between some of the more sophisticated and attractive (in terms of character) Iranians and myself, and I became aware of the naturalness of the non-mythologized, worldly, liberalized sensibility, and that this point of view, of conditioning had its own universe, and when that universe was juxtaposed with the universe of pure mythology, otherworldliness, puritanical morality, then the incommensurability of both universes declared itself.

I felt my fortune in being able to move within both worlds, and although I regretted these people being unable to identify with the supreme integrity and spiritual beauty of Imam Khomeini I nevertheless saw that they were performing their lives within what they had determined was, and had chosen to be, the good life. There was nothing manifestly decadent, distorted, sinister about many of these Iranians; they were innocently experiencing the horror of what had happened to Iran; they simply saw it as the most bizarre and fanatical turn of events, a turn of events that made their own style of living, their own attitudes completely incompatible with the prevailing mood in Iran. They were in a sense martyrs, although I wished for them to have been able to know the validity, the necessity for what their simple, devoted countrymen now gave themselves utterly to. And the Iranian Muslims who looked with disdain upon these people as simply being unable to make the sacrifices required for Islam, as being unable to adjust their own selfish habits, as being too corrupted to be brought into the divine truth of the revolution, these Iranians would not have the imagination to be able to see that however much the revolution was pure and necessary, it was not at all true that every person who did not receive that simple faith and transfusion of love from the Imam was evil or even unGodly; but it was in the nature of the script that these two divergent forces would not reach any sort of agreement; it was in the destiny of things that they would even be driven further apart. Religious intuition was almost all or nothing; either one knew immediately that this revolution was divinely inspired, or one experienced it as utterly ridiculous, dangerous, and atavistic, the final spasm of fanatical religion attempting to impose itself on the irreversibly modern, secularizing twentieth century.

Once having crossed the borders of Iran all the wealthy Iranian women removed their scarfs and visibly became more expansive, carefree, and individualistic in their conversation and suggested behaviour. There was a sudden sense of relief, of deinhibition, and they relished living once again in the civilized world. They were out of hell and could adopt the customs of the detribalized, demythologized, defanaticized modern world. The Iranian Muslims on board, on the other hand, were leaving the incipient paradise of Iran and entering into the vast territories of the infidels. I sat there and saw my journey coming to its proper conclusion in the revelation of this necessary ambivalence.

What Will Happen When Khomeini Dies?

The underlying assumption of this book is that reality is structured by a deftly beneficent intention: i.e. a God who is supremely aesthetic when it comes to the details (however gruesome they may appear) of the script of history and human existence. Therefore, since Ayatollah Khomeini is an individual who is carrying out purely a particular historic, moral, and dramatic function within the script (because his own individual intention has become taken over by the intention of the force of cosmic evolution) it is inconceivable that he will pass away from the earth until such time as the revolution is so firmly rooted in the soul of Iran that nothing will be able to dislodge it or take it off course. However, in order for the revolution to continue to prosper (at least in the religious and spiritually unifying sense) there would have to be a successor who was as 'enlightened' as Khomeini himself, for it is in the center of that creative improvisation of Khomeini that the revolution has its stability, its surety of purpose. Khomeini will, in my estimation, live for many more years— perhaps as many as ten. It will be part of the design of things (unless the revolution is to achieve its dramatic significance in the loss of grace and power when Khomeini leaves, thus indicating the primacy of the role Khomeini's consciousness played in the whole successful institution of Islam) that someone—perhaps even Khomeini's son—will be so filled with, so imbibed with the heart and mind of Khomeini, that he will transcend that ego functioning that will interfere with, or distort the cosmic purpose, and thus begin to (although in a more diluted sense) enact the same impulses of efficient action as Khomeini.

164

In other words, it is my firm belief that despite the integrity, that is to say, the coherent, unified, inwardly consistent mythology of Islam—and its absolutist application to Iran—the death of Khomeini in the absence of a leader who has attained the same level of selfhood and ontological mode of being will be subtly disastrous for Iran; it will lose its center, it will gradually become a victim of dogma applied in the absence of mystical cognition, and this will erode the power of the revolution and it will never become a serious factor in the world—at least in other Middle East countries. That, it seems to me, is the fate of religion in the world today: without an individual capable of embodying the truth of religion (as Khomeini does, as the Dalai Lama does) that religion cannot survive the challenge of pluralistic, individualistic, relativistic intention. Iran may have become an Islamic Republic, Iran may have organized all the structures that would ensure its doctrinal, social, legal, and even economic survival; however, without the finessed sensitivity and intuition of Imam Khomeini there would be that inevitable gap that would start to open up between the dogmatic understanding of life and the actual impulses of life. This would mean the revolution could come under the influence of forces that, however sincere, lack that magnificent dignity and wisdom that guarantee a mythology such as Islam can be a viable form of response to the pressures of Western secular consciousness. The pure life force of the revolution would die with Khomeini, and the subsequent record of the Iranians—in battle, in culture, in social and moral cohesion—would be unmiraculous, and subject to the same laws of relativism as the rest of the countries of the world, although the spiritual power that has come through such sacrifice and purity of intention would still exert a considerable force against the tendencies of entropic consciousness. Nevertheless the grace would attenuate, until it became quite legitimate to contemplate the possibility of a change and a withdrawal from the pure Islam of the Imam. That withdrawal would not come about through any lack of enthusiasm for or commitment to Islam, but rather as an indirect outcome of the revolution—at the point of Khomeini's death—failing to be attuned perfectly to the intention of aesthetic evolution. Only Khomeini is capable of keeping the revolution perfectly on course, and this is not because of his devotion to Islam, but because his consciousness has its living power and purpose in the consciousness which is carrying out the power and purpose of Creation itself.

Although talking with many members of the Mujahaddin e Khalq in Evin Prison, nearly all of these people had either renounced their allegiance to the Mujahaddin or were unable to defend the actions of the Mujahaddin (and attack the government) with the intensity that would make them just the right example of the anti-Khomeini political thinking that I was looking for. Now I had heard that the most active group of Mujahaddin sympathizers abroad were located in London, that the subways were filled with Mujahaddin slogans, that the opposition to Khomeini was fierce among university students. The thought had come to me that it would be valuable to make contact with this dissident element while I was staying in London before returning to Canada. I did not have to seek the Mujahaddin out. While returning to my hotel just past Piccadilly Circus a young student was hawking his propaganda leaflets and shouting out, "Khomeini is a butcher," encouraging people who passed by to sign a petition aimed at the United Nations denouncing Khomeini and the executions. All kinds of accusations were contained in his petition, and in the newspaper produced by the Mujahaddin—and there were hundreds of endorsements from British M.P.'s, civic leaders, and political writers on the left. The charges were almost too wild to be believed: Khomeini encouraged raping of women prisoners in Evin Prison; Khomeini had executed dozens of pre-teenage boys; torture was a systematic and legalized part of the regime, and these abuses were described in graphic detail, making any other descriptions of torture seem benign—even the Shah's; Revolutionary Guards were granted permission by Khomeini to practise sexually perverted acts against women prisoners; high school students were regularly rounded up and shot on the spot;—the litany of outrage went on and on. Now curiously enough I had wanted to determine what support, what forces of moral power were coming to the cause of the Mujahaddin and I intuitively determined that this one individual (with whom I professed a certain detached sympathy—in the interests of getting the most candid response from him: for instance I did not tell him I had just been to Iran) would tell me a great deal about the character of the Mujahaddin. Well, as it happened, the student was filled with a hatred of Khomeini, but he utterly lacked any sort of focused and eloquent intensity to his judgements, and he became the perfect contrast to the Revolutionary Guards I had met on the war front. He was a young man, seemingly alienated and uprooted; however sincere he was he did not understand the revolution; he did not understand Islam; he did not possess that matured vision of political realities that would give a cogency to his perceptions, and most of all, he floundered around in a spiritual void, unable to command any kind of inspired argument that came to terms with the objective facts. I felt more pity than anything else; I had looked forward to meeting a passionate, articulate revolutionary, someone who would make my account of Iran more interesting by a presentation of the opposing view that had conviction and moral resonance. Alas, if the opposing view did carry some moral weight in the universe, this student could not partake of that support, and he seemed to be just another manifestation of the diminishing power of the Mujahaddin who, now that Khomeini had announced the release of over 7,000 prisoners as a general amnesty in celebration of the success in the war with Iraq (and I knew that most of these 7,000 people were now more pro-Khomeini than they had ever been pro-Rajavi), were gradually losing all political credibility.

Now I suppose that my own intuition about this student, and my analysis, reflects a simple bias that I have: that when the issues are absolute: Khomeini is evil or Khomeini is a saint (and I doubt that there could be a more polarized moral and political reality in the world today), then whichever (especially if the drama of human existence is to be affected profoundly by the outcome of two rival views) point of view is correct (i.e. congruent with the intention of the evolutionary unfolding of the Script) the person who is the proponent of one view or the other will be speaking against the background of the moral reaction of the universe. Alas, this Mujahaddin student was denied all form of assistance by the universe, and his performance, and his newspaper, were sorry examples of a rather deluded and hopelessly prejudicial perception of the revolution and of Iran. Not that a case cannot be made against Iran (and within this book I have presented the alternative view) but in this particular instance, when the Mujahaddin are the only viable alternative to the Khomeini regime, it seemed significant that I should run into an individual who utterly lacked that charge of pure feeling and light that so movingly ordered the consciousness of the Iranian martyr, that supreme dignity of purpose that embodied itself in the personhood of Imam Khomeini.

Understanding the Revolution Through a Visit to Westminster Abbey and St. Paul's Cathedral

It may seem out of place to discuss bloody and revolutionary Iran within the context of the soaring, magnificent splendour of London's two most famous churches; however, once inside these awesome monuments I glimpsed, I felt, the pure power of mythology, the imaginative force of God working through man to project the divine meaning of Creation. No, it was not possible for man himself to dream these feats of architectural richness and beauty through his own imagined idea of a Creator. God himself had manifested through the piety of man, through the surrender of man to God, through his need to praise God. Within the atmosphere of Westminster Abbey and St. Paul's Cathedral was that religious reality that absolutely silences the aesthetic metaphysic of communism, or secular scientism. One would have to have been anaesthetized to the living breath of God not to experience a power beyond man, beyond the architect (Christopher Wren for St. Paul's), beyond the human ego. No, what was contained within these monuments was the still living force of Western mythological intuition, and I defy any architect not able to touch the experience of divinity to approach the spiritual aura that has been created inside these cathedrals. Iran had found its mythology; we had lost the source of inspiration of our own mythology; these great cathedrals were hymns to the glory of God; our civilization could no longer make such hymns (evangelical Christianity has never produced the architectural or aesthetic forms that exalt God the way God has been exalted in these cathedrals). What Iran had found on the battlefield through martyrdom, what Iran had found in its devotion to Imam Khomeini, what Iran had found by submitting absolutely to Allah was reflected, albeit in a very different manner, in these cathedrals. It would not be possible to return as the Iranians had, to our mythological purity, but we could, if we were innocent enough, if we were sensitive enough, realize the grace that had left our civilization in taking ourselves out of the traditions of revelation passed down to us from our own prophet, Jesus Christ. The essential transcendent reality of mythology, the Christian mythology, was preserved by God through the structures through which I walked and contemplated; here, and only here, could one sympathetically understand how a mythology could so grip the consciousness of man that he would rise up towards the heavens and offer his life only to his God. I also thought how desirable it would be for all true Muslims—especially those Muslims who lacked an aesthetic sensibility—to walk through these cathedrals; even Imam Khomeini, were his eyes to see the magnificence of God here below the vaulted arches, the richly painted domes, would bow down in humbled wonder that Western man, through devotion to God, was capable of creating such beauty and power. Truly the final declaration of God was in the perception of the artistry of God, the perception of how beautifully designed was the whole cathedral of Creation itself.

The Meaning of
The Islamic Revolution

I have written this book in the attempt to describe as carefully as possible, the actual events and forces which are at work in Iran, free of any sort of opinion. While I cannot pretend to have that ultimate spiritual disinterestedness of Thomas à Kempis who declared

The Holy Spirit has freed me from a multitude of opinions.

(And many readers will think this, rather than a statement of disinterestedness, is the most intensely irrational opinion of all.) I can at least claim that what I have presented in terms of my reflections on the revolution constitute the experience of one individual who seeks to know precisely what are the facts, the tendencies, the conclusions to be made; however these facts, tendencies, conclusions are seen to be already existing within a dramatic structure, an allegory, if you will, that is defined not just by man, but by the very power that has brought Creation into being and which has created the possibilities of major conflict, tension, suffering, and yes, a multitude of opinions. Thomas à Kempis's declaration is not unrelated to Plato's idea of opinion as the evidence of lack of knowledge. For à Kempis and Plato the universe has an a priori order which it is man's duty (and perhaps destiny) to know; that knowingness is the basis of the purely religious experience, the basis of all scriptural revelation, the basis of the great mythologies, and the basis of any final judgement about the significance of the events of the world itself. Now if one subscribes to the idea that the universe is orderly, is purposeful, is beneficently intentional, then one is forced to interpret the meaning of various events taking place on the stage of the world. The Islamic Revolution is one of the most enigmatic events taking place on that stage, an event subject to the most violent disagreements, opinions, criticism. It is an event, however, that cannot be understood except in terms of a sensibility that is essentially intuitive and not rational or intellectual—and certainly not political. What is happening in Iran, according to the thesis developed in this book, is the expression of a consciousness that lies wholly outside of the grasp of man's faculties. It is something very absolute; that absoluteness is such as to confound the analysis of all political pundits, and virtually every intelligent and educated Westerner. The basis of that absolutist fact (that the revolution is being conducted by a force that transcends the rational, the known, the familiar, the analyzable) is found in the awareness of something needing to happen on the stage of the world which will remind man of his spiritual origins, that, as someone said, "the dice are loaded," that secular, liberal, Marxist, mechanistic views of the universe are ultimately unable to explain what happens, that a cause beyond man's calculations ultimately decides the course of history, that at this moment in history the spiritual, the mythological, the transcendental needs a regeneration, not a regeneration that will vitiate the discoveries of science, nor indeed the pluralistic freedoms and individualism that have emerged in the breaking down of the rigid metaphysical codes imposed upon man through the major mythologies, but a regeneration that awakens man to a sense of the sacred.

Now what is essential to grasp (if one accepts my own a priori assumptions about this revolution) is that the reality out of which Creation, man, and the drama of human existence has come, is ultimately unable to hide itself from itself; this means that no matter how much one of the contingent agents within that drama takes upon himself the appropriation of his own identity, purpose, and nature (i.e. assumes that he is created out of the random movement of amino acids, that his own existence is independent of any inherent purpose to the universe, that the existential fact of his own utter isolation is the final meaning of his experience), there will eventually be that revelation which will make it impossible for man to get away with thinking and knowing that he is essentially isolated, a law unto himself, an agent of action that has no interrelatedness with the rest of the cosmos.

Islam—especially the form of Islam regnant in Iran (and I am holding to the view that it is the purest expression of Islam that is conceivable at this time in man's development, due in the main part to the leadership of Imam Khomeini)—is the single most dominant expression of a reality that is in absolute opposition to the prevailing view of modern man: that there is no God, that man is free to manipulate the universe with impunity, that there is nothing intrinsically purposeful or meaningful about this universe. Islam demands total obedience to God; Islam is based upon the absolute necessity that man totally surrender up his life to God; Islam is based upon the affirmation that man must live according to the laws of God, and that these laws have been revealed by a prophet who represents the final and perfected will of God; Islam declares that all of Creation has its existence by virtue of being surrendered to God; and finally Islam divides Creation into the forces of good and evil and sees the final good of man in the realization of his own potential perfection. Now in the present context—the revolution in Iran—we can see how the doctrine of Islam is asserting itself without any attempt to dilute, compromise, or amend any of the fundamental principles; there is no attempt to espouse an Islam that takes into consideration the revolutionary facts of science, art, technology, literature that have surfaced since the Renaissance—or rather the Islam that is being expressed today in Iran has as its cornerstone belief the notion that it must resist all tendencies to adjust itself to the modern world, that it is precisely in relationship with the demonic powers of Western secularist, materialist, egocentric thinking that it has its survival, and its purifying purpose.

Islam, under Ayatollah Khomeini, is the expression of a power and ideology that will consistently defy all the persuasive powers of reasonableness, moderation, and modernism; the very moment that it does not affirm that the essential facts (the spiritual facts, which are of course the only significant facts) have not changed over fourteen centuries when the Prophet received his revelations, the Islamic Revolution will disintegrate—at least in its current archetypal meaning and impact.

Islam as it is being enacted through this revolution represents the countervailing force that confronts the dangerous excesses of modern civilization—both on the left and on the right (and, perhaps especially in the middle—the once "vital center")—, and in the unfolding of events in Iran we find a reality that defies the indices that were once sufficient to comprehend all political, not to mention social, moral, and religious events. Iran—or rather this Islamic Revolution—represents the means through which modern man is confronted by a phenomenon that will not submit to the control, the manipulable categories of analysis, the unconscious and conscious paradigms of modernist thought that characterize the whole methodology and *Weltgeist* of an age which is demythologizing itself—or which has reached the extreme point of such alienation from its sources of spiritual vitalization. The Islamic Revolution in Iran will never—certainly while Imam Khomeini lives, and he may live long enough to see a world profoundly altered in terms of its political and spiritual complexion—become comprehensible except to those whose intuition is developed enough to recognize the profound purpose embodied in that articulation of that revolution, the purpose of confronting modern man with the arrogance of his assumptions of the knowability of the universe, the knowability of the why of political (and all other) events, the ontological premise of non-intrinsic meaning and intention within the universe. The Islamic Revolution in all its excesses, delirium, and inhibiting dogmatism, will never move towards a pattern that will fit into the calculations of those who now are thought to understand what happens in our world. As far as I know only one scholar in the whole Western world was able to correctly anticipate the events of modern Iran—in terms of the resistance to the Shah, the paramount role of Shi'a martyrdom, the mystique of Imam Khomeini[63]; at present there is no evidence that Western analysts have reached a consensus as to the meaning or the future of this revolution, although the successful ousting of the Shah and the systematic defiance of both superpowers ("Neither East nor West... but Islam") have made scholars attach much more importance to the role of religion. It is my intuition that the revolution will not be subject to any sort of threat from the left—or from the military; the actual impulses of the revolution have gone so far down into the consciousness of most Iranians (while awakening latent impulses of religious devotion as well) that nothing other than the precise, pure formulations of Islam enunciated and embodied by Imam Khomeini will have any hold over the Iranians. The intensity of the feeling for Islam, the intensity with which this loyalty to Khomeini and the Revolution expresses itself is the most intense expression of political feeling in the world. Indeed, because of the significance of the factors I have outlined—the need for demythologized man to be confronted by mythological purity that implies the a priori order of the universe, contrary to all the paradigms employed currently to understand political realities—this intensity of commitment and feeling goes beyond any commitment or feeling in the world, for it has the support of the cosmos itself. It is, therefore, the only fundamentally inviolable political reality extant.

Something so primary is at stake in this revolution: the final elimination of God from the stage of international reality—or the resurrection of God, the proof that belief in God, the leadership of a purely devoted, realized human being, that these factors bring about a sequence of events that cannot be explained by a universe which is indifferent to the beliefs of man, a universe which has not been created to fulfill a final purpose. Islam, the leadership of Imam Khomeini, has created a consciousness of bravery, surrender, and faith whose power has generated results—a revolution, the successful pursuit of war—against all odds, a power that, once witnessed by those willing to receive its distinctive resonances, convinces one that Imam Khomeini is not just hallucinating wildly when he talks about the revolution in terms of the grace of Allah.

[63] Hamid Algar, "The Oppositional Role of the *'Ulama* in Twentieth-Century Iran," *Scholars, Saints, and Sufis: Muslim Religious Institutions Since 1500*, ed. Nikki Keddie (Berkeley: University of California Press, 1972), pp. 231-58.

The behaviour of the Islamic fighters on the battlefield against Iraq—
the manifestation of martyrdom—comes about not just through faith,
but through a force which makes that 'faith' a living, empirically felt
reality. At the basis of this revolution is a grace; however impoverished,
unsophisticated, and narrow-minded may appear the vision of the world
held by the rabid Muslim yearning for the exalted station of martyrdom,
that vision is sacred in the mind of this universe—sacred enough to allow
more than small miracles to take place. Once touched by this mood of
surrender to what is transcendent of all material reality, once having
absorbed this mood into one's being (whether one is secularist, believer,
agnostic or what) one finds one's own consciousness altered, and one is
at the edge of the harrowing thought: could it be that the Creator of this
universe—through the inspired and absolutist integrity of a single
Muslim leader—seeks to demonstrate a final truth to man, and that
therefore this Creator, this Absolute, creates a particular chemistry of
feeling within the Iranian Muslim such that he touches the reality of
transcendence?

Such is the thesis of this writer. There are many other important
struggles, conflicts, movements going on in this world; in America itself
since the sixties, there has been a kind of spiritual renaissance (for
instance, the interest in Eastern religions, meditation; the yearning for
conservative values; the resurgence of evangelical Christianity—although
in the case of the latter one senses the absence of that universality of
religious sensibility which is the touchstone of authentic religious experience); the affirmation of the existence of order, purpose, and lawfulness in the universe (also being implied by post-Einsteinian physics) will
never finally challenge the paradigm that determines the attitudes
towards political realities until such time as a competing paradigm—like
Islam—demonstrates a cause (faith in God) and effect (success against
the enemy) relationship that is as triumphant as Kissinger-styled *Realpolitik*, Guevaran radicalism, Marxist-Leninist materialism, or Haigian
toughness. In the assortment of metaphysical styles that are brought to
bear upon the political circumstances of our world, the Iranian martyr
who inscribes his tank with verses from the Qur'an, stops everything for
midday prayers, and then resumes his fighting, charged with the anticipation of deathless bliss, achieves a meaning which will be defiant of all
our expectations, a meaning that threatens to force itself upon our
unIslamic (i.e. unsurrendered, disbelieving) consciousness. This revolution will go on until these ancient archetypes—perhaps eternal archetypes—go down so deep into the consciousness of man, that he recovers
the balance of himself, and comes to know his own boundaries are
supported by what is unbounded, to know that his own life is the unique
experiment of that consciousness which is absolute, and which seeks to

make consciousness become conscious of itself. The Islamic Revolution in Iran will continue to confound us until we accept the metaphysical challenge which is posed in all its frenzied, apocalyptic grace. Islam exists—at least at this moment—to restore the spirituality of the West. The progress of this revolution will itself dictate to us the reckoning of ourselves. We must never ignore the weaknesses, the excesses, the distortions of this revolution, but when we meet the eyes of the martyr and sense the fragrance of his faith, we are meeting and sensing the manifestation of the universe as it balances the anti-mythological with the beatitudes of the mythological.

This book is written in the conviction that the lines of the drama in which we are participants have a meaning determined by that intention which seeks to both universalize man's consciousness, while at the same time acquainting him with the perfected expression of his own uniqueness, the perfected expression of the drama through which he is enacting his (and God's[64]) own conscious and unconscious desire. To adapt a phrase by a famous English poet, man's life is a continual allegory—and very few eyes can see the Mystery of this life—a life like the scriptures, figurative. The Islamic Revolution in Iran is a potent expression of that intention to have us realize the allegorical, scriptural reality of our lives—and the collective life of man.

[64] This flow of creation, from where it did arise,
   Whether it was ordered or was not,
   He, the Observer, in the highest heaven,
   He alone knows, unless...He knows it not.

                       Rig-Veda, X, 129.7

Hymns from the Rig-Veda, trans. Jean Le Mée (New York: Alfred A. Knopf, 1975), p. 32.

174

Appendices

An Open Letter to *Ayatollah Khomeini* From the Author

Dear Respected Leader of the Iranian People,   June 24, 1981

Since November 4, 1979 when I first experienced the intrinsic lawfulness of the lawless act of seizing the diplomatic personnel from the United States Embassy (the intuition of the great purity and idealism of your revolution manifested in my heart the moment when the Muslim students were interviewed on television) I have looked with considerable satisfaction on the unfolding of the events in Iran, and have, as a non-Muslim and Westerner, defended the revolution there and the powerful mythopoeic integrity of Islam as it was re-vitalized by the revolution, your leadership, and the deaths of all the martyrs.

During the confrontation with the United States and immediately after the imposed war with Iraq there seemed little resistance to the flow of logic and analysis that made the essential position of your government and its brave people the right one. As someone with a profound trust in the pure wellsprings of Tradition as originally conceived (or received) by the prophets of each major religion, and as someone who had undergone my own sense of the fundamental wholeness and sacredness of existence, I knew the religious context of your revolution to be absolutely genuine. And when I visited Iran and walked through Beheshte Zahra Cemetery I did not need my guide to explain to me the significance of this holy sanctuary: the essence of Shi'a Islam, the sense of immortality, charged the atmosphere with an energy and feeling that authenticated the reality of martyrdom. (And this experience is described in detail in my second book on Iran.)

I also had the opportunity to meet with many Iranian Muslims both in Iran and here in Canada. I even had the opportunity to witness an hour-long prayer service conducted by a group of devout Muslims here under the guidance of Mohammed Hossein Adeli, the Iranian chargé d'affaires for Canada.

My association with these Muslims (and supporters of the Islamic Revolution in Iran) was wholly satisfying, even inspiring to me, for I sensed the intensity of commitment, the totality of surrender that true Islam demanded of each believer. And I felt the grace, the tenderness, that seemed to flow so spontaneously from so many of these Iranian

Muslims, and I could perceive the causal relationship such spirituality had with the nature of Islam. The apparent lack of egotism and narrow selfhood that characterized my experience of course was a refreshing change from one's normal relations with Westerners, who by and large possess a strong sense of ego isolation and are much more competitive and neurotic in their personal relations. One has to be careful about making generalizations, but bowing down to the ground five times a day and giving oneself to the possibility of martyrdom seemed to result in a religious consciousness distinct from my Judaeo-Christian experiences, where Sunday morning worship could never exact that ceremony of purification and egolessness that seemed collectively expressed in the tens of thousands of Muslims whom I watched praying toward Mecca— this during the celebration of Now-Ruz in Beheshte Zahra.

Most importantly in reading the Holy Qur'an and Nahj al-Balagha (sermons, letters, and sayings of Imam Ali) I felt the essence of God as he chose to have himself known and understood through Islam. And I felt, as I watched your revolution progress, the utterly authentic relationship between these scriptures and what was happening in Iran. This was no ordinary revolution, made in the name of freedom, nationalism, or Marx; it had its own rhythm, its own personality, its own grace, and this was the impulse that emerges out of the mythological power that Marx or Rousseau knew nothing of, for Islam was not just an idea; it had been written into the consciousness of Man through a divine intervention and, in the case of Shi'a Islam, it had been sustained through the miraculous character of the twelve Imams and the archetype of martyrdom. Your people had managed to—in their resistance to the Shah, in their defiance of American aggression—make of history an allegory where truth and purity seemed supported by the universe itself, while falsehood and cruelty were punished. Truly your revolution had been a miracle completely defying all CIA probabilities—and confounding the atheists to the north. And throughout all this I also became aware of the special nature of your own integrity as the embodiment of Islam: no matter how viciously you were attacked and ridiculed in the West, no one who had any sense of judgement of strength and integration of character could doubt that your motives, your deeds, warranted your supreme position in the hearts of Iranians and all true Muslims in the world.

But somewhere some of this grace and nobility of purpose has gone astray—or so it seems to me in my reading of present events and tendencies in your country. In the interests of preserving the absoluteness of Qur'anic law, in the interests of preserving the foundation of Islam, there seems to be a movement towards the inhibition of the soul, towards the suppression of all impulses that do not strictly and dogmatically accord with the literal application of religious precept. Thus the former President Abolhassan Bani-Sadr is stripped of his command, thus all those who counsel moderation are persecuted (such as Mehdi Bazargan), thus every form of dissent is suppressed (increasingly so; at first there seemed to be the genuine signs of a democratic dialogue, the healthy acting out of the prerogative to disagree in such a young republic still learning the best way to apply religious truth to statehood).

And those on the left are ruthlessly dealt with as subversives, as infidels, as the violators of the Prophet's will. They are looked at as trying to destroy the revolution—and no doubt many of them desire to manipulate events so as to make the revolution fall into the pattern that fits their own materialist view of things. But must they all be—including now your president, elected by seventy percent of the people—hunted down like dogs and summarily executed? Do you realize what this looks like to the civilized world? You may be absolutely right in administering the law in the punitive, divinely deadly way laid down by Mohammad himself, but you must realize that even divinely sanctioned penalties can be carried out by persons whose hearts are frozen and cruel. Surely the experiment with subjectivity and individuality that is at the heart of the Western experience since the ending of a theocratic rule cannot be all the work of Satan. Granted, the failure of Western man to embrace an absolute-like surrender to God and obedience to a perfect Tradition has wreaked havoc with the psyche and destroyed the spiritual equilibrium of a whole civilization. Western man is no doubt cut off from his roots, and his reading of Kafka (an artist who takes subjectivism to its demonic extremes) is not likely to bring him into harmony with the universe—or himself. Islam sets out to do this, and, as I have already mentioned, it seems to have accomplished something remarkable in empirically demonstrating its spiritual efficacy.

But you, who has taught mysticism and philosophy, must know that absolute obedience to dogma is only the first step to freedom (conceived in its spiritual sense), that at some point in the evolution of the soul it becomes possible to conceive of the sacredness of impulse as opposed to the sacredness of law. Even the Creator has created out of the Law of Love and Imagination, not out of shibboleth or conformity. And you are aware of what happened to Jesus when he invoked the spirit rather than the letter of the law.

Now these leftist groups have not been given the grace to believe in Islam with the same fervency as others more loyal to you and the revolution have. And yet some of the more moderate groups surely are sincerely attempting to bring about justice and truth. (At this point I must draw attention to the utterly hypocritical Western press which decries the "barbarism" of the present government in Iran while only intermittently addressing itself to the massive slaughter carried out by military dictatorships with interests favourable to the United States. When twenty-five people are executed in Iran, this is a monstrous act. When 350 Salvadoran peasants are massacred while trying to cross the border—by government troops—we are largely immune to this act of unspeakable horror.) But since your revolution contains so much more of what is eternal and potentially healing to man, since your revolution has been waged in the name of God, since your revolution looks to set an example to all nations, it becomes important to assess the application of Islamic law in the context of a world that must see the working out of an integrity that in and of itself—outside of its Islamic content—carries the resonance of justice and compassion.

What I am trying to get at here is the idea that no matter what law is invoked to justify persecution, repression, or execution, it is finally the act itself that carries with it the vibration of good or evil, and the right law applied in a spirit of vengefulness or sadism becomes an act of evil equivalent—or perhaps worse since it is done in the name of righteousness—to the transgression of the accused. The Shah created his system (with the assistance of the CIA) of terror and torture, and most of the world was silent. Now, because of the challenge to Western values and cultural dominance, there is a predisposition to seize upon any behaviour that seems to fit into the thesis that you are a madman, that this regime will outdo even Hitler. I lament this, especially because in my lengthy interviews with the student leaders inside the embassy, with young Revolutionary Guards, with even the president, I sensed the presence of something that transcended the context of mere revolution; —I sensed the sanctity of religious truth. Now, however, there is the increasingly uneasy feeling that the imagination of the revolution is being attenuated and the simple solution to all dissent is liquidation, or the rigid reflex of Islamic justice without a sensitivity to the overall context of this historical moment.

Now before I go any further, I wish to make one thing clear: I realize absolutely the necessity of not compromising with anything that smacks of relativism, secularism, Westernized assumptions; I know that your people need to see that Islam is being carried out to the letter, and that the whole pattern of religious law is being stitched into the consciousness of the whole society. It is just that recent events give me the strongest feeling that the mere dogmatic and ruthless impulses of those who are now empowered to expedite Islamic justice are not participating in the currents of truth and integrity which gave birth to your revolution, which have created such a fresh (and ancient) model of civilization. Since Bani-Sadr and his followers have indicated in the past their allegiance to Islam, since there are moderates currently under seige by

180

the *'ulama* and Majlis who have fought hard for the revolution and are decidedly anti-communist, it seems there are signs from within the drama that a gathering of opposition to the policies of the Islamic Republican Party may not after all be motivated by anti-Islamic ideas; in other words the sincere and orthodox clergymen who oppose the former president and his followers seem to me to be bent upon exercising their power in the absence of a sense of moral imagination. I can even see certain members of the ruling authority getting some perverted satisfaction now that they seem to have been given the green light to round up and execute who they wish.

Despite all the millions marching and demanding Bani-Sadr's head (I saw one portrait of the former president, with half his face cut away, and replaced with the half face of the Shah) I sense they too have become partial to a perception that spares them the necessary complexities of working out this unprecedented blueprint of an Islamic Republic. Is each individual critical of the present situation manifestly evil? No, I don't think so, and I intuitively feel that there must be some other way to bring in the next phase of the revolution. If these critical, even counter-revolutionary forces in Iran must be eliminated, then let us see this done within the spirit of wisdom and dignity. As it is now, the continued polarization is playing into the hands of those who would compromise the vision of Islam, since the Party of God and its leaders can credibly be seen to be fanatical and primitive in their demands for swift punishment of all wrong-doers.

If Islam is right then surely what it means is that the obedience to its spirit brings with it the sense of an intrinsic morality and wholeness that exposes the shallowness of secularized, desacralized morality and values.

Do those who call for Bani-Sadr's head now possess the requisite inner purity and wisdom to be so righteous in their judgement of the wrongs of others? Is there the sufficiently Islamic consciousness to make of these deeds (the punitive ones) an organic connection with the spirit behind the law of Islam? Is God acting through the agents of Islamic justice as it now applies to those who support Bani-Sadr? I am afraid that the events in Iran now seem to give the lie to the continued emphasis of mine that a civilization can be reborn in the sacredness of a mythology and possess thereby an inner beauty and strength that would make the de-mythologized civilizations envious—eventually at least.

As someone who values tradition, ceremony, and custom, I am partial to the idea that an ancient myth such as Islam holds within itself the seed for the redemption of much of mankind. As I have brought out in my two books and in this letter I am thoroughly convinced that a great archetype of the human soul is enacting itself through your revolution and that the outcome of this revolution portends a transformation of man. However, as someone ultimately devoted to the individualistic tendencies of what is universal—and to the intelligence of the heart—I must issue my concern at the potential negativism that could seize your revolution and bring about its destruction. For surely a revolution made in the name of God must reflect the presence, and intention of God. Therefore if a revolution is informed by divinity it will, in its actions, carry a vibration that distinguishes it from all other revolutions, not to mention all other societies. And we can assume that God has an integrity beyond that of that which would deny Him (such as Western politics does, implicitly). Is that integrity now manifesting in the tactics of the *'ulama*, in the persecution of the followers of Bani-Sadr?

One of the aspects of Islam that I found most impressive was set off against the character of so many of the Christian evangelists that currently dominate the airwaves here in the West (and most of whom have of course seen you and your revolution as wicked—satanic!); this was the sense of surrender and personal grace that seemed to make the Iranian Muslims I talked with more intuitive, more effortlessly attuned to the impulses of each moment. The evangelists here seemed brutally arbitrary in their judgements of political events, seeming to assume that in heaven there is one big American flag and that the angel Gabriel is a capitalist-militarist who dispenses celestial rewards according to how many nuclear warheads you were prepared to vote for. Is that same intuition now being applied in the current unrest and upheaval? Something in my heart says not. It is too simple to see all the problems simply as the result of deviants wrecking the divine efficiency of Islam. But is it correct to assume that those who now are bent upon ridding Iran of all opposition are endowed with the requisite innocence and imagination to fulfill a mandate from heaven—i.e. to build an Islamic society that can be a model for the rest of the world?

I have said enough about all this. I do hope that I am wrong and that history will show that the glory of this revolution could only be achieved by the present actions of the clergy and the Islamic courts—and the breaking of all opposition. But somehow I cannot believe that the only challenge to your republic is coming from the devil; somehow there is some truth on the other side, and it just will not do to think of the solution to all this in terms of annihilation of the opposition. Where will the flower of Persian culture, art, character, subtlety go when all that is left are those who cling to a fundamental idea of Islam without the necessary inner development to justify their denunciation of those who prefer to see the acting out of history in more complex and challenging forms? One specific area of concern to me—and millions of others here in the West—is the position your government (and your constitution) has taken on the issue of Baha'ism. Whatever the links Baha'ism in Iran had to Israel and SAVAK, whatever way in which the Baha'is demonstrated in support of the Shah, whatever way in which certain individuals used Baha'ism as a means of weakening Islam, you must know that here in the West there are thousands of absolutely sincere practitioners of this faith, persons who cannot be accused of any of the things the Baha'is there are accused of. Indeed I have known several dozen members of this church here in Canada and almost without exception their devotion to Baha'ism produced a religious consciousness much more vital than that which characterized most Christians. Now perhaps this comes about because of the partially Islamic roots within Baha'ism; whatever the case you must know that the people here are innocent of any wrongdoing and experience their religion to be the ultimate truth. Religious truth is surely not just a question of what you believe in; it is a question of what that belief does to one's heart, to the deeds of one's life. By any kind of criterion many Baha'is here fulfill the definition of the sincere believer and have, as I have said, a special kind of devotion that is not surpassed by the other traditional religions.

Now I realize that one of the biggest objections to Baha'ism is that Baha'u'llah proclaimed himself to be directly connected to the Twelfth Imam, that he had succeeded the Prophet and was henceforth the final translator of God's will, thus making Mohammad but the penultimate prophet and not the final one as believed by Muslims. Baha'ism must seem from this point of view to be the worst kind of heresy and damaging to the continued strength of Islam. However, based upon its teachings, in the West at least, there can be no question about its authentic claims for justified eminence, and the extraordinary efforts being made in Iran to eradicate its influence merely feed into the conception and prejudice that so many people have here of the bigoted nature of your government. Perhaps Baha'ism is a Zionist plot to weaken the hold of Islam in the world, but for me, in my encounter with the proponents of this faith, my criterion was simply: is it an inspired and integrated vision of God. By itself it is this, and whether it has aligned itself to movements and thinking that are inimical to Allah and the Islamic Republic of Iran is a point that will never hold up in an argument with a dedicated Baha'i here in the West. Granted it is the supreme heresy. Can we therefore assume that God blesses those who would destroy any remnant of its existence? Is every Baha'i merely deluded or consciously plotting against Islam?

I acknowledge the evidence of the perfidious relationship between SAVAK and Baha'is in Iran—and even the possibility that this religion was exploited by certain interests favourable towards Israel; this does not destroy the final credibility of Baha'u'llah, nor the sincere intentions of thousands of Baha'i followers here in the West. What does happen is that persons and organizations interested in discrediting your revolution seize upon whatever evidence exists of the persecution in Iran and use that evidence to defile the character of Islam, and your revolution— the Islamic Revolution.

I suppose this comes down to the same issue that I have been harping upon throughout this letter: that the mandate of Islam does not preclude the creative responsibility of applying that mandate within a context of intuition, reasonableness, and spiritual intention. Religious dogma cannot be the excuse for an individual not having to accept responsibility for having each act he performs pass through his heart. You are the inspiration to a whole people, a human being who will take your place in history as a truly remarkable leader who personified one of the great religions of the world and achieved a vision of human civilization that represented a genuine alternative to that of Western capitalism or Eastern socialism. And I cannot help but think that deep down you are aware of what is happening and are taking the secret steps to make certain that these things that I have spoken of are approached in a manner so as to ensure the quality of your revolution, for the final truthfulness of what is happening in Iran cannot be measured ideologically, it must be measured by the organic, spiritual power (*barakah*) that flows from the hearts of your people.

As the Qur'an says:

Lo! Allah changes not the condition of a people until they (first) change that which is in their souls.

XIII,11

This surely implies the actual transformation of the nature of the people and not the mere repetition of slogans or the enactment of a ritual. When that change is rooted in the souls of the people a radiance will shine out towards the world and then we shall see the signs of the promised perfection for which the angel invaded the vision of Mohammad.

In absolute sincerity,

Robin Woodsworth Carlsen

Letter to the Author
From *Mehdi Bazargan*

Dear Mr. Carlsen,

I had received a copy of your open letter of June 24 to the leader of our Islamic Revolution, Ayatollah Khomeini, which I had the chance to translate and read a few months ago, and now I am happy to have the chance to respond to it and talk with you.

...Now that for the first time I have heard about you and your sincere, deep and sympathetic letter, it was very enjoyable for me for several reasons, and for my part I thank you for that.

Your favourable opinion, with moral graciousness and submission before the truth, that you have indicated about Islam and the spirituality of the Iranian Revolution, your praise of the eminence and influence of its leader and your statement about the faith and sincerity of our youth are the salient points in the first part of your letter, which was completed by your impartial view about the deviations of western civilization and by the false accusations made in the west about the Islamic Revolution of Iran and its leader. I feel, indeed, very happy and consoled to find a commiserator of the same mind overseas. I also see a live evidence in your thought and words of the Holy Quran, which says:

"...and nearest among them in love to Believers wilt thou find those who say, 'We are Christians': because amongst these are men devoted to learning and men who have renounced the world, and they are not arrogant."   (V:85)

"And when they listen to the revelation received by the Apostle, thou wilt see their eyes overflowing with tears, for they recognize the truth..."   (V:86)

I hope that you enjoy the last of the verses which he included about the "People of the Book":

"And for this their prayer, hath God rewarded them with Gardens, with rivers flowing underneath,—their eternal home. Such is the recompense of those who do good."   (V:88)

Because I have spent a few years in France during my higher education, I am a little familiar with western thought and knowledge, and there I have seen the best examples of humanity, truth seeking and virtue; therefore, your views were not unprecedented and surprising for me.

Sighting the meaningful Quranic verse at the end and statements of Imam Ali in other parts of your letter, made me very glad to see that you are fortunately, in reach of the clear springs of the sea of Islam, i.e. Quran and Nahjul-Balagha, and that you get your information from the original sources.

But my admiration and gratitude is for your reminding me, your regrets and your advice, which arises from your fine feelings and deep understanding of divine customs, in which, with a lot of care and great endeavor, while confirming the religious justice and the necessity of carrying out the spiritless, and perhaps, merciless penal orders, you have wanted to condemn the revengeful and sadistic mentality which is parallel to satanical laws. You have tried to prove that destruction and negation of lives and superficial supression of non-party movements does not agree with the spirituality and ideals of religion, and because our revolution has been generated with the name of God, it must be a model combined with justice and mercy.

I noticed the points which you had made about the treatment of some individuals and different Iranian and non-Iranian political and ideological groups, on which points I agree with you completely, and I have repeatedly said and written that the magnificence and greatness of our revolution can be presented only by the correct actions of our responsible authorities, and that not all of the difficulties of our Republic are created by Satan and that the solution for all of them is not through the destruction of opponents.

What I would like to add as my present to you is that fortunately the Divine norms and Islamic penal laws, as shown in the Holy Quran, as well as the traditions of the holy Prophet (may peace be upon him!) and his true successors, are not compatible with hostility, coercion, revenge, and destruction. Rather, they are perfectly coordinated with the pure nature of man and with the Divine graciousness and excellence of God. Priority is given to freedom, tolerance, compassion, and virtue before justice, equity, and retaliation. The relation between Satan and man is that of enemy, and the relation between God and man is based on kindness, so much so that the names of God in the Holy Quran, and the advice to the believers are clearly indicative as such. Unfortunately, some actions and words which appear in our Revolution have not shown such features of Islam—words appearing in and out of Iran, which must be attributed to losses and damages of any political revolution; and the ignorant tradition of man, Marxist mentality and teachings are the main causes of this.

... With hopes for the victory of truth over falsehood and the establishment of one just and universal government, I wish from the one God health and success for you as my brother in faith.

Mehdi Bazargan

Letter to the Author
From *Ali Quli Qarai,*
Editor of *The Message of Peace*

Dear Mr. Carlsen:

... A few days ago I received your 'Open letter to Ayatollah Khomeini' which I read and reread with interest and the intention behind this letter is to convey what I feel about things you have talked about. You have expressed your fears thus: "But somewhere some of this grace and nobility of purpose has gone astray ... there seems to be a movement towards the inhibition of the soul, towards the suppression of all impulses that do not strictly and dogmatically accord with the literal application of religious precept ... thus all those who counsel moderation are persecuted. ..."

I think the young Islamic Republic has been gracefully tolerant of any form of impulses that not only did not sympathize with the aims and ends of the present regime or the revolution but on the other hand directed venomous propaganda at it and condemned its every move. Here what you are implying is not suppression of critical impulses but suppression of armed rebellion by a handful few against a revolution and a government established at the price of more than seventy thousand martyrs and many more disabled youths. The Mujahedeen-e-Khalq have carried on a relentless war of propaganda and criticism for more than two years not for the sake of helping or guiding the young government but for the sake of overturning it. Such were also other leftist groups. But during the last week of Khordad [1981; May 22-June 21], the Mujahedeen-e-Khalq formally declared armed rebellion against the government charging its members to hold armed demonstrations attacking people and revolutionary guards with knives and guns. They not only declared open war against the Islamic Republic but followed their declaration with assassinations, bombings and street killings. They were not hunted down like dogs by some SAVAK-like organization but handed over by people who cooperated zealously in revealing their hideouts. Do not the public or government have a right of self-defence? Islam and its teachings do not leave Muslims or an Islamic Government helpless against wolves. It was no longer a matter of dissent but of armed rebellion.

Divinely sanctioned penalties are for the sake of defending and protecting sublime values and wholesomeness of society. If they are deadly in some cases, it is because of the deadlier nature of the crime. It is not for the sake of depriving men of life but for the sake of giving strength to Life itself. If divinely sanctioned penalties can be carried out by persons whose hearts are frozen and cruel, then surgeons must be without exception cruel people. I do not say that carrying out such penalties is not a difficult task (on the other hand it can be a shocking experience), for it is related that at times when the Prophet himself decreed a death penalty, his complexion would pale as if his body were dripped of its last drop of blood. Divine justice is not opposed to the demands of compassion or mercy but on the other hand it is only through implementation of divinely sanctioned laws that the demands of mercy in its fullest, most comprehensive sense are satisfied, since it is justice that is 'potentially healing to man'. A compassionate gardener is not the one who allows weeds to destroy his trees. It is not administration of divinely sanctioned penalties that make hearts cruel and frozen. Rather it is blind attachment to material aspects of life and destruction of life for the sake of selfish interests that corrupts, deadens and freezes the hearts and infests them with cruelty.

As far as I am concerned, I think most of the executions and death penalties dealt by the Islamic Revolutionary courts have been the 'best' of executions anytime, anywhere (if one were allowed to use the word in this context). I regard these executions to be the highest form of 'mercy killing' that has taken place in the interest of human society; because I sense what kind of monsters that were those who were destroyed.

There is something in this matter of defending or condemning death penalties and executions that the defender by his defence makes a butcher out of himself and the one who condemns by definition projects himself as a humane person. That is probably why everybody wants to take this honour and no one [is] prepared to accept this apparent discredit. In any case, the matter was not of dissent by a political group or two, but a common plot to liquidate the revolution itself and its leadership, and very unfortunately, Bani Sadr has played an evil subversive role, having located himself consciously, or fallen unconsciously into the very nucleus of conspiracy against the revolution.

You will notice that the word 'moderation' used in this context is similar to 'modernisation' being used formerly during the days of the fall of Shah's regime. For Muslims, the word 'moderation' can be meaningful only in the context of Islam. How can a Muslim accept moderation or be advised moderation against Islam? Does it not imply that Islam by definition involves fanaticism, so that moderation has necessarily to come from outside? When the opponents of Ulema are depicted as 'moderate', whose nomenclature are we adopting? Is it the

188

nomenclature put forth by the enemies of Islam or its friends? Is it moderation to obey God and implement His laws or is it moderation to try to break this obedience? Why is deviation the necessary condition for moderation? If I say that five and five are eleven and you claim stubbornly that they add up to ten, which of us according to the above method of nomenclature is a moderate? Shall I say that you are a radical or what is more befitting a fanatic mathematician and I a moderate?

You have posed the typical Western question: "Do you realize what this looks like to the civilized world?" Will you permit me to ask as bluntly, "Where is this civilized world?" Of course civilization is supposed to be a monopoly of the West; but you here forget that the Islamic Revolution in Iran has called into question the authenticity of this very pretension. You have forgotten that we have not yet agreed with the West about the meaning of the words the Westerners are fond of using such as 'modernisation', 'civilization', 'wisdom', 'barbarism', 'dignity' and 'honour'. Does not the West regard itself as being more civilized compared to the rest of the world due to its advanced technology, scientific knowledge and industry? If this is civilization what did Hitler lack? Why is the West so forgetful of the deadly nuclear missiles under its arm. Have not the Western leaders put the majority of mankind only a pressing of a button away from annihilation? Certainly a civilized man can never become a threat for himself or others? Have the Westerners not fought two world wars only seventy years ago? One may also argue that those missiles are intended only as a deterrent and will never be exploded. Shall we then take up the argument later after those buttons have been pressed and missiles been fired? Do such problems belong in a 'civilized world'?

I would like to use this opportunity to object to your usage of the word 'mythology' and 'myth'. Islam is not a 'mythology'. It is a God-revealed Truth. Myths are fabrications of men. They are like the works of Kafka adopted and practised by men in serious life. You are not right in talking of the West as a de-mythologised civilization. In fact the West is a prisoner in the Web of its fabricated myths: the Myth of Western Materialism and the Myth of Marxism. These Myths have divided the world and threaten to destroy it. The progress of physical sciences has been paralleled by a joint venture in myth-making in the so-called human sciences: thanks to men like Darwin, Freud and Marx, the glorious myth-makers.

Your continued mention of 'myth' and 'mythology' (in a very special sense that is distinctly your own) seems to be yet another adventure in the field of myth-making. With what seems to be an admixture of your own special mythology, and pragmatic theory of truth (or shall I say myth?) you seem to be suggesting to your western audience that Islam can serve as a potent, useful myth that would substitute [for] what you misleadingly refer to as a de-mythologised vacuum. Or you seem to imagine that Islam would be more easily swallowed when sugar-coated as myth rather than as (an unpleasant term for a common Westerner) a God-revealed Truth and Religion. But I think that God or Islam cannot be smuggled. One can mislead away from truth but I doubt if there is a way to 'mislead' people towards truth. Is there a back door to Paradise? Or a way to mislead them through its front doors? Do the Western ideas of marketing assist the purpose of propagation of Islam? Or basically is it a matter of open-eyed conscious choice? Quran does not make any such attempts. It squarely declares:

Say: 'O unbelievers, I serve not what you serve and you are not serving what I serve, nor am I serving what you have served, neither are you serving what I serve.
To you your religion and to me my religion!'

You seem to dismay: "Where will the flower of Persian culture, art, character, subtlety go when all that is left are those who cling to a fundamental idea of Islam without the necessary inner development to justify their denunciation of those who prefer to see the acting out of history in more complex and challenging terms?" There is a blunt way of answering this question: Is it necessary to be a biologist to kill a snake?

Here I presume you have been misled by the Western media (though I can understand that you are always on your guard), struggling to depict Islamic revolutionaries as people given to crude, simplistic and monolithic ways of thinking, devoid of wisdom and maturity, taste and dignity, in effect totally unsophisticated.

I think the revolution has made the nation more mature, bringing entirely new and sophisticated ways of thinking to the Iranian mind. To quote just an example, the Iranian people have shown great understanding and political sophistication in the Bani Sadr affair.

You shall agree that cultural forms, art forms, character forms, and varieties of "subtlety" depend on the substratum which in the case of Iran is Islam. The revolution has tried to re-establish and re-consolidate this substratum. It is steadily driving out any impure material that might have crept in through the course of centuries. The leadership of the revolution has been determined to preserve this intention which was the very aim of the revolution. The types represented by Bani Sadr and to some extent Bazargan by the very virtue of their 'impurity' have failed and demonstrated their bankruptcy. In other words their rejection was an inevitable step in the march of the revolution towards its goal of purification. That is why I do not see this process in terms of breaking and "annihilation of the opposition". The opposition was opposed to this process of purification and broke as a result of its failure to interrupt the process of purification of the revolution. Shah, Bakhtiar and Bani Sadr are milestones on this road. History will wonder at the understanding of the Iranian nation of complex historical situations and the right choices it made and how it defeated the plots of scheming enemies through its right choices and timely admission of mistakes (election and rejection of Bani Sadr). Is it not possible to see in the determination to fight the present war to the point of victory the preference of the people to "see the acting out of history in more complex and challenging forms?"

The biggest objection to Baha'ism is that Baha'u'llah and his like, like the Mohammad ibne Abdul Wahab in Iraq, and Ghulam Ahmad Qadiyani in India have not been sent by Allah but by the British Foreign Ministry of the time. All the above three British-made brands of Islam have been propagated in Muslim countries for the sake of de-politicizing, de-legalizing Islam and dividing Muslims. Had they succeeded there would never have been the kind of Islamic revolution as we witness.

The recent ties with Israel have been only the latest in the chain of relations with foreign governments.

As to "the sincere intentions of thousands of Baha'i followers" in America and Europe, I don't know what to say. Somebody has said that the road to hell is paved with good intentions. I have seen thousands of sincere American and European followers of Dubious Hindu sadhus in America and India—poor folk—who had somehow fallen perhaps in search of a better, more satisfying 'myth'. Some turn away after seeing their Gurus from near. Perhaps 'inspired visions' are not enough. Good intentions are not enough. Having a religious consciousness much more vital than that which characterizes most Christians is not enough; just as it is not enough as a sign of health to look less pale and warmer than most dead bodies.

Should not the followers also examine the 'saint' behind the 'inspired visions'. We must do a lot of hard work and search before we make a selection, before we choose a 'myth' to wrap our minds and souls in. This is more important than other kind of work we have to do for making a living. We cannot bypass our freedom, neither pretend that we have not chosen at all.

I did not intend to write such a long letter as this. I hope all your fears come out to be unfounded and that this revolution shall successfully cover the journey to the end of night until daybreak when the Sun of Imamate will rise whose light as it is illumines the dark panorama around us.

Sincerely,

Ali Quli Qarai